The Ultimate Collection
Confident Communication

From Everyday Conversations to Public Speaking & Presentations

Unlock the power to speak with impact, build genuine connections and captivate any audience!

Anne McKeown

©Copyright Anne McKeown 2025 - All rights reserved.

The content within this book may not be reproduced, duplicated or transmitted without direct written permission from the author or the publisher.

Under no circumstances will any blame or legal responsibility be held against the publisher or author for any damages, reparation, or monetary loss due to the information contained within this book. Either directly or indirectly. You are responsible for your own choices, actions, and results.

Legal Notice:

This book is copyright-protected. This book is only for personal use. You cannot amend, distribute, sell, use, quote or paraphrase any part of the content within this book without the consent of the author or publisher.

Disclaimer Notice:

Please note the information contained within this document is for educational and entertainment purposes only. We have made every effort to present accurate, up-to-date, and reliable information. No warranties of any kind are declared or implied. Readers acknowledge that the author is not engaging in the rendering of legal, financial, medical or professional advice. The content within this book has been derived from various sources. Please consult a licensed professional before attempting any techniques outlined in this book.

By reading this document, the reader agrees that under no circumstances is the author responsible for any losses, direct or indirect, which are incurred as a result of the use of the information contained within this document, including, but not limited to, — errors, omissions, or inaccuracies.

Contents

How To Talk To Anyone: From Small Talk To Big Impact

1. Introduction to Powerful Interactions — 3
2. Managing Social Anxiety — 7
3. Building a Foundation of Confidence — 16
4. Mastering Small Talk — 30
5. De-coding Non-Verbal Communication — 40
6. Empathy and Active Listening — 51
7. Balancing Speaking and Listening — 61
8. Networking and Career Advancement — 72
9. Enhancing Memory and Recall — 81
10. Cultural Sensitivity in Communication — 90
11. Special Considerations for Introverts — 101
12. Advanced Psychological Insights — 111
13. Sustaining Long-Term Growth and Connection — 120
14. Final Word — 131
15. Make a Difference with Your Review and Unlock the Power of Connection — 133

| 16. References | 136 |

Public Speaking : From Stage Fright to Spotlight

1. The Power of Public Speaking	140
2. Conquering Your Fear of Public Speaking	142
3. Finding Your Distinct Public Speaking Voice	158
4. Crafting Compelling Content	171
5. Mastering the Art of Storytelling	185
6. Body Language and Nonverbal Communication	200
7. Vocal Techniques for Maximum Impact	213
8. The Art of Audience Engagement	225
9. Effective Use of Technology and Visual Aids	240
10. Tailoring Your Message Across Various Contexts	252
11. Specialized Techniques for Different Audiences	266
12. Pursuing Growth as a Public Speaker	278
13. Setting Yourself Apart as a Public Speaker	290
14. Final Word	303

How To Talk To Anyone

From Small Talk to Big Impact

Communicate with confidence,
create instant connection and master
every social & professional conversation
even if you're an introvert!

Anne McKeown

1

INTRODUCTION TO POWERFUL INTERACTIONS

"Be who you are and speak from your guts and heart. It's all one has."
Hubert Humphrey

Communication is at the heart of human interaction, yet it remains an area where many of us stumble. Whether at work or in social settings, we can often find ourselves on the outside looking in, unsure of how to connect.

Many years ago, not long after starting a new job, I was invited to a drinks evening with colleagues who had worked together for many years. I remember entering the room and feeling hesitant. I hovered at the edge of the conversation, wrestling with the dilemma: how do I break into this circle? This simple yet profound moment sent me down the path of learning everything I could about communication and social skills.

This book is about those moments. It's about the fear of rejection that keeps us silent, the awkwardness of small talk that makes us stumble, and the misreading of social cues that can lead to misunderstandings. I've repeatedly seen people struggle with these challenges in my many years as a communications coach. Anxiety does not discriminate; it affects corporate leaders, small business owners, and individuals from all walks of life. I know because I've coached them!

My goal with this book is clear: to equip you with practical tools and techniques to communicate with confidence. I want you to create connections that feel genuine and for you to enjoy every interaction, whether it's a casual chat or a critical business meeting. This is not just about talking to anyone; it's about feeling good while doing it.

Let me introduce myself. I'm Anne McKeown, and I've dedicated my career to helping people like you step up, speak up, and show up with confidence. Communication is not a one-size-fits-all skill. It requires understanding your strengths, your fears and your unique voice.

Here are some questions clients have asked me and I've answered throughout this book:

- What techniques can help me manage anxiety during important social interactions?

- How do I make a memorable impression when meeting someone new?

- What are some effective conversation starters for networking events?

- How can I keep a conversation flowing naturally without awkward pauses?

- What strategies can I use to overcome my fear of speaking up in meetings?

- How do I read body language to understand what someone is really thinking?

- What are practical ways to boost my self-confidence in social settings?

- How do I connect on a deeper level with acquaintances and build lasting relationships?

- How can I handle miscommunications or misunderstandings?

- What tips can help me remember names and details about people I meet?

- How do I engage introverted individuals in conversation without overwhelming them?

- What are the best ways to express disagreement without causing conflict?

- How can I tailor my communication style to suit different cultural contexts?

- What should I do if I feel ignored or unheard in a group discussion?

- How do I politely exit a conversation that isn't going well?

If you aspire to connect more deeply with others, to be heard and understood, discover your unique communication style, build your inner confidence and manage social anxiety then this book is for you.

If you are looking to grow personally and professionally, want to master small talk, understand body language, emotional intelligence, attentive listening and networking with ease, look no further.

Each chapter builds on the next and provides insights and strategies tailored to your needs. Whether you're an introvert seeking to navigate extroverted spaces or someone looking to refine your communication skills, there's something here for you.

What sets this book apart is its focus on authenticity. We won't just skim the surface; we'll dive deep into what makes communication meaningful. We'll explore strategies that honor who you are, especially if you're more reserved. You'll learn to communicate in a way that feels true to you.

ANNE MCKEOWN

As we begin, I invite you to see this as more than a book. It's a step-by-step guide, a companion and a source of encouragement.

Let's start this journey together.

2

MANAGING SOCIAL ANXIETY

"Communication is a dance between risk and reward." Anne McKeown

This chapter delves into the multifaceted topic of social anxiety, exploring its origins and manifestations. We look at the genetic and experiential factors that shape it, recognize the societal pressures that amplify it, and introduce the self-awareness needed to navigate it. This journey of understanding lays the foundation for a deeper exploration of techniques and strategies designed to manage and alleviate the impact of social anxiety.

For many, the anticipation of social interactions triggers a flow of physiological reactions that can feel overwhelming. Sweaty palms, a racing heart, and an inexplicable urge to flee are common indications of this invisible burden. Though often unseen by others, these symptoms can significantly influence your life. They can lead to avoidance behaviors, where the desire to escape discomfort overrides the opportunity to connect.

Understanding the roots of social anxiety requires looking at both genetic and environmental factors. Research, including a significant genome-wide association study[1] highlights that social anxiety is often inherited and linked to neurobehavioral traits. Some individuals are naturally more sensitive or introverted, making them more susceptible to anxiety in social settings. Yet, genetics is only a part of the puzzle. Past social experiences also play a crucial role. Negative encounters, such as bullying or rejection, can imprint lasting scars, reinforcing the fear of future interactions. These experiences shape our social blueprint, dictating how we perceive and respond to the world around us.

Societal and cultural influences can further compound these challenges. We live in an era where social media dictates norms and shapes self-perception[2]. Many social media platforms offer curated glimpses of idealized lives, amplifying the pressure to conform. This digital arena blurs the line between genuine connection and superficial interaction. For those with social anxiety, the constant comparison to seemingly perfect lives can exacerbate feelings of inadequacy and fear. The need to project a polished image online often leads to a disconnect between one's true self and the persona they present, further fuelling anxiety. Additionally, cultural expectations often demand adherence to specific behaviors, pressuring individuals to navigate social norms that may not align with their natural personality.

Self-awareness becomes a vital tool in managing these complex layers of social anxiety. It begins with recognizing your patterns and triggers. Are there specific situations that heighten your anxiety? Do certain people or environments make you feel more vulnerable? I recommend documenting your experiences to track these triggers and creating a record to help you identify patterns and recurring themes. Set aside dedicated time each day to journal about your social interactions. Focus on moments that felt particularly challenging. What were the circumstances? Who was involved? How did your body react? Over time, this practice will reveal underlying patterns, offering a roadmap to better understand and manage your anxiety. Reflective practices, such as meditation or quiet contemplation, also offer a space to explore these insights further. They encourage a deeper understanding of your responses and help foster a mindset of acceptance and growth. Mindfulness can also be a powerful ally against anxiety, providing a buffer against the stresses that accompany social interactions.

Mindfulness Techniques for Anxiety Reduction

Imagine you are in a busy room with conversations swirling around you. Your thoughts race, and your breathing quickens, but amid this chaos, there's a tool that can help stabalize you: mindfulness.

At its core, mindfulness is about being present, truly present, in the moment. It involves paying attention to your thoughts and feelings without judgment, allowing you to experience them without being overwhelmed. It encourages a state of calm and clarity, enabling you to navigate social engagements with greater ease. The principles of mindfulness focus on grounding yourself in the present moment, which can significantly reduce anxiety. By centering your attention on the here and now, mindfulness helps break the cycle of relentless worry about what might happen or what others might think.

Deep Breathing

It's easy to integrate simple mindfulness exercises into your daily life. One such exercise is deep breathing. When anxiety strikes, your breath often becomes shallow and rapid, exacerbating feelings of panic. By consciously slowing and deepening your breath, you signal your body to relax, reducing physical symptoms of anxiety. Try inhaling deeply through your nose, holding your breath for a count of four, and exhaling slowly through your mouth. Talk to yourself when doing this, say "I am breathing in calm." Then, "I am breathing out peace." This simple practice can help calm your nerves, allowing you to regain control.

Grounding Techniques

Grounding techniques play a crucial role in anchoring your attention. When you feel overwhelmed, focus on your surroundings. Notice the texture of the chair you're sitting in, the sensation of your feet on the ground, or the sounds around you. These techniques divert your mind from anxious thoughts, helping you remain in the present moment.

Self-Compassion

Mindfulness isn't just about reducing anxiety; it also fosters self-compassion. As you practice mindfulness, you learn to view your thoughts and feelings with a non-judgmental mindset. This shift in perspective encourages a kinder relationship with yourself. Instead of berating yourself for having anxious thoughts, you begin to accept them as part of your experience without letting them define you. Developing self-compassion involves exercises that promote self-acceptance and understanding. One approach is to practice self-kindness. When you notice a critical thought, pause and consider how you would respond to a friend in the same situation. Offer yourself the same empathy and support you'd extend to others. Over time, this practice builds a reservoir of self-compassion, reducing the impact of anxiety on your self-esteem.

Incorporating mindfulness into your daily routine can transform how you experience social interactions. Consider setting aside time each day for meditation or reflection. This practice doesn't have to be lengthy; even five minutes of focused breathing or mindful observation can set a positive tone for your day. As you do your daily tasks, look for opportunities to infuse mindfulness into routine activities. Whether it's savoring the taste of your morning coffee, feeling the water on your skin in the shower, or listening to a loved one, these mindful moments can create pockets of calm throughout your day. By making mindfulness a regular part of your life, you cultivate a sense of peace and presence that extends beyond individual exercises, ultimately enhancing your ability to manage anxiety in all areas of your life.

Strategies for Building Social Confidence

Imagine for a moment your thoughts are the scriptwriters of your life. They craft narratives about your interactions, shaping how you feel and act. As a coach, I help people manage their anxiety by teaching various techniques; one such method is altering these scripts. I examine the intricate relationship between your thoughts, feelings, and behaviors. For instance, consider how a thought like, "I'm going to embarrass myself," can spiral into feelings of panic, leading you to avoid speaking up. We can work together to identify these negative thought patterns, challenging their accuracy and reframing them into supportive, realistic appraisals.

Thought Stopping

Another simple technique is referred to as thought-stopping. This involves mentally halting negative thoughts as they arise. Picture yourself watching a movie on TV where the story is becoming dark and negative. It makes you feel anxious; you don't want to see the ending. All you have to do is take the remote control and press the pause button. By recognizing these thoughts early, you can disrupt the cycle of negativity before it escalates.

Exposure Therapy

A technique, known as exposure therapy, is a method that involves gradually facing anxiety-inducing situations to build confidence. Imagine creating a ladder of social challenges, each rung representing a different level of anxiety. Start by listing situations that trigger your anxiety, ranking them from least to most intimidating. For instance, if public speaking is your greatest fear, you might begin with small group discussions, progressing to larger audiences over time. By practicing exposure in controlled, incremental steps, you gradually desensitize yourself to the fear, proving to your mind that these situations are manageable.

Celebrate Small Wins

As you climb each rung, self-reward plays a crucial role in cementing these positive behavior changes. Celebrating progress, no matter how small reinforces your efforts and enhances motivation. Set achievable goals for each step on your ladder and choose meaningful rewards for reaching them. Perhaps after successfully speaking in a meeting, you treat yourself to a favorite activity or indulge in a special meal. These rewards create positive associations with the experience, encouraging further growth. Over time, this cycle of exposure, achievement and reward nurtures a newfound confidence, transforming how you perceive social interactions.

Rewrite Your Script

I invite you to become an active participant in reshaping your social experiences. By understanding the power of thoughts and behaviors, you can rewrite the script of anxiety that has held you back. With practice, patience, and a willingness to face discomfort, you'll be more equipped to engage authentically and confidently.

Overcoming the Fear of Rejection

Every time we step into a room full of strangers or prepare to speak our minds, a familiar knot tightens in our stomachs. It's the fear of rejection, a profoundly ingrained anxiety that whispers caution in our ears. This fear isn't just about the immediate sting of someone turning away; it's rooted in our evolutionary past. Once upon a time, being accepted by our tribe was a matter of survival. Rejection could mean isolation, and isolation spelled danger. Fast forward to today, and our minds still cling to this ancient instinct, even though the stakes have changed. In modern society, rejection rarely threatens our existence, yet it continues to wield enormous influence over our actions and decisions.

Think about this: you're in a meeting, eager to share a new idea. But doubt creeps in, and you stay silent, fearing others might dismiss your thoughts. This scenario is all too common. The fear of rejection can paralyze us, causing us to miss opportunities to connect and grow. However, understanding this fear is the first step toward managing it. Recognizing that it's a natural response can help diminish its power over us.

Cognitive Reframing

To manage rejection fear, several strategies can be incredibly helpful. One technique I find to be extremely effective is cognitive reframing. This involves identifying negative thoughts about rejection and deliberately shifting them to more positive or neutral perspectives. For instance, instead of thinking, "They'll think I'm foolish," you might reframe it as, "This is an opportunity to share my perspective, and it might be valuable."

Vizualisation Techniques

As humans, our imagination creates pictures of every scenario that could unfold. Unfortunately, most of these pictures are negative. The subconscious tries to keep us safe by warning us that unfamiliar territory is ahead. I suggest using conscious visualization techniques to foster positive outcomes and counteract this. Before entering a potentially daunting situation, envision a successful interaction. Picture yourself speaking confidently, see the nods of agreement from those around you, and feel the satisfaction of being heard. This mental rehearsal can prepare you for real-life situations, reducing anxiety and boosting self-assurance.

Embrace Rejection

Embracing rejection itself can be a powerful tool for growth. Many renowned individuals have faced rejection on their paths to success. Consider Steve Jobs, who was once ousted from the very company he founded. His story is a testament that rejection, rather than an end, can be a catalyst for new beginnings. It teaches resilience, sharpens focus, and redirects us toward better opportunities. Lessons learned from rejection are invaluable; they instil humility, encourage adaptability, and can lead to unexpected triumphs.

Lean Into Discomfort

Taking risks in conversation is essential to overcoming the fear of rejection. By stepping out of your comfort zone and initiating challenging dialogues, you build a tolerance for discomfort and learn to navigate it easily. Start by choosing safe environments for practice, like discussion groups or classes where open dialogue is encouraged. Here, you can experiment with expressing your ideas and receiving feedback in a supportive setting. These experiences bolster your confidence and prepare you for more challenging interactions.

In the end, communication is a dance between risk and reward. By understanding the roots of rejection fear and employing strategies to manage it, you can transform potential barriers into building blocks. Embrace the discomfort, take calculated risks, and remember that each conversation is an opportunity to learn and grow. The more you practice, the more adept you will become at turning fear into fuel for connection.

Cultivating a Growth Mindset for Social Success

In your mind's eye, see yourself at a social gathering, surrounded by people effortlessly engaging in lively conversations. You want to join in, but a nagging voice in your head tells you that you're not naturally sociable. This is where the concept of a growth mindset becomes crucial. Coined by psychologist Carol Dweck[3] a growth mindset involves the belief that abilities can be developed through dedication and hard work. It's the opposite of a fixed mindset, which views traits like intelligence and social skills as static. A growth mindset opens doors, allowing us to see setbacks not as failures but as opportunities to learn and improve. In communication, this mindset translates to seeing each interaction as a stepping stone, not a test.

Consider two people at that same gathering. One with a fixed mindset might think, "I'm just not good at small talk," and retreat to a corner. The other, embracing a growth mindset, thinks, "I can get better at this," and seeks out conversation, eager to improve. This mindset shift impacts learning and development significantly. By acknowledging that our abilities aren't set in stone, we free ourselves to experiment, make mistakes and grow. It encourages us to step out of our comfort zones, transforming how we approach communication challenges.

Developing a growth mindset involves specific, actionable strategies. Start by setting achievable communication goals. These could be as simple as initiating one new conversation each day or practicing active listening in meetings. By setting targets, you create an outline for improvement, allowing you to track progress and celebrate small wins.

Befriend Feedback

Embracing feedback is another critical component. Feedback from colleagues or friends provides invaluable insights into your communication style. Use it as a tool for refinement, not a critique of your abilities. Reframe mistakes as learning opportunities rather than failures. When a conversation doesn't go as planned, ask yourself, "What can I learn from this?" This reflection turns each interaction into a chance to grow.

Consistent Practice

Persistence and effort are the backbone of any growth mindset. Consistent practice is vital to enhancing communication skills. A client of mine who was initially terrified of public speaking committed to presenting at a local event every month despite her fear. She signed up to speak at local Probus clubs, Toastmasters, storytelling events, and libraries in her area. Her persistence paid off, and she gradually became a sought-after speaker. Her transformation was a pleasure to watch and highlights the power of effort and the resilience it builds.

The path to improving social skills is not a straight line; it's a series of gradual improvements that compound over time. Each effort, no matter how small, contributes to growth.

3

BUILDING A FOUNDATION OF CONFIDENCE

"Great communication begins with connection." Oprah Winfrey

Years ago, during a workshop, I watched one of the attendees, Paul, struggle to speak up. He sat quietly, his eyes darting between his colleagues as they engaged in animated discussion. Having worked with Paul previously I knew he had brilliant ideas, but his words seemed stuck somewhere between his mind and his mouth.

This struggle is more common than you may think. Regardless of our skills or intellect, many of us have encountered situations where our confidence wavers. We hesitate to speak up, fearing judgment or rejection. This chapter aims to dismantle those barriers, empowering you to find and use your voice.

Confidence in communication is about more than just speaking loudly or often. It's about knowing who you are and expressing that with conviction.

It involves understanding your unique communication style and how it influences your interactions. This self-awareness is the first step in building a solid foundation for confident communication.

Understanding Your Unique Communication Style

Communication styles are diverse and shaped by our personalities, upbringing and experiences. They dictate how we express ourselves and interpret others. Broadly, communication styles fall into four categories: assertive, passive, passive-aggressive and aggressive.

- Assertive communication, the gold standard, involves expressing your thoughts and feelings honestly while respecting others. It promotes healthy interactions and builds trust.

- Passive communicators, on the other hand, often hold back, avoiding conflict at the expense of their own needs. This can lead to misunderstandings and resentment.

- Passive-aggressive style is where individuals express negative emotions indirectly, often leading to confusion and tension.

- Aggressive communicators are confrontational, using anger and dominance, which can create fear and hostility.

Recognizing your communication style is crucial. It helps you understand why you interact the way you do and how others perceive you. To identify your style, consider reflecting on past interactions. Do you often avoid conflict, or do you tend to dominate conversations? Do you express your needs directly, or do you hint at them? To discover your communication style, complete the quiz at the end of this chapter.

Each communication style has its strengths and weaknesses. For example, assertiveness fosters respect and clarity but requires balance to avoid appearing aggressive. Passivity may maintain peace but as said before, often ignores personal needs. Passive-aggressiveness can mask emotions, leading to unresolved conflicts. Aggressiveness might get results but at the cost of relationships. Understanding these dynamics and being open to addressing your weaknesses allows you to leverage your strengths.

For instance, an assertive communicator can enhance their approach by incorporating empathy, ensuring their message is heard and felt.

Flexibility is key, allowing you to navigate different scenarios effectively. You might need to be assertive in negotiations at work but adopt a more passive approach in a supportive role. Sometimes, you may need to blend styles. In some professional settings, assertiveness paired with diplomacy can enhance leadership and teamwork. In personal relationships, balancing assertiveness with compassion can foster deeper connections.

Self-awareness and reflection are the cornerstones of confident communication. They encourage growth and adaptability. Regularly assessing your interactions makes you more attuned to your communication patterns and their impact.

I encourage you to set aside time each week for reflection. Note any significant conversations, your feelings at the time, and any lessons learned. Over time, this practice will produce patterns that help enhance your communication skills and build your confidence to engage fully and authentically in every interaction.

Harnessing the Power of Authenticity

Imagine stepping into a room where every conversation feels like a performance, where each word is carefully crafted to fit an image that isn't yours. We've all been there, feeling the pressure to conform, to say what we think others want to hear. But what if instead of playing a part, you could show up as yourself, genuine and unfiltered?

Authenticity in communication is about being true to who you are, and it's crucial for building meaningful connections. When people sense genuineness, they feel they can trust you, and trust is the foundation of all lasting relationships. It's like opening a window to who you are, inviting others to see the real you rather than just a reflection.

Being authentic also means allowing yourself to be vulnerable. It means admitting that you don't have all the answers or that you're unsure, and that's okay. Vulnerability isn't weakness; it's an invitation for others to engage with you on a deeper level. When you share your struggles or uncertainties, you create space for others to do the same, paving the way for genuine connections. Consider the people you admire most. Often, it's not their successes that resonate with us, but their humanity, their willingness to show their imperfections. This openness encourages others to open up, fostering a sense of community and understanding.

Being authentic breaks down barriers and brings people closer. I know from personal experience. When starting my business many years ago, I was invited to a breakfast meeting with other professional women. We were asked to introduce ourselves one by one; the women before me spoke of their important roles and achievements; they were lawyers, accountants, doctors, and professors. When it was my turn, I didn't want to lie so I told them that I was starting out in my coaching business and I thought I was in the wrong room because I wasn't as successful in my endeavours as the accomplished women who spoke before me. I immediately regretted being so honest and could feel my body shrink back into the chair. But then an incredible thing happened. The next woman to speak said that her business was going into liquidation, and she couldn't sleep at night worrying about it. The woman after her shared that she was trying for a baby and wished she could work part-time and was jealous that my business wasn't taking up my whole life. And so, the stories continued around the table. Each woman taking off her mask, showing their true selves and sharing their struggles. The organizer later told me that in my openness, I had unwittingly given everyone permission to be authentic, and we all benefitted from a more profound connection. To this day, I am still friends with many of the women that were in that room.

Authenticity doesn't mean airing every thought that crosses your mind. It's about sharing the parts of yourself that are true and relevant to the situation. It's a delicate balance. You want to be honest without being rude and open without oversharing. Start by using "I" statements to express your thoughts and feelings. This way, you take ownership of your words, making it clear that you're speaking from your perspective. When you disagree, do so respectfully, acknowledging the other person's viewpoint. It's about being honest while maintaining empathy and respect for others.

Challenges to authenticity abound, especially in a world that often values conformity. Societal norms and expectations can pressure us to hide our true selves. The fear of judgment looms large, making authenticity seem risky. But these challenges can be overcome. Begin by questioning the norms that don't serve you. Ask yourself why you need to conform and whether those expectations align with your values. Strategies for overcoming fear of judgment include surrounding yourself with supportive people and practicing self-compassion. Accept that not everyone will appreciate authenticity, but many will; those are the connections worth fostering.

We can see authentic communication shine through real-world examples. Oprah Winfrey's authenticity has made her a trusted figure worldwide. Her willingness to share personal stories and vulnerabilities has created a profound connection with her audience. Authenticity might mean admitting a mistake at work and proposing a solution rather than brushing it under the rug. Or it could be speaking up about your needs in a relationship, even if it feels uncomfortable. These acts of honesty, though small, have the power to transform interactions from superficial exchanges to meaningful dialogues.

As we explore the power of authenticity, remember that it's not about perfection. It's about showing up as you are, embracing your imperfections and inviting others to do the same. As you can see from my earlier story, authentic communication creates a ripple effect, encouraging those around us to communicate more openly and honestly. It builds trust, deepens relationships and enriches every interaction. As you continue to express yourself authentically, you'll find that your connections become more genuine, your conversations more rewarding and your interactions more fulfilling. Each step toward authenticity is a step toward more profound, meaningful communication.

Building a Supportive Social Environment

Creating a supportive network is very important in building social confidence. Imagine stepping into a space where people understand your challenges and where sharing your experiences feels natural. Having friends or groups who share similar struggles can significantly alleviate the weight of social anxiety. It's about finding those who resonate with your journey, those who nod knowingly when you express your fears.

Engaging with supportive online communities or forums can also be a lifeline. These digital spaces offer anonymity and a platform to connect with others facing similar issues. Here, you can exchange stories, offer advice, and celebrate small victories without fearing judgment. In these interactions, you realize you're not alone; a whole world of people is navigating similar paths, ready to offer a listening ear and a compassionate heart.

Cultivating positive social connections requires intentionality and openness. It's about seeking out environments that feel safe and nurturing, where interactions are genuine and supportive. Initiating conversations with like-minded individuals can form the bedrock of such connections. Start by attending events or joining groups that align with your interests. Whether it's a book club, a sports team, or an art class, shared passions often pave the way for deeper connections. These activities provide a natural context for conversation, reducing the pressure to perform or impress. As you engage, focus on building relationships that are nurturing, where you can be yourself without fear of judgment. Approach these interactions with kindness and authenticity, allowing them to unfold naturally.

Communication plays a vital role in expressing your needs and boundaries within these relationships. It's about asserting yourself respectfully and ensuring your comfort and well-being are prioritized. This might mean saying no to invitations that feel overwhelming or asking for support when you need it. Learning to express your feelings openly can strengthen your connections, as it encourages honesty and transparency. When you articulate your needs, you give others the opportunity to understand and support you. This exchange fosters trust and mutual respect, creating a foundation where both parties feel valued and heard. Practicing these communication skills can transform your interactions, making them more fulfilling and less anxiety-inducing.

Building a personalized support system involves identifying reliable and empathetic individuals who can offer encouragement and accountability. These are the people who will check in with you, celebrate your successes, and lend a shoulder when times get tough. Consider creating a regular schedule to connect with them through phone calls, texts, or in-person meetings. These check-ins provide a consistent source of support, helping you stay grounded and motivated. Share your goals with them and invite their feedback and encouragement. A network like this bolsters your confidence and reminds you that you're part of something larger than yourself. It's a reminder that even when anxiety feels insurmountable, you're never alone.

As you navigate building this network, remember it's an evolving process. Relationships take time to develop, and it's okay to start small. Trust grows with each interaction, blossoming into a network of support that empowers you to face challenges head-on. Surrounding yourself with understanding individuals can be transformative, turning anxiety from an isolating experience into one of shared understanding and camaraderie.

Quiz : Discover Your Communication Style

Instructions: Answer each question honestly. Choose the option that most closely aligns with how you usually respond in the situations described.

When someone interrupts you while you're speaking, how do you typically react?

A. I stop talking and let them speak.

B. I express my frustration either then or later in an indirect way.

C. I point out the interruption and ask to finish what I was saying.

D. I might snap at them or interrupt them back.

How do you handle criticism from others?

A. I tend to stay quiet even if I disagree.

B. I say nothing but later complain about it to someone else.

C. I listen, ask questions, and try to use the feedback constructively.

D. I often feel attacked and respond defensively.

What is. your approach to expressing disagreement?

A. I rarely express disagreement to avoid conflict.

B. I might not say anything but will show my displeasure in other ways.

C. I clearly state why I disagree in a respectful manner.

D. I am very direct and can get loud or demanding.

In a group decision-making process, how do you contribute?

A. I tend to go along with what others decide.

B. I might not voice my opinion and possibly resent the decision later.

C. I share my opinions and consider others' points of view as well.

D. I push hard for my ideas and struggle to accept other perspectives.

How do you feel about asking others for help?

A. I hesitate to ask for help as I don't want to bother others.

B. I complain about my situation hoping someone will offer to help.

C. I comfortably ask for help when needed and offer help in return.

D. I demand help from others and might get impatient.

When you're angry about something, how do you express it?

A. I keep it to myself to avoid confrontation.

B. I might not say anything directly but will make sarcastic comments.

C. I calmly explain why I'm upset and discuss possible solutions.

D. I often let others know exactly why I'm angry in a heated manner.

What do you do if you need something from someone who is busy?

A. I wait until they are free, even if it takes a long time.

B. I wait. I might make passive comments about how busy they always are.

C. I ask them when would be a good time to talk or help.

D. I insist they make time for me as soon as possible.

How do you respond when you feel you're being treated unfairly?

A. I often don't speak up to avoid making things worse.

B. I may not confront the issue directly but hold a grudge.

C. I address the issue directly and seek a fair resolution.

D. I get angry and demand an explanation.

What's your usual way of handling a conflict with a friend?

A. I try to smooth things over, sometimes ignoring my own feelings.

B. I give them the silent treatment until they figure out what's wrong.

C. I discuss the problem openly and seek a mutual understanding.

D. I confront them aggressively to make my point.

How do you express appreciation or gratitude to someone?

A. I feel it, but don't always say it directly.

B. I might send a message later instead of saying it in person.

C. I openly express my gratitude and appreciation.

D. I might not say thanks unless it's a big favor.

How do you deal with being given tasks you feel are beneath you?

A. I do them quietly without complaint.

B. I might do them but not without expressing some sarcasm.

C. I discuss the assignment with the person to understand their rationale.

D. I refuse or argue about the appropriateness of the tasks.

When someone shares good news, how do you respond?

A. I might smile, but I'm quiet.

B. I say congratulations, but I might not seem enthusiastic.

C. I respond enthusiastically and encourage them to tell me more.

D. I might make a quick comment, then switch the conversation to my experiences.

Scoring Guide:

Mostly A's: Passive Communication Style

Mostly B's: Passive-Aggressive Communication Style

Mostly C's: Assertive Communication Style

Mostly D's: Aggressive Communication Style

A: Passive Communication Style

Strengths:

Good at listening and avoiding conflicts.

Often perceived as easy-going and approachable.

Weaknesses:

May not express personal needs or opinions, leading to potential misunderstanding and resentment.

Can be overlooked in personal and professional settings due to a lack of assertiveness.

Improvement Tips:

Practice stating your needs and opinions in small, non-threatening settings to build confidence.

Work on setting and respecting personal boundaries. Remember, it's okay to say no.

Enhance your self-esteem through affirmations and positive self-talk to support more assertive behavior.

B: Passive-Aggressive Communication Style

Strengths:

Can be highly diplomatic, managing to navigate through difficult situations subtly.

Often creative in expressing feelings without direct confrontation.

Weaknesses:

Indirect communication can lead to misunderstandings and unresolved conflicts.

May harbor resentment and cause others to feel frustrated when the real feelings are masked by sarcasm or backhanded comments.

Improvement Tips:

Aim for direct communication about your feelings and needs. Be honest and open to prevent misunderstandings.

Reflect on the reasons behind your indirectness; understanding these can help you address issues more directly.

Learn to manage anger and frustration through healthier outlets like exercise, journaling, or speaking with a therapist.

C: Assertive Communication Style

Strengths:

Generally clear, direct, and respected for honest communication.

Good at negotiating and expressing needs without infringing on the rights of others.

Weaknesses:

May sometimes come off as too blunt or straightforward, which can be perceived as insensitivity.

Risk of overconfidence which might lead to less compromise.

Improvement Tips:

Focus on maintaining empathy and consider others' emotions when you communicate.

Practice active listening to ensure that you understand others' perspectives and needs as well.

Continue to practice self-awareness to ensure that assertiveness does not slip into aggressiveness.

D: Aggressive Communication Style

Strengths:

Very clear about personal wants and needs.

Can be highly effective in leadership roles where decision-making and direction are required.

Weaknesses:

Often seen as overbearing, which can alienate others and create hostility.

Might overlook others' needs, leading to poor relationships and team dynamics.

Improvement Tips:

Work on emotional regulation skills to handle conflicts calmly and without aggression.

Practice active listening to understand and validate others' points of view.

Focus on collaborative problem-solving techniques to ensure all voices are heard and integrated into decisions.

By identifying your primary communication style, you can leverage your strengths and actively work on your weaknesses to improve your overall effectiveness in both personal and professional interactions.

Are you ready to master small talk? You will be once you realise how valuable it is? Turn the page because that's what we're discussing in the next chapter.

4

MASTERING SMALL TALK

"Small talk, though often dismissed as trivial, serves a vital purpose."
Anne McKeown

Picture yourself at an after-work networking event. Mingling voices surround you. You're holding a drink, glancing around and you notice a familiar feeling creeping in—a mix of excitement and anxiety. You want to connect, to join in, but the right words seem out of reach. We've all been there, standing at the threshold of interaction, where small talk acts as the bridge.

This chapter is about perfecting the art of starting conversations, turning that initial awkwardness into ease. Small talk, though often dismissed as trivial, serves a vital purpose. It sets the stage, breaking down barriers and laying the groundwork for deeper connections. Effective icebreakers are the key to this process. They open doors, inviting others into conversation with warmth and curiosity.

Icebreakers are more than just a tool; they're a way to transform the social environment. When used effectively, they ease tension and invite genuine engagement. They help you move past the initial stiffness, setting a tone that encourages openness. Icebreakers can dissolve the invisible walls that separate us, whether at a networking event, a casual gathering, or a business meeting. They are the first step in building rapport, signaling you're approachable and interested. The right icebreaker can turn a room full of strangers into a group of potential connections within minutes.

At networking events full of professionals from all walks of life, I've asked, "What brings you here today?" It's perfect for this situation. It's open-ended, inviting the other person to share their motivations and interests, creating a natural segue into a more detailed conversation. In a more casual setting, like a party, I've asked, "Have you tried the [food/drink]? What do you think of it?" This approach is light and engaging and taps into the shared experience of the event itself. Or perhaps you're catching up with someone you haven't seen lately. "What's been the highlight of your week so far?" is a question that opens the door to personal stories and shows genuine interest in their life.

Building a toolkit of versatile icebreakers is like having a Swiss Army knife for social situations. These questions and statements are adaptable, suitable for different contexts, and can be tailored to reflect your personality. They serve as reliable starting points while allowing flexibility to adjust based on the setting and the person you're speaking with. The goal is to engage without overwhelming and to pique curiosity without prying. A well-chosen icebreaker can be the difference between a fleeting exchange and a memorable connection.

As you engage, it's crucial to read the room—literally. Pay attention to body language and facial expressions, as they can reveal more than words. Are they leaning in, making eye contact, or smiling? These are signs of interest and receptiveness. Conversely, crossed arms, glances around the room, or monosyllabic answers might indicate discomfort or disinterest. Listening for verbal cues and tone of voice also provides insight. Are their responses enthusiastic or hesitant? Do they mirror your energy, or are they holding back? Adjust your approach by shifting topics or asking more open-ended questions to encourage participation.

Creativity and personalization are your allies in crafting unique icebreakers. Let your personality shine through, using humor or shared interests to make the conversation yours. If you share a love for a particular hobby or current event, weave it into your opening line. Humor, when used mindfully, can break the tension and invite laughter, a universal connector. A well-timed joke or witty observation can disarm and delight, making the interaction memorable. However, it's important to gauge the appropriateness of humor, ensuring it aligns with the setting and the individual's comfort level. This blend of creativity and personalization not only differentiates your approach but also enhances the authenticity of the exchange.

Craft Your Own Icebreakers

Take a moment to jot down three icebreakers that resonate with you. Consider your interests, recent experiences, or current events that intrigue you. How can these be molded into engaging opening lines? Reflect on past interactions—what worked well, and what fell flat? Use these insights to refine your approach, creating a personal repertoire of icebreakers that feel natural and inviting. As you practice, notice how these openers influence the flow of conversation and the connections you form.

Transforming Small Talk into Meaningful Dialogue

Small talk can often feel shallow, a necessary but mundane start to conversations. Yet, the beauty of small talk lies in its potential, a stepping stone toward more profound, more meaningful dialogue. It's an opportunity to transition from surface-level chatter to conversations that leave you feeling enriched and connected.

Active listening is key to this transition, an often-underestimated skill that transforms interactions. By truly listening, you catch nuances and unspoken cues hinting at someone's passions or interests. Follow-up questions play a vital role too. They show you're engaged and willing to explore beyond the initial topic. When someone mentions their recent vacation, don't just nod. Ask about their favorite moment or why they chose that destination. These questions invite elaboration, nudging the dialogue into more substantive territory.

Transitioning to deeper discussions requires an eye for opportunities. Spotting these moments is like reading between the lines. A casual mention of a hobby might be an invitation to delve into a shared passion. Recognizing these cues, you can smoothly guide the conversation to topics that resonate more deeply. This requires a blend of curiosity and intuition, allowing the conversation to evolve naturally. Steer discussions toward meaningful subjects using open-ended questions. These questions can't be answered with a simple yes or no, encouraging others to share more. Instead of asking, "Do you like your job?" try, "What do you find most rewarding about your work?" This invites the other person to reflect and reveal more, setting the stage for a richer dialogue. Sharing personal insights or anecdotes also deepens the conversation. By offering a glimpse into your own experiences, you create a space where others feel comfortable doing the same. It's about creating a dialogue that is reciprocal and genuine.

Empathy and curiosity are your allies in this endeavor. They fuel your interest in others, allowing you to see things from their perspective. Empathy involves more than just understanding; it's about conveying that understanding in your responses. Instead of a generic "I see," try something like, "That sounds challenging, how did you manage it?" This acknowledges their experience and encourages them to open up further. Curiosity drives you to ask questions that matter, ones that reveal stories and insights. It's about showing genuine interest and a desire to learn and connect. Encouraging others to share their stories is crucial. Often, people hold back, unsure if their experiences are worth sharing. By expressing curiosity, you signal that you're not just listening but eager to understand their world.

Consider a networking event where you're speaking with a colleague about a recent industry conference. Instead of sticking to the basics, you ask, "What was the most surprising thing you learned there?" This question transitions the conversation from mere information exchange to a discussion about insights and learning. The colleague shares an innovative idea they encountered, sparking a dialogue about industry trends and personal growth.

Think about a casual chat with a neighbor. They mention their garden, and instead of just commenting on the weather, you ask about what they enjoy growing the most. This leads to a conversation about sustainable living and personal values, topics that might not have surfaced otherwise.

These examples illustrate the power of transitioning small talk into meaningful dialogue. They show how simple questions can uncover layers of experience and understanding. The conversations we cherish are often those where we feel heard and valued, where the exchange moves beyond the mundane. Small talk is the gateway, but the empathy, curiosity and willingness to explore deeper turn ordinary exchanges into significant connections.

Finding Common Ground

Imagine you're at a friend's dinner party, surrounded by unfamiliar faces. The conversation ebbs and flows around you, and you search for a way to connect with the person beside you. In such moments, discovering common ground becomes a lifeline. It transforms strangers into acquaintances and acquaintances into friends. Shared interests serve as the glue that binds us, turning fleeting exchanges into meaningful connections. When you identify a mutual hobby, a recent news event, or even a shared acquaintance, you create a bridge that spans the gap between you and the other person. This connection fosters rapport and lays the foundation for deeper engagement, making the conversation feel less like an obligation and more like a shared adventure.

Topics with universal appeal offer a reliable starting point. Travel, for example, is a rich vein to mine. Whether it's the destinations you've visited, dream of seeing, or simply the allure of exploring new places, travel stories are laden with vivid imagery and personal insight. Discussing recent books or movies can also ignite a spark. Narratives often reflect our values and experiences, providing a canvas for dialogue. "Have you read anything interesting lately?" or "What movie has caught your attention?" are questions that invite others to share their tastes and opinions.

Food, too, is a universal connector. Given our shared love for culinary delights, conversations about favorite meals, new recipes, or memorable dining experiences will likely resonate with almost anyone.

Uncovering commonalities is an art, one that involves curiosity and a dash of storytelling. As you engage, ask open-ended questions that invite others to share their experiences. "What inspired your love for travel?" or "How did that book change your perspective?" are inquiries that encourage others to open up. Sharing your own stories in response creates a reciprocal and engaging dialogue. This exchange of narratives not only highlights similarities but also builds a sense of camaraderie.

Humor can be particularly effective in uncovering common ground. Light-hearted jokes about shared experiences or playful banter about everyday mishaps can make the atmosphere more relaxed and enjoyable.

Navigating conversations requires an awareness of potential pitfalls. Certain topics, like politics or religion, can be divisive, especially in initial interactions. Such subjects often evoke strong opinions and emotions, risking conflict in an otherwise pleasant exchange. It's wise to steer clear until you know the other person better and feel confident that the conversation can remain respectful and balanced. Similarly, overly personal questions can intrude upon privacy, making others uncomfortable. Striking the right balance involves gauging the other person's openness and comfort level, ensuring that your questions invite rather than intrude.

Finding common ground is a delicate balance of curiosity and empathy.

It requires an openness to explore new perspectives and a willingness to share your own. As you navigate these conversations, remember that the goal is not to agree on everything but to find those precious moments of connection that make the dialogue worthwhile. By focusing on shared interests and avoiding contentious topics, you create a space where genuine rapport can flourish, transforming simple exchanges into enriching experiences.

Navigating Awkward Silences with Confidence

There you are, mid-conversation, when suddenly the words dry up, leaving a silence hanging between you and the other person. It's a moment we've all experienced, one that can make your heart race and your mind scramble for the nearest exit. But what if these pauses aren't the conversational villains, we often make them out to be? Silences in conversation can serve as valuable moments of reflection or transition, offering a break for both parties to process what's been said. They provide the opportunity to gather thoughts and consider the next direction the conversation might take. Instead of viewing these silences as uncomfortable voids to be quickly filled, recognize them as natural pauses that are part of any dialogue.

Managing pauses with ease involves a mix of humor, observation, and a touch of creativity. When the silence stretches, sometimes a light-hearted comment can ease the tension, inviting a shared laugh and shifting the focus away from the awkwardness. You might comment on something amusing in your surroundings, like the quirky art on the wall or the peculiar choice of music. This not only fills the silence but can also redirect the conversation towards a new topic. Alternatively, use the silence as a moment to make an external observation. Perhaps you notice a beautiful sunset outside or the bustling energy of the café. These observations can inspire a fresh angle for the conversation, guiding it naturally into new territory without forcing the flow.

Patience and composure are your allies during these moments. Staying relaxed and present allows the conversation to evolve at its own pace, without the pressure to rush or force words. As mentioned previously, simple breathing exercises can help maintain calm. Try inhaling deeply through your nose, holding for a moment, and then exhaling slowly and quietly. This practice calms your nerves and enables you to stay grounded in the moment. Focusing on the other person's non-verbal cues, can also keep you engaged without feeling the need to fill every pause with words. By embracing the silence, you demonstrate confidence and comfort in the conversation, allowing both parties the space to think and reflect.

I've found that silences have punctuated some of my most memorable conversations. There was a time I sat across from a friend at a café, where a sudden pause led us both to gaze out the window. The shared silence was filled with an unspoken understanding, and when we resumed talking, it was about something entirely different—deeper, more personal. That pause had allowed our thoughts to wander and reconnect on a new level. Another incident was during a recent family gathering where a lull in the conversation allowed my aunt to share a story we hadn't heard before, the content of which brought us all closer.

Remember that silences are not your enemy. They can be moments of introspection and opportunities for new beginnings. Embrace them with patience, use them to your advantage, and let them guide you to connections that resonate. Silences needn't be feared; they can bridge understanding and depth. As we move forward, consider how pauses can enhance your interactions, offering clarity and insight. Each pause is a chance for a new beginning, a fresh perspective, or a deeper connection.

Social ice-breakers to help you start a conversation.

"Have you read any good books lately?"
This can be a gateway to talking about common interests in literature or recommendations.

"What's the best movie you've seen recently?"
Movies are a popular topic and can lead to longer, engaging conversations.

"Are you a cat person or a dog person?"
This question is light-hearted and can lead to funny stories about pets.

"What's your favorite travel destination?"
Travel elicits memories of good times and dreams of future adventures."

"Do you have a favorite local restaurant or coffee shop?"
Recommendations for food or hangouts often lead to mutual interests or plans to visit them together.

"What kind of music do you like to listen to?"
Music is a universal language and discussing favorite genres or artists can be very bonding.

"Have you picked up any new hobbies recently?"
This can uncover new activities they are passionate about or challenges they've taken on.

"What's the best piece of advice you've ever received?"
This question can lead to meaningful conversations about life lessons and personal philosophies.

"If you could learn one new professional or personal skill, what would it be?"
This opens up a conversation about aspirations and interests.

"What's your go-to comfort food?"
Food often connects people and talking about comfort foods can be a warm and friendly topic.

Professional ice-breakers to help you facilitate conversation in a workplace or networking environment.

"How did you start your career in this industry?"
Understanding someone's professional journey can offer insights and shared experiences.

"Have you attended any interesting webinars or conferences lately?"
Sharing knowledge gained from industry events can foster learning and partnership opportunities.

"What trends do you see shaping our industry?"
Discussing future predictions can show their insight into industry dynamics and their forward-thinking mindset.

"What do you enjoy most about working in this field?"
This can highlight the positives of the industry and what motivates them professionally.

"What's the last professional book you read and would recommend?"
Recommendations can lead to shared learning resources and further discussion on professional growth.

"What project are you currently excited about at work?"
This question directly relates to their professional interests and can spark a conversation about shared areas of expertise or different fields.

"Who in your field do you most admire and why?"
This can lead to discussions about industry leaders, inspirational figures, and the qualities valued in your shared profession.

"What's one piece of technology you can't work without?"
Discussing tools of the trade can lead to practical tips and mutual interests in tech.

"What professional achievement are you most proud of?"
This allows them to share successes, which can be inspirational and enlightening.

"What's the best career advice you've ever received?"
Sharing and receiving advice can build a foundation for a mentorship-like relationship.

5

DE-CODING NON-VERBAL COMMUNICATION

"You can't not communicate. Everything you say and do sends a message."
James Borg

Imagine you're at a friend's birthday party, trying to converse with someone new. The words come easily, but something feels off. You can't quite put your finger on it, yet an invisible barrier seems to linger. This is the silent interplay of body language—an unspoken dialogue that shapes our interactions profoundly. While we often focus on what we say, how we say it can be just as important, if not more so.

The 7-38-55 Rule

Dr. Albert Mehrabian, a researcher and professor emeritus of psychology at UCLA, studied human communication patterns in the 1960s. His research[4] specifically focused on inconsistent messages involving feelings and attitudes. He concluded that the interpretation of a message is 7 percent verbal (words only), 38 percent vocal (tone of voice, inflection, and other sounds), and 55 percent non-verbal (body language, facial expressions, posture, etc.). This breakdown is commonly summarized as the "7-38-55 Rule." It's important to note that this statistic applies primarily to situations where someone communicates feelings or attitudes; it isn't a general rule that applies to all types of communication. Having said that, it is a statistic we can't ignore. Understanding non-verbal communication allows you to read between the lines, offering insights into emotions and intentions that might otherwise remain hidden.

Body Language Basics

Body language basics begin with posture and stance, foundational elements conveying openness or defensiveness. An open posture, characterized by uncrossed arms and a relaxed stance, signals receptivity and ease. It invites others in, creating an atmosphere of approachability. Conversely, crossed arms or a rigid posture can suggest defensiveness or discomfort, erecting an invisible wall between you and the other person. This is not just about physical positioning; it's about the emotional message you project.

Our gestures also play a crucial role in communication. They can emphasize spoken words, adding clarity and passion, or contradict them, leading to confusion. For instance, a nod while saying "yes" reinforces agreement, while a shrug might suggest uncertainty, even if you are verbally saying "yes".

Observing body language cues requires attention to detail and context. Signs of interest or disengagement can be subtle yet telling. Leaning in, maintaining eye contact, and nodding are indicators of engagement and interest. They show that the person is present and actively participating in the exchange. On the other hand, glancing around the room, fidgeting, or checking a phone can signal disengagement, suggesting that their mind is elsewhere. Stress or discomfort often manifests through physical cues such as clenched fists, tense shoulders, or rapid blinking. These signs reveal underlying emotions that words might not explicitly express. You gain a deeper understanding of the emotional landscape within interactions by tuning into these cues.

Practical Applications

Your body language can significantly influence the outcomes of any meeting or discussion. Consider the two following examples:

Workplace Interaction:
In a team meeting, a manager is discussing the rollout of a new project. Sarah, a team member, has concerns about the timeline, believing it to be too aggressive. During the meeting, Sarah sits with her arms crossed, leaning slightly back in her chair, and avoids eye contact with her manager. Her facial expressions are flat with occasional frowns.

Influence of Body Language:
Sarah's body language signals disapproval and disengagement. The manager, picking up on these cues, might perceive Sarah as resistant or uncooperative. This could lead the manager to dismiss her concerns without fully understanding them, potentially missing out on valuable feedback that could improve the project's success. Conversely, if Sarah maintained open body language—leaning forward, nodding, and maintaining eye contact—it might encourage a more constructive conversation and willingness from the manager to consider her feedback.

Negotiation Interaction:
Alex is negotiating a contract with a potential new client. The stakes are high, and Alex wants to secure a profitable and fair deal. Throughout the negotiation he uses open palm gestures, maintains good eye contact and nods when the client speaks, signaling attentiveness and openness. When discussing terms, Alex's posture is upright but relaxed, and he uses his hands to emphasize key points gently.

Influence of Body Language:
Alex's body language conveys confidence and sincerity, making the client feel respected and valued. This approach fosters a positive atmosphere and encourages the client to be more open and transparent about what they need from the deal. As a result, both parties are more likely to find a mutually beneficial agreement.

These examples illustrate how subtle non-verbal cues can significantly affect the dynamics and outcomes of professional interactions.

Learning From Experts – Oprah Winfrey's Interview Techniques

Oprah Winfrey, renowned for her empathetic and effective interview style, employs body language to connect deeply with her guests. She often leans forward slightly, signaling interest and engagement. Her facial expressions mirror those of her guest, which helps to establish a rapport and shows empathy. For instance, during a poignant interview with Lance Armstrong, Oprah's use of nodding and maintaining consistent eye contact encouraged him to open up about his use of performance-enhancing drugs—a topic he had long denied publicly.

Oprah's body language sends a powerful message of trust and sincerity to her interviewees, often leading them to share more freely and deeply than they might in a more conventional interview setting. This technique not only enhances the quality of information received but also deeply engages the audience, making her interviews memorable and impactful.

This example highlights how non-verbal cues can be strategically used to enhance verbal communication. It shows that good interviewers do more than just ask questions; they communicate through their posture, expressions, and gestures to create an environment where open and honest dialogue can flourish.

Context is Key

Context is key when interpreting body language. The same gesture can carry different meanings depending on the setting. In a casual environment, slouching might indicate relaxation, while in a formal setting, it could be seen as disrespect or lack of interest.

Environmental factors also shape physical expression. A crowded room, for instance, might lead to more constrained body movements, whereas an open space might encourage expansive gestures. Understanding the nuances of context allows you to interpret body language more accurately, avoiding misinterpretations that could lead to misunderstandings.

People Watching

Practice is essential to develop your reading body language skills. People-watching can be fun and valuable, offering a real-world classroom where you can observe interactions and note various cues. Visit a park, café, or mall, and watch how people communicate without words. How do they express interest or boredom? What physical signals accompany their emotions? I've created a guide for you to follow at the end of this chapter.

You could also try analyzing body language in films or TV shows. These visual mediums provide rich examples of non-verbal communication, allowing you to pause, reflect, and dissect interactions in detail. Observing fictional characters can hone your ability to recognize body language signals in your own life.

The Subtleties of Facial Expressions

Imagine sitting across from someone, conversing, when their face subtly shifts. Perhaps it's the flicker of a smile or the brief furrow of a brow. These fleeting moments, often overlooked, hold immense power in revealing emotions and intentions.

Facial expressions are a universal language that transcends words, offering insights into the emotional undercurrents of our interactions. Even when words fail or deceive, expressions like happiness, sadness, and anger speak clearly and honestly. These basic expressions are recognized worldwide, serving as a shared human vocabulary. However, the human face is also capable of complexity, expressing mixed emotions that can convey nuanced feelings.

Understanding these facial nuances requires a keen eye and a willingness to look beyond the obvious. Micro-expressions, for instance, are brief, involuntary facial movements that occur in less than a second. They offer a glimpse into a person's true emotions, often before they have time to mask them. Recognizing these micro-expressions involves paying attention to quick changes in facial muscles, such as fleeting lips tightening.

Eye contact is another critical element. It can signal interest, confidence, or challenge, while avoidance might suggest discomfort or deceit. Observing these eye movement shifts and subtle changes in eyebrow positioning can reveal much about a person's emotional state.

Emotional congruence is at the heart of effective communication. When facial expressions align with spoken words, they create a harmony that feels authentic and trustworthy.

However, discrepancies between words and expressions can signal deception or hidden feelings. Imagine someone saying, "I'm fine," while their eyes dart away and their mouth tightens; such mismatches alert us to underlying emotions that contradict the verbal message. Conversely, when verbal and facial cues are consistent, they enhance the message, reinforcing sincerity and openness. Recognizing these cues helps us navigate conversations with greater empathy and understanding, allowing us to respond appropriately to the unspoken feelings of others.

Train Your Brain to Read Facial Expressions

Improving your ability to read facial expressions is a skill that can be cultivated through practice. One effective method is using flashcards with different facial expressions. By repeatedly identifying the emotions depicted, you train your brain to notice subtle differences and improve your recognition skills.

There are some great interactive apps available that offer training in recognizing micro-expressions, providing real-time feedback as you practice. I've played around with these two:

Face Reader - this software is often used in academic and professional research settings.

Humintell Mix – this app was developed by a team of psychologists and offers a mix of training on micro-expressions, body language, and lie detection.

Engaging with tools like these regularly will enhance your sensitivity to the emotional states of those around you, enabling you to connect more deeply and authentically. Each smile, frown, and glance tell a story, and with practice, you'll become adept at reading the narratives written across the faces of those you encounter.

Understanding Cultural Nuances in Non-Verbal Cues

Stepping into a new culture can feel like walking into a room where everyone speaks a different language, yet no one utters a word. Non-verbal communication is woven with gestures, expressions and spatial dynamics that vary significantly across cultural contexts.

In some cultures, personal space is almost sacred, with invisible boundaries that dictate comfort levels. Stand too close, and you might inadvertently step into someone's bubble, causing discomfort. In others, close proximity might signify warmth and friendship, an invitation to closeness. Understanding these differences is crucial, as missteps can easily lead to awkwardness or offense.

Gestures, too, carry a spectrum of meanings. A simple thumbs up, which might be seen as a positive affirmation in one culture, could be interpreted differently in another, perhaps even as an insult. Each gesture carries a history, a cultural context that shapes its interpretation.

Navigating these cultural differences requires a combination of research and mindfulness. We delve deeper into this topic in chapter ten.

Using Your Own Body Language to Build Rapport

You can foster trust and build rapport with others by consciously using body language. One effective technique is mirroring, subtly reflecting the other person's posture and movements. This isn't about mimicry; it's about creating a rhythm that resonates with the person you're interacting with. When done naturally, it signals alignment and understanding, making others feel more comfortable and valued.

Open gestures play a crucial role in appearing welcoming and approachable. Think of gestures as the punctuation marks of non-verbal communication. They add emphasis and clarity to your message. Open palm gestures, for instance, suggest honesty and inviting others into the conversation. Avoiding closed-off gestures, like crossing your arms or turning your body away, can prevent the creation of barriers. Instead, face the person fully and use expansive and inclusive gestures. This openness is a non-verbal invitation to engage, signaling you're present and interested in the interaction.

Maintaining positive body language throughout a conversation enhances your presence and impact. Eye contact is a powerful tool here. It demonstrates engagement, showing the other person you're attentive and invested in their words. However, it's important to balance eye contact to feel natural, avoiding an intense stare that might appear intimidating.

Alongside eye contact, controlling nervous habits is vital. Fidgeting, tapping your foot, or playing with your hair can distract from the conversation and convey anxiety. Knowing these habits allows you to manage them, reinforcing a calm and confident demeanor.

To refine your skills in using body language, practice through role-playing scenarios. This exercise allows you to test different approaches and receive feedback on your perceived non-verbal cues.

You might play the role of a leader in a meeting or engage in a casual conversation with a friend, experimenting with various gestures and postures. Recording these interactions and reviewing them offers valuable insights. It allows you to see yourself from an outside perspective, highlighting areas for improvement and reinforcing effective techniques. By practicing regularly, you'll build a repertoire of non-verbal skills that enhance your communication in diverse situations.

Body Language in Leadership

In leadership, body language becomes a foundation of influence and authority. Effective leaders use authoritative gestures to assert confidence and command respect. These gestures include standing tall, using deliberate movements, and occupying space confidently.

Amy Cuddy, social psychologist and author of "Presence," says, "Our bodies change our minds, and our minds can change our behavior, and our behavior can change our outcomes. In her book she discusses how adopting powerful, expansive poses can increase feelings of confidence and can impact our chances of success—a concept she calls "power posing."

Most successful leaders know how to balance this authority with approachability. They combine assertive gestures with warmth, using open postures and genuine smiles to convey strength and empathy. This blend of qualities fosters trust and inspires those around them, creating an environment where people feel guided and supported.

Step-by-Step Guide to Body Language Observation

Step 1: Select the Right Location

Choose a public place where people frequently interact, such as a park, cafe or shopping mall. Ensure the location provides a good vantage point from which to observe without intruding on privacy.

Step 2: Prepare for Observation

Bring a notebook and pen to record your observations or use a digital device.
Settle yourself where you can watch without being noticed, as natural behavior is more likely when people don't feel watched.

Step 3: Decide on Focus Areas

Before you begin, decide what specific aspects of body language you want to focus on. This could be gestures, facial expressions, postures, or interpersonal distances.
You can start with one focus area and gradually add more as you become more experienced and comfortable with observation.

Step 4: Observe and Record

Spend at least 30 minutes observing people. Note down key behaviors.

Gestures:
Are they expansive or restricted?
Do they seem to match the verbal communication?

Posture:
Is it open or closed?
How does it change in different interactions?

Facial Expressions:
What emotions are being displayed?
How do these relate to the conversation?

Eye Contact:
Is it direct or avoidant?
What might this indicate about the person's comfort level or interest?

Try to see if there's a pattern or trigger that changes a person's body language.

Step 5: Analyze Context

Reflect on how the context might influence the body language you observed. Consider factors like the setting, the number of people and the apparent relationships between individuals.

Step 6: Reflect on Your Observations

After your observation session, spend some time reflecting on what you noted. Ask yourself:
What surprised you?
Were there any interactions that were particularly informative?
How did the context appear to affect people's behavior?

Step 7: Apply What You Learned

Think about how you can apply your newfound insights into body language in your daily interactions.
Practice being more mindful of your own non-verbal cues and how they could be perceived.

Step 8: Repeat and Expand

Regular practice will enhance your observational skills. Repeat this exercise in different settings to broaden your understanding.

As you become more skilled, try to observe more subtle aspects of non-verbal communication, such as micro-expressions or the synchronization of movements between people in conversation.

By following these steps, you will develop a deeper understanding of body language and its impact on communication.

6

EMPATHY AND ACTIVE LISTENING

"Empathy is seeing with the eyes of another; listening with the ears of another and feeling with the heart of another." Alfred Adler

The room is filled with laughter and chatter at a family gathering, and you notice your cousin sitting quietly in the corner. Something inside you shifts as you approach, sensing the weight of words unsaid.

This instinctive pull towards understanding is empathy—a profound yet often misunderstood component of human connection. Empathy transcends mere sympathy; it is the ability to step into another's shoes and perceive the world through their eyes. It is the cornerstone of effective communication, bridging the gap between individuals and fostering a sense of shared humanity. Empathy transforms superficial interactions into meaningful dialogues that resonate long after the conversation ends. It's not just about understanding others; it's about being understood.

Empathy plays a pivotal role in building relationships, acting as a catalyst for trust and rapport. Consider a friend confiding in you about a recent struggle. An empathetic response would involve listening intently, acknowledging their feelings, and offering support without judgment. This approach contrasts sharply with a non-empathetic reaction, where the focus shifts to offering unsolicited advice or dismissing their emotions as trivial. When empathy is present, it fosters an environment where individuals feel valued and heard, laying the groundwork for more resilient relationships.

The impact of empathy extends beyond personal connections, influencing professional interactions as well. Empathy can enhance collaboration and understanding in the workplace, allowing teams to function more effectively and with greater cohesion. When colleagues feel understood, it fosters an atmosphere of trust, encouraging open communication and sharing ideas.

Developing Empathy

Developing empathy requires intentional practice, and the rewards are immeasurable. One effective strategy, known as perspective-taking, is the exercise of stepping into someone else's shoes. This involves setting aside personal biases and judgments to fully embrace another person's experience. It requires an open mind and the willingness to see beyond your own viewpoint.

Another powerful tool for cultivating empathy is reflective listening. By actively listening and reflecting back what you've heard, you signal understanding and validation. This practice deepens the conversation and strengthens your connection with the speaker. For example, saying, "It sounds like you're feeling frustrated because of the deadline," shows empathy by acknowledging the other person's emotional state and helps clarify their message.

Role-playing scenarios can further enhance empathy by allowing you to experience diverse perspectives firsthand. These exercises increase awareness of others' emotions and experiences, fostering a more empathetic approach to communication.

Despite its importance, maintaining empathy can be challenging, especially when personal biases or emotional fatigue intervene. Barriers like these can cloud our judgment and limit our ability to connect.

Overcoming these obstacles begins with self-awareness—recognizing the biases that shape your interactions and taking conscious steps to set them aside.

In demanding environments, emotional fatigue and burnout can hinder empathy. Here, self-care and boundary-setting become essential. Ensuring you have the emotional resources to engage empathetically without depleting yourself allows for more meaningful connections with others.

Everyday Empathy

The Dalai Lama's teachings and actions reflect his deep commitment to empathy. He often speaks about the importance of understanding others' suffering and perspectives, stressing that this is the foundation of compassion. His ability to listen actively is evident in his interactions with people from various walks of life, from world leaders to ordinary citizens, where he engages with genuine curiosity and concern.

His empathetic leadership style has allowed him to advocate effectively for the rights of the Tibetan people and promote global peace. His message resonates in numerous international forums, where he speaks about the importance of emotional and spiritual well-being, fostering an environment of mutual respect and understanding across diverse global communities.

Everyday interactions offer countless opportunities to practice empathy, turning routine exchanges into moments of genuine connection. For instance, engaging in empathetic conversations with colleagues can transform the workplace into a supportive and collaborative environment. Similarly, demonstrating empathy in customer service interactions enhances the customer experience, fostering loyalty and trust. These moments, though seemingly small, have the power to ripple outward, creating a culture of empathy that extends far beyond the individual interaction.

By embracing empathy daily, you contribute to a world where understanding and compassion are the norm, not the exception.

Empathy in Conflict Resolution

In conflict situations, especially those involving deep emotions or differing viewpoints, empathy can help transform adversarial interactions into more co-operative and solution-oriented discussions. When individuals in conflict empathize with each other, they are more likely to listen actively, acknowledge the emotional stakes, and be open to compromise rather than becoming defensive or entrenched in their positions. One key aspect of empathy in conflict resolution is that it shifts the focus from a "win-lose" mentality to a more collaborative "win-win" approach. Rather than seeing the other person as an opponent, empathizing allows one to perceive them as a human being with valid experiences and feelings, which can defuse tension and pave the way for constructive dialogue.

An empathic approach involves not just hearing the words the other person is saying but also understanding their underlying emotions, fears, and needs. This is essential for addressing the root causes of the conflict rather than just the superficial symptoms. Empathy enables individuals to step outside of their own perspective and gain insights into the experiences and motivations of others. By doing so, they can identify common ground and find solutions that meet the interests of both parties rather than settling for a solution that benefits only one side. In addition, empathy can lead to more positive and lasting resolutions because it fosters mutual respect and builds trust between the parties involved.

A real-life example of empathy in conflict resolution can be seen in the process of restorative justice, particularly in the context of criminal justice. Restorative justice focuses on repairing the harm caused by criminal behavior through dialogue between the victim and the offender, often with the help of a mediator. In many cases, the victim feels anger, betrayal, or fear, while the offender may struggle with guilt or defensiveness. Through the process, both parties are encouraged to share their feelings and perspectives in a safe, structured environment. The mediator facilitates this exchange by encouraging active listening and empathy, helping each side understand the other's emotional experience. For instance, in a therapeutic justice session involving a victim of theft and the offender, the victim might express feelings of violation and loss. In contrast, the offender might explain their struggles, such as poverty or addiction, which led to the crime. By recognizing the humanity in both parties, empathy allows them to move beyond the anger or resentment that typically fuels conflict and open up to mutual understanding and healing. This empathetic exchange can result in agreements about how to make amends, whether through apologies, restitution, or community service and can reduce the likelihood of reoffending. The success of restorative justice illustrates how, when applied thoughtfully in conflict resolution, empathy can foster healing, accountability, and stronger relationships in the aftermath of a dispute.

The Science of Active Listening

Imagine sitting across from a friend, nodding as they share a story about their day. You're present, but your mind drifts, caught in the web of your own thoughts. This is where active listening comes in—a skill that transforms passive hearing into meaningful engagement. At its core, active listening is about fully immersing yourself in the conversation, focusing entirely on the speaker rather than planning your response.

Active listening is an essential expression of empathy, enabling you to understand better and connect with others. It involves several key components:

- **Minimizing distractions**—putting away your phone, turning off the TV, and making eye contact signaling your commitment to the conversation.

- **Verbal affirmations**, such as simple nods or exclamations like "I see" or "Go on," encourage the speaker and show that you are engaged.

- **Non-verbal cues** such as leaning forward, maintaining an open posture, and mirroring the speaker's expressions reinforce the connection.

Mastering active listening requires intentional practice. One effective method is mindfulness—taking a moment before entering a conversation to center yourself. Focus on your breath to clear your mind of distractions. This mindfulness practice grounds you in the moment, enhancing your ability to listen with intent.

Additionally, techniques for avoiding interruptive thoughts are key. When your mind begins to wander, gently redirect your focus back to the speaker, using their words as an anchor. Recognizing these moments without judgment allows you to return to the conversation with renewed attention.

Tone & Inflection in Active Listening

Tone and inflection are critical elements in active listening because they influence how messages are received, interpreted, and responded to. These vocal cues can either enhance or hinder the communication process, shaping the emotional quality of the interaction and contributing to its success or failure.

Tone refers to the overall quality or character of one's voice, which can convey a range of emotions such as warmth, aggression, sarcasm, enthusiasm, or indifference. In active listening, the listener's tone can signal to the speaker whether they are engaged, open and empathetic. For example, a soft, calm and steady tone indicates attentiveness and reassurance, while a harsh or dismissive tone might suggest judgment or impatience. When listening actively, a listener's tone of voice can help reassure the speaker that they are in a safe and non-judgmental space, which is essential for fostering trust and open dialogue.

Conversely, inflection refers to the rise and fall in pitch while speaking, and it can dramatically affect how a message is perceived. A listener's inflection can signal interest, surprise, confusion, or agreement, depending on how the voice rises or falls in response to the speaker. For instance, if a listener's voice increases slightly at the end of a sentence, it can indicate curiosity or a desire for clarification, whereas a downward inflection can signal understanding or affirmation. When a listener adjusts their inflection to reflect the emotional undertones of the speaker's message, it helps to validate the speaker's feelings and encourages them to continue sharing. This kind of vocal responsiveness demonstrates that the listener is not only hearing the words but also attuned to the speaker's emotional state and the nuances of their message.

Together, tone and inflection help convey non-verbal feedback, which we know is often more powerful than the words themselves. When these vocal cues align with the content of the conversation, they create a sense of connection and mutual respect. For example, if a speaker is discussing a sensitive or painful topic, a listener who responds with a gentle, warm tone and uses soft, understanding inflections can make the speaker feel supported and validated. On the other hand, a tone that is abrupt, dismissive, or monotone can cause the speaker to feel disregarded or frustrated, even if the listener's words are neutral or polite.

Feedback and Clarification

Feedback is a vital component of active listening. Paraphrasing and summarizing what you've heard confirms your comprehension while allowing the speaker to clarify or expand on their points. For example, you might say, "So what I'm hearing is..." or "It sounds like you're saying..." This shows your engagement and ensures that the message has been accurately received.

Asking clarifying questions further deepens the conversation. Questions like "Can you tell me more about that?" or "How did that make you feel?" show a genuine interest in their perspective, inviting them to elaborate.

Responding with Emotional Intelligence

In a world where emotions often drive our interactions, emotional intelligence (EI) is a linchpin for effective communication. EI refers to the ability to recognize, understand, and manage your own emotions while also comprehending the feelings of others. This dual capability forms the foundation for meaningful, empathetic responses in conversations.

Recognizing your emotions provides insight into the triggers that evoke certain feelings and reactions. This awareness helps regulate your responses, preventing impulsive actions that might escalate a situation. Understanding the emotions of others further enhances this process by allowing you to tailor your responses to their emotional state, fostering a deeper connection.

When responding, validating the other person's feelings is an essential emotional intelligence skill. For example, saying, "I can see you're upset about this," acknowledges their emotions without judgment. In difficult conversations, compassion is key. Compassionate responses, characterized by empathy and support, can de-escalate tension and encourage collaboration. Instead of jumping into problem-solving, you might say, "How can I support you right now?" This shifts the focus from fixing the problem to offering emotional support.

Building Trust Through Empathetic Engagement

In relationships, trust is built on empathetic interactions. When you consistently demonstrate empathy, you show others that you value their feelings and perspectives. This fosters a sense of safety and openness, encouraging honesty and vulnerability. For example, in one of the teams I worked with, we had a member named Helen who had been unusually quiet in meetings. Her ideas were often overlooked, and while she seemed to withdraw, she had relevant insights to contribute. One day, during a particularly tense brainstorming session, I noticed her reluctance to speak up. Rather than pressuring her to share, I approached her privately after the meeting, acknowledging that she seemed hesitant to contribute and asking if something was on her mind.

She opened up about feeling dismissed in earlier discussions, where her ideas hadn't been given proper consideration, making her less confident in speaking up. Rather than defending the team's behavior, I listened, validating her feelings. I said, "I can understand why you'd feel that way. It must be frustrating to feel your input isn't valued." By giving her the space to express her frustrations and showing empathy, I helped her feel heard. At the next meeting, Helen felt empowered to share her thoughts, and her contributions turned out to be a pivotal turning point for the project. From then on, Helen was much more engaged in discussions, and her trust in the team grew, leading to stronger collaboration.

Empathy is not just about listening—sometimes, it's about creating the right environment for someone to feel comfortable opening up. This simple act of recognition, validation, and encouragement can transform someone's relationship with the group.

Building trust through empathetic communication requires consistency. Keeping promises, no matter how small, reinforces reliability and integrity. When you follow through on commitments, you show others they can count on you, deepening their trust.

However, trust can be fragile, and breaches—whether intentional or accidental—can damage relationships. To repair trust, acknowledge mistakes, take responsibility, and make amends. Balancing openness with appropriate boundaries is also important, ensuring that trust evolves without overexposure or discomfort.

Building trust through empathetic engagement is an ongoing process. By practicing empathy in every interaction, you strengthen your connections with others, creating relationships that are resilient, open, and built on mutual understanding. In the next chapter, we will explore the balance between speaking and listening, further enhancing your communication skills and deepening your relationships.

Checklist for Empathy & Active Listening

Use this checklist as a guide to assess your empathetic engagement in conversations.

- I created a safe space for the other person to express themselves.
- I actively listened without interrupting or planning my response while they spoke.
- I acknowledged the other person's feelings or experiences without judgment.
- I avoided jumping to conclusions or offering advice too quickly.
- I shared my feelings or vulnerabilities to create a reciprocal, trusting environment.
- I asked open-ended questions to encourage deeper dialogue and understanding.
- I used reflective listening (e.g., paraphrasing or summarizing their words) to confirm understanding.
- I validated the other person's perspective, even if I didn't fully agree.
- I showed patience and gave the other person the time they needed to articulate their thoughts.
- I followed up with actions or promises to show that I value their trust.

7

BALANCING SPEAKING AND LISTENING

"Listening is not a skill, it's a discipline. All you have to do is keep your mouth shut." Peter Drucker

You will notice that I touch on the topic of 'attentive listening' in both chapters 6 and 7. This is deliberate, because 'attentive listening' plays a very important role in all conversations. It is a key lesson that cannot be emphasized enough. I have put a different slant on each example to enhance the message. I hope you will agree that repetition is beneficial when learning something new.

Picture yourself at a dinner party, engaged in a lively discussion about a recent film. As the conversation flows, you notice one person dominating the dialogue, leaving little room for others to contribute. You want to interject, to share your thoughts, but you're unsure when or how. This common scenario highlights the delicate relationship between speaking and listening that defines effective communication. Achieving this balance is crucial. It ensures all voices are heard, ideas are exchanged, and connections are formed.

Conversations are not just about speaking or listening but about knowing when to do each.

When we fail to maintain this equilibrium, misunderstandings arise.

Imagine a team meeting where one member speaks over others, pushing their agenda without pause. Important ideas are lost, and frustration builds. This imbalance not only stifles creativity but also strains relationships. On the other hand, a conversation where everyone is given space to contribute fosters a sense of inclusion and respect. Equal communication creates an environment where people feel valued and understood, laying the groundwork for stronger connections. It transforms dialogue into a collaborative exchange, where each participant's insights enrich the discussion.

Deciding when to speak involves assessing the relevance and value of your contribution. Ask yourself, "Does this add to the conversation?" or "Is this the right time to share?" Consider whether your input will enhance the dialogue or shift it off course.

Timing is crucial. Speaking up at the right moment can emphasize a point, while poorly timed interjections may disrupt the flow.

Context also matters. In professional settings, concise and relevant contributions are often more impactful. In casual conversations, sharing personal stories might foster deeper connections. Balancing these elements ensures your voice is heard without overshadowing others.

Recognizing when to listen is equally important. Pay attention to verbal cues that suggest openness or the need for further exploration, such as pauses or questions. As mentioned previously, non-verbal signals, like nodding or leaning forward, indicate engagement, suggesting the speaker values your input. Observing the dynamics of the conversation helps gauge when listening is more beneficial. If someone is sharing a personal experience or complex idea, your role may be to absorb and understand rather than respond immediately.

This attentiveness deepens your understanding and strengthens the relationship, demonstrating respect.

Practicing Balance in Conversation

Engage in a role-playing exercise with a partner, alternating between speaker and listener. Choose a topic of mutual interest. As one person speaks, the other practices active listening, offering feedback and asking questions. Afterward, switch roles and reflect on the experience. Discuss what techniques helped maintain balance and what could be improved. This practice enhances your awareness of conversational dynamics, helping you find the right mix of speaking and listening in future interactions.

Participating in group discussions with a focus on balance also hones these skills. Encourage each member to share their thoughts, promoting an environment where all voices are valued. This collaborative approach enriches the discussion and builds a culture of mutual respect. As you practice, notice how the balance of speaking and listening influences the quality of the conversation. Embrace the pauses, the exchanges and the insights that emerge when dialogue flows naturally.

Techniques for Encouraging Others to Share

Imagine yourself in a room where everyone's thoughts hang in the air, waiting to be spoken. It's a space where encouragement isn't just a nicety but a tool for connection. Inviting others to share their thoughts nurtures inclusivity, creating an environment where everyone feels valued. This encouragement fosters a supportive atmosphere where ideas flourish and relationships deepen. When people feel encouraged to speak, discussions become richer, more dynamic, and filled with diverse perspectives. It's like adding different colors to a painting, each hue contributing to a more vibrant picture. Encouragement allows us to hear voices that might otherwise remain silent.

To prompt others to share, start with open-ended questions that invite elaboration. Instead of asking yes-or-no questions, consider, "What are your thoughts on this?" or "How do you feel about that?" These questions open the door for others to express themselves freely without the constraints of a limited answer. They show genuine interest in the other person's perspective, encouraging them to contribute more deeply to the conversation. Non-verbal cues also play a crucial role. Simple actions like nodding or maintaining eye contact signal that you're engaged and receptive. These gestures create a sense of safety, reassuring the speaker that their words are welcome and valued.

Creating a safe space for sharing is vital for encouraging openness. This involves demonstrating empathy and understanding through active listening as discussed in the previous chapter. When someone speaks, listen not just to reply but to understand. Acknowledge their feelings and thoughts without judgment, creating an environment where they feel comfortable sharing more. Avoiding interruptions is important. Allow pauses in the conversation to unfold naturally, giving the speaker time to gather their thoughts. Patience in these moments shows respect and encourages others to express themselves without fearing being cut off.

I recently coached a teacher who couldn't get classroom interaction off the ground. He was unaware that he always asked the same students for a response. As a result, others remained silent, believing he wasn't interested in their input. His classroom discussions transformed when he invited every student to share their diverse opinions and ideas. These conversations led to a series of stories that brought the class closer together, revealing insights that might have otherwise remained hidden. This illustrates how encouragement can empower individuals to speak up, turning conversations into vibrant exchanges.

Managing Dominance in Conversations

I'm sure we've all been in a meeting where one person talks incessantly, leaving no room for others to contribute. This is conversational dominance, where a single voice overshadows the rest, often stifling dialogue and creativity. It can turn a collaborative environment into a one-sided monologue, where diverse ideas and perspectives are lost.

Dominance can be subtle, such as interrupting frequently or steering every topic back to oneself. It can also manifest overtly, like dismissing others' opinions or speaking over them. These behaviors disrupt the balance necessary for effective communication, leading to participant frustration and disengagement. The effects on group dynamics are profound. When one person dominates, others may retreat, feeling their contributions aren't valued. This imbalance hinders the flow of ideas and impacts morale as people become reluctant to share. Over time, this can erode trust and cooperation within a group, stalling progress and innovation.

To manage dominance, self-awareness is key. It's important to recognize when your voice is overpowering the conversation. This requires honest reflection on your communication habits. Are you speaking more than listening?
Do you often interrupt or redirect discussions back to yourself?
By acknowledging these patterns, you can begin to adjust your approach.

One technique is to set personal limits on your speaking time, allowing space for others to share. This might involve consciously pausing after making a point and inviting others to contribute. It could also mean actively listening more, focusing on understanding rather than responding immediately. Creating a mental checklist can help keep these goals in mind, fostering a more inclusive dialogue.

Facilitation plays a crucial role in mitigating dominance. A skilled facilitator can guide discussions, ensuring all voices are heard. This involves redirecting focus to quieter participants and encouraging them to share their insights.
Phrases like "I'd love to hear your thoughts on this" or "What do you think about this perspective?" can be powerful invitations for those who hesitate to speak up. Encouraging equitable contribution from all members diversifies the conversation and enriches the dialogue with various perspectives and ideas.

Practicing non-dominance can be developed through specific exercises. Group activities where roles rotate between speaker and listener can provide valuable practice. Each participant takes turns speaking and listening in these scenarios, offering feedback on the experience. This highlights the importance of balance and enhances understanding of the dynamics at play.

Observing and reflecting on personal communication habits is another effective strategy. Keep a journal of your interactions, noting moments where you felt dominant or where others were. Reflect on what triggered these behaviors and how you might adjust.

By addressing conversational dominance, we pave the way for richer, more inclusive interactions. It requires a commitment to self-awareness, a willingness to adapt, and a focus on fostering a collaborative environment. The benefits are manifold, from improved group dynamics to enhanced creativity and innovation. As we learn to manage dominance, we create spaces where every voice is valued, every idea is heard, and every conversation becomes an opportunity for connection and growth.

Handling Conflict in Communication

Conflict is an inevitable part of life, whether in personal relationships, the workplace, or everyday interactions. While conflict itself isn't inherently negative, how we handle it can determine the outcome. If approached thoughtfully and with a focus on resolution, conflict can lead to greater understanding, stronger relationships, and creative solutions. However, when emotions are high, conflict can quickly escalate if we don't take care to balance speaking and listening. In these situations, managing our emotional responses and maintaining composure is crucial for keeping the conversation productive and resolving the issue effectively.

When emotions run high, the instinct is often to defend ourselves or react to perceived attacks. However, reacting impulsively can escalate the conflict, making it more difficult to reach a resolution. Instead, focusing on listening first—without interruption—helps defuse tension and allows for a more rational conversation.

For instance, imagine a workplace disagreement between two colleagues, Anna and Mike, over a project. Anna feels that Mike has not been pulling his weight, while Mike believes that Anna is micromanaging and undermining his ideas. If both start defending their positions immediately, the conversation will become combative and unproductive. However, if Anna listens attentively to Mike's concerns without interrupting, she might understand the deeper reasons for his frustration. This allows both to move toward a solution without needing to "win" the argument.

Active listening in conflict resolution means paying full attention, acknowledging the other person's feelings, and reflecting back their concerns to show that you understand. It can be as simple as saying, "I hear you're frustrated because you feel like your contributions aren't being valued." This step can calm the emotional temperature of the conversation and open space for dialogue.

De-escalating Tension in Heated Conversations

Learning to de-escalate tension is an invaluable skill. When emotions are high, responding with anger or defensiveness only fuels the fire. Instead, pausing before responding can help maintain control of the conversation. Taking a moment to breathe deeply and collect your thoughts helps avoid impulsive reactions that might escalate the situation.

For example, in a heated discussion about household chores between two roommates, one person might raise their voice and express frustration about not being helped enough. The other might feel attacked and instantly respond with anger. However, if the second roommate pauses, takes a breath, and chooses to react calmly, both individuals can reconsider their approach. Saying something like," I understand you're upset about the chores, and I want to find a way to work this out together," can create a shift in tone and open space for compromise.

Conflict resolution is not about winning or being right; it's about understanding the issue, acknowledging emotions, and working together to find a solution. By focusing on listening, de-escalating tension, and staying composed, we can resolve conflicts to strengthen relationships and promote understanding.

Cultivating a Dialogic Mindset

Think of conversations like a dance, where both partners move in harmony, responding to each other's cues. This is the essence of a dialogic mindset—viewing conversations as cooperative exchanges rather than combative encounters.

In this approach, the goal is not to win or dominate but to understand and connect. We open the door to richer and more meaningful interactions when we foster a cooperative communication environment. Dialogic conversations thrive on mutual engagement, where each person is both a speaker and a listener, contributing to a shared understanding. This stands in stark contrast to adversarial interactions, where the focus is on outtalking or outsmarting the other person. In such cases, the conversation becomes a battleground, with each party trying to assert their point rather than seeking common ground.

Shifting to a dialogic mindset requires consciously prioritizing mutual understanding over individual agendas. One way to develop this approach is by practicing curiosity and open-mindedness in discussions. Enter conversations with the intention to learn, asking questions that invite exploration rather than confrontation. This might involve setting aside preconceived notions and allowing yourself to be surprised by the other person's perspective.

Prioritizing shared goals also plays a crucial role. When you focus on what you and the other person are trying to achieve together, aligning your efforts and working collaboratively becomes easier. This shift from a "me" mindset to a "we" mindset transforms the dynamic, fostering cooperation and connection.

Flexibility and adaptability are key components of a dialogic mindset. Being open to changing perspectives enhances dialogue by allowing space for new ideas to emerge. It's about remaining receptive to what you hear, even if it challenges your beliefs. Techniques for staying open include active listening, focusing intently on the speaker without planning your response, and reflective thinking, considering how new information might alter your views. Numerous examples illustrate flexibility leading to innovative solutions. In a team meeting, for instance, a manager might initially resist a new strategy but, through open dialogue, realize its potential and decides to implement it. Such adaptability enriches the conversation and fosters a culture of innovation and growth.

Reflecting on your communication style is an important step in cultivating a dialogic mindset. Start by journaling reflections on past interactions, focusing on the quality of dialogue. Consider questions like:
Did I approach this conversation with an open mind?
Was I more interested in understanding or being understood?
This self-reflection can reveal patterns and areas for improvement.

Seeking feedback from peers is also valuable. Invite trusted colleagues, friends or your coach to share their observations of your communication style and be open to their insights. This external perspective can highlight blind spots and offer guidance on how to enhance your dialogic skills.

A dialogic mindset transforms conversations into opportunities for connection and growth. By approaching dialogue as a collaborative exchange, you create a space where every voice is valued and every perspective is considered. This mindset enriches your interactions and deepens your relationships, fostering a sense of unity and understanding. As you embrace this approach, you'll find that your conversations become more fulfilling and impactful, setting the stage for richer connections and more significant insights.

With this foundation, you're ready to explore the next chapter, where we delve into the complexities of networking and career advancement.

Self-Assessment : Balance of Speaking & Listening

Instructions: For each question, rate yourself on a scale from 1 to 5

1 = Rarely 2 = Occasionally 3 = Sometimes 4 = Often 5 = Always

Do I allow others to finish their thoughts completely before responding?

Do I find it difficult to listen without mentally preparing my response?

Do I reflect on or paraphrase what the speaker has said to confirm my understanding?

Do I prioritize the quality of listening over the need to express my opinions in discussions?

Do I actively listen for both verbal and nonverbal cues to understand the whole message being communicated?

How often do I find myself dominating conversations by speaking more than listening?

How frequently do I ask follow-up questions to clarify or deepen my understanding of what others are saying?

When someone is speaking, how often do I notice myself becoming distracted or thinking about unrelated topics?

How often do I interrupt others during conversations to share my own thoughts or opinions?

When I disagree with someone, how likely am I to listen fully before explaining my perspective?

How often do I offer verbal affirmations (like "I understand" or "Tell me more") to show I am engaged in a conversation?

When a conversation ends, how often do I feel that both parties had an equal opportunity to speak and be heard?

Scoring and Reflection
Add up your scores for a total out of 60.

48–60: You likely have a strong balance between speaking and listening.

36–47: You may strike a balance occasionally but could improve active listening or speaking behaviors.

12–35: You might benefit from focusing more on either listening or limiting interruptions.

8

NETWORKING AND CAREER ADVANCEMENT

"What makes networking work is that it sets up win-win situations in which all parties involved get to take something home." Earl G Graves Snr

You are standing in a crowded elevator surrounded by colleagues and strangers. The space is tight, everyone is silent, and you have only the duration of that elevator ride to make an impression. This is where the elevator pitch concept originates—a brief, impactful introduction designed to spark interest and initiate further conversation. Crafting an elevator pitch that resonates is an art, and it starts with understanding the core components:

a crisp introduction
a compelling value proposition
a clear call to action

These elements must fit seamlessly into a 30-second narrative, capturing attention without overwhelming the listener.

Your introduction is the first handshake, even if it's just verbal. It sets the tone, offers a glimpse into who you are, and establishes the initial connection. Think of it as the opening line of a novel—it should intrigue and invite curiosity. The value proposition is where you shine, illustrating what you bring to the table. It's about articulating your unique strengths and skills, which differentiate you in your field or industry. This isn't just about listing achievements but weaving them into a story that speaks directly to the needs or interests of your audience. Finally, the call to action is your invitation, whether it's a request for a meeting, a suggestion for collaboration, or a simple invite to continue the conversation. It guides the listener on what to do next, ensuring the dialogue doesn't end with the ding of the elevator doors.

Identifying your unique value proposition requires introspection and honesty. Start by pinpointing your core skills and strengths. What do you excel at? What comes naturally to you? Reflect on past experiences where you've made a significant impact. These moments often hold the key to your unique value. Consider how these strengths align with the needs of your audience. Tailoring your pitch involves adapting language and examples to suit the context, ensuring relevance and clarity. Avoid industry jargon that might alienate or confuse. Instead, focus on clear, relatable language that resonates with your listener's experiences and challenges. Consider how your skills can solve a problem or enhance an opportunity specific to them.

Practicing and refining your elevator pitch is essential for polish and confidence. One effective technique is to record your pitch and review it. Listening to your delivery can reveal areas for improvement, whether in tone, pace, or emphasis. Role-playing scenarios with peers or mentors offer another layer of feedback. Choose different contexts, such as a networking event or a casual meet-up and adjust your pitch accordingly. This exercise helps refine your message and builds adaptability for real-world applications. By rehearsing in varied situations, you hone your ability to pivot and personalize your pitch on the spot, making it both engaging and effective.

The elevator pitch is more than a professional necessity; it's a personal declaration of who you are and what you aspire to achieve. It distills your essence into a concise narrative, inviting others to join you on your journey. In crafting and delivering your pitch, you gain clarity about your goals and the value you offer, empowering you to navigate networking and career advancement confidently and purposefully.

Exercise: Perfecting Your Elevator Pitch

Grab a notebook and jot down the main elements of your pitch: an engaging introduction, your unique value proposition, and a clear call to action. Record yourself delivering this pitch. Listen critically, focusing on clarity, tone and timing. Adjust where necessary and then rehearse with a trusted friend or mentor. Ask for honest feedback, and refine your pitch based on their insights. Repeat this process until your elevator pitch feels natural and compelling. I've created an Elevator Pitch Template for you to follow at the end of this chapter.

Building a Professional Network Strategically

Networking is often likened to an intricate and interconnected web where each thread strengthens the overall structure. Strategic networking, however, is about creating that web with intention. Instead of casting a wide net haphazardly, it involves pinpointing opportunities that align with your goals and values. For example, attending an industry seminar where every conversation holds potential. Here, networking isn't just about collecting business cards; it's about forging relationships that matter.

In today's fast-paced world, where career advancement hinges on who you know as much as what you know, understanding the role of networking is pivotal. A robust network opens doors to opportunities, offering support, guidance, and access to resources that can propel your career forward. It's the difference between passively hoping for connections and actively cultivating them.

You must identify these opportunities to build a network that genuinely supports your ambitions. Industry conferences and seminars are fertile grounds for meeting like-minded professionals. These events are designed to unite individuals with shared interests, creating a space ripe for connection. Engage actively in discussions, attend workshops and participate in panels. Each interaction is a chance to learn, share and find those who resonate with your professional journey.

Online platforms, too, offer vast potential. Professional communities and forums allow you to engage with peers globally, breaking geographical boundaries. Through these digital spaces, you can join conversations, contribute insights and expand your network beyond physical confines.

Making meaningful connections requires more than just showing up; it demands genuine curiosity. Approach new contacts with an open mind, eager to understand their experiences and perspectives. Ask questions that encourage dialogue, not just responses. Finding common ground through shared challenges or aspirations creates a foundation of mutual respect and interest. As you engage, look for ways to contribute value. Identifying how you can support others fosters a sense of community and collaboration. It's about building relationships where both parties feel enriched, paving the way for long-term connections.

The role of giving in networking cannot be overstated. Offering value to your contacts through sharing resources, insights, or introductions strengthens your network, encourages reciprocity and enriches everyone's experience. If someone mentions a challenge they're facing and you have relevant expertise, offer your insights or suggest resources that might help.

Introducing new contacts to beneficial connections is always appreciated and can open doors for them and enhance your network's diversity. It's a reciprocal exchange where each party contributes to and benefits from the collective knowledge and opportunities. By focusing on what you can give rather than what you can gain, you build a network founded on trust and collaboration that will last.

Navigating Networking Events with Ease

Walking into a networking event can feel like stepping into a whirlwind. Preparation is your ally in navigating this type of environment.

Before attending, take a moment to set clear objectives for what you hope to achieve. Are you there to meet potential collaborators, explore career opportunities, or gain insights into industry trends? Knowing your goals helps direct your focus and energy. Crafting a practical introduction and conversation starters tailored to the event can also ease initial interactions. Think of a few key points you'd like to convey about yourself or your work and be ready with questions that invite others to share their experiences.

Once inside, engaging with confidence becomes the name of the game. Approach groups and individuals openly, signaling your willingness to connect. A warm smile and genuine interest in others go a long way in breaking the ice. When initiating conversations, remember that active listening is your greatest tool. It keeps you grounded and fosters a deeper connection with those around you. Listen intently to what others say and respond thoughtfully, weaving shared interests or goals into the dialogue. This approach builds rapport and makes interactions more memorable for both parties. As you engage, be mindful of the natural flow of conversation, allowing it to evolve organically rather than forcing it in a particular direction. This flexibility eases the pressure on you and creates a relaxed atmosphere for everyone involved.

While rich with opportunity, networking events come with their challenges. Anxiety or nervousness is common, especially in large gatherings where the sheer number of people can be overwhelming. Take a moment to breathe and remind yourself of your objectives. Visualize successful interactions, focusing on the positive outcomes you hope to achieve.

Navigating cliques or exclusive groups can be confronting. These tight-knit circles may seem impenetrable, but approaching them with humility, respect and a smile can open doors. Introducing yourself and expressing interest in their conversation can gradually break down barriers. It's about finding the right moment and showing genuine interest in what they say.

I remember being introduced to an event organizer at a coaching conference a few years ago. We chatted briefly, but he had to leave in a hurry. At first, I thought he wasn't interested in talking to me. I was hesitant to ask for his business card, but I did before he darted off. Even though I felt nervous, I contacted him the next day and we arranged a coffee meeting. We kept in touch online and a few months later, he offered me the opportunity to speak at his firm. I was surprised and delighted. This transformation from a casual encounter to a career opportunity underpins the importance of being present, staying in touch and remaining open to possibilities.

When my daughter finished university, I encouraged her to attend a local networking event for young entrepreneurs because I know the power of such gatherings. She was nervous and unsure of what to expect but went armed with a few questions and genuine enthusiasm. Her proactive engagement caught the attention of a leading industry expert who after chatting with her, recognized her potential and offered her a coveted internship.

These true stories highlight how networking can be a catalyst for growth, turning fleeting exchanges into lasting relationships and wonderful opportunities.

The Art of Follow-Up: Sustaining Connections

You've just left a networking event with a stack of business cards in your pocket. Each one represents a potential relationship, a door left ajar. But without follow-up, these opportunities can fade into oblivion. Timely follow-up is crucial; it solidifies the initial impression and demonstrates sincere interest. It prevents those connections from slipping through the cracks, ensuring the dialogue continues beyond that fleeting first encounter. Without it, even the most promising introductions can wither, leaving untapped potential.

Crafting effective follow-up communication is an art and must not be ignored. A personalized follow-up email or message is more than a courtesy; it's a reaffirmation of interest and a gentle nudge toward further engagement. Begin by referencing your previous conversation, showing you were genuinely interested in what was shared. This helps jog their memory and re-establishes the context of your meeting. Then, suggest specific reasons for future collaboration or meetings. Perhaps you discussed a shared interest, a project that aligns with your goals, or an event that could benefit you both. Highlighting these points provides a reason to reconnect and underscores the value of your budding relationship.

Balancing persistence with patience is critical in follow-up communications. While staying on their radar is important, you must avoid appearing overly eager or intrusive, which can be off-putting. Timing is everything. Gauge the appropriate follow-up interval based on industry norms and the nature of your initial interaction. In some fields, a week might be customary, while a more immediate follow-up could be expected in others. If you're anxious, do it immediately before you change your mind. That's what I do.

Recognize when it's time to pause or shift focus to other opportunities. If a contact doesn't respond after a couple of attempts, it might be wise to step back and revisit the connection later. This demonstrates respect for their time and space, preserving the relationship for future re-engagement.

Long-term relationship building requires a system for nurturing and maintaining your network over time. Regularly checking in with contacts through updates or shared content keeps you relevant in their minds without the need for constant direct communication. Whether it's sharing an article that might interest them, congratulating them on a recent achievement, or simply sending a friendly message during the holidays, these touch points strengthen the foundation of your relationship. Celebrating achievements and milestones together fosters a sense of camaraderie and mutual respect. Acknowledging their successes shows that you value them beyond the professional sphere, enriching the connection and laying the groundwork for deeper collaboration.

I know networking events can be stressful, especially for those of you who feel overwhelmed by large groups or find it challenging to converse with strangers. I understand that the pressure to make a good impression, navigate small talk, or advocate for yourself can feel daunting. However, these events are crucial for personal and professional growth. It's okay to acknowledge your anxiety—it's a natural response to stepping outside your comfort zone. But rather than avoiding the discomfort, I encourage you to lean into it. Remember that every interaction is a chance to learn; the more you show up, the easier it will become. Courage grows with action, so take a deep breath, go, and trust your ability to navigate the experience.

Here's the elevator pitch outline – remember you only have 30 seconds to connect with everyone and let them know who you are, what you do and why they should take your business card or meet you for coffee next week. Learn it off by heart so you don't sound nervous or forget what to say.

Elevator Pitch Template

Introduction: Start with your name and your role.

Example: "Good evening, my name is Anne McKeown, I'm a Communication Coach who empowers people to step up, speak up and show up with confidence in business and life."

Engagement: Open with a question or statement that highlights common challenges.

Example: "Have you ever felt overlooked in conversations or struggled to articulate your thoughts in high-pressure situations?"

The Need: Describe the common issues people face that your business addresses.

Example: "Many talented professionals find themselves unable to speak up in meetings, manage small talk, or connect deeply with colleagues and clients."

Your Approach: Explain your unique answer or philosophy.

Example:"Using a blend of personalized strategies and practical exercises, I help clients find their authentic voice and communicate with clarity in all situations."

Success Stories: Briefly mention a success story or a general outcome experienced by your clients.

Example: "Clients who have worked with me have gone on to lead teams more effectively, engage more confidently in networking events, and even excel in public speaking."

The Benefit: State the direct benefits your role/company provides to potential clients.

Example: "With my coaching, you can expect to feel heard and understood, build stronger relationships at work and home, and finally feel at ease in conversations, no matter the setting."

The Ask: Conclude with what you seek, such as new clients, a workshop opportunity, or a speaking engagement.

Example: "I'm looking to expand my client base with professionals eager to transform their communicative abilities."

Closing: Thank the listener for their time and suggest a way to continue the conversation.

Example: "Thank you for your time. I'd love to exchange contact information and learn more about your business."

And remember to smile.

9

ENHANCING MEMORY AND RECALL

"A person's name to them is the sweetest sound." Dale Carnegie

You're at a lively gathering and as you circulate the room, you meet several new people. Each introduction feels like an opportunity, yet you struggle to remember their names moments after they've spoken. It's a common scenario that can unsettle even the most confident of us.

The ability to remember names isn't just a party trick; it's a crucial skill that can forge stronger personal connections and leave lasting impressions. Recalling a name is a simple yet profound gesture that shows respect and attentiveness. We all love it when the local barista remembers our name and coffee order; this recognition makes us feel a sense of belonging.

In professional settings, this ability becomes even more essential. Remembering colleagues' and clients' names can set the tone for future interactions and foster trust and connection.

Mnemonic Techniques for Name Recall

So, how can we remember the names of multiple people? My secret weapon is alliteration. I pair a person's name with an easily memorable characteristic or profession. For instance, "Tom the Teacher" or "Lisa from

London" creates a catchy phrase that links the name to something tangible and makes it much easier for me to remember.

Associating names with visual imagery is another excellent technique. If I were to meet someone named Rose, I'd picture a rose flower alongside her face. A vivid image like this anchors her name in my memory, making retrieving it later easier. These devices act as mental shortcuts, transforming abstract names into memorable concepts your brain can easily access.

Another thing I do is repeat the person's name several times during the initial conversation to embed it in my brain. I greet them using their name, include their name when asking them questions, and I even mention it as we part ways to reinforce it in my memory. Writing down names immediately after introductions can also strengthen recall, whether in a discreet notebook or a notes app on your phone. The more you practice these strategies, the more natural they will become.

Attentiveness plays a big role in remembering names. When someone introduces themselves, focus on their name as if it's the most vital part of the conversation. This requires minimizing distractions and giving them your full attention. Listen with intent and maintain eye contact. Reduce distractions by putting your phone away, avoid letting your gaze wander, and center your attention on the person and create a mental space where their name can take root. This practice of mindfulness not only aids memory but also demonstrates genuine interest, setting a positive tone for the interaction.

Creating Mental Hooks: Associative Memory Techniques

Associative memory is a fascinating aspect of our cognitive function, intertwining different pieces of information to make them easier to recall. Imagine your brain as a vast library, where each piece of information is a book on a shelf. Associative memory acts like a librarian who remembers where each book is and how they relate to each other. This ability to create mental links between concepts helps us store and retrieve information effectively. For instance, think about how a familiar song can instantly transport you back to a specific moment, evoking vivid memories and emotions. This is the power of association at work, creating a web of connections that your mind can easily navigate.

To develop personal mental hooks, consider linking new information with personal experiences. This approach transforms abstract concepts into relatable ones, making them more memorable. For example, if you're learning about a historical event, try associating it with a personal memory from a related location or period. This creates a unique anchor in your mind, allowing the new information to latch onto something familiar.

Rhymes and wordplay can also serve as effective mnemonic devices, turning complex information into catchy phrases that are easier to remember. Creating a rhyme or using alliteration can provide a rhythmic cue that jogs your memory when needed. These techniques tap into your brain's natural affinity for patterns and rhythm, making information stick.

Visualizing a "memory palace" is another technique that uses associative memory. This method involves mentally placing pieces of information within a familiar setting, like rooms in a house you know well. As you walk through the memory palace in your mind, each room or object you encounter triggers a specific piece of information, creating a vivid mental map.

Associating names with famous people or characters also works. Connecting a new name to someone well-known creates a mental shortcut that makes the name easier to recall. For example, if you meet someone named Albert, you might link them to Albert Einstein. This association provides a memorable reference point, helping the name resurface when needed.

I've created a Memory Palace Description and Quiz for you to try at the end of this chapter.

Implementation in Daily Life

Incorporating associative techniques into daily interactions can significantly enhance memory retention. Try creating associations for frequently encountered names or concepts, weaving them into stories or scenarios that resonate with you.

Practicing associations with lists or sets of new information can also be beneficial. When you encounter a list of items to remember, imagine them interacting in a creative scene. For example, you need to buy milk, potatoes, eggs, and bananas. Create a picture of bananas in pyjamas, Humpty Dumpty, and a couch potato crying over spilled milk. This transforms a mundane task into an engaging mental exercise that reinforces the connections you've made. Practicing these techniques regularly trains the brain to make associations naturally, turning memory retention into a fluid, intuitive process.

Memory, at its core, is about making connections. By harnessing the power of associative memory, you can transform how you store and recall information. These mental hooks make learning more engaging and enhance your ability to remember details that matter. Whether it's a name, a concept, or a set of instructions, associative memory techniques offer a dynamic way to deepen your understanding and retention.

Practicing Active Recall in Conversations

Have you ever been in a conversation where, halfway through, your mind draws a blank? And you struggle to remember the details you want to share, leaving you flustered? This is where active recall is terrific, offering a way to strengthen memory retention. Unlike passive review, which involves simply reading or hearing information multiple times, active recall pushes you to retrieve information actively from memory. This method engages your brain more deeply, reinforcing neural connections and making the information easier to recall later. Studies have shown that active recall significantly enhances memory retention compared to passive study methods[5]. It turns learning into an active process, requiring effort and engagement, which in turn cements the information in your mind more firmly.

Incorporating active recall into your conversations can transform how you remember details and engage with others. One effective technique is to summarize prior conversations before starting new ones. This practice reinforces your learning and prepares you for the next interaction. Imagine revisiting the main points of a previous discussion as you get ready to meet someone again. This habit keeps the information fresh and relevant, allowing you to build on it confidently. Quizzing yourself on key details after interactions is another powerful method. After a meeting or chat, take a moment to review the main topics discussed mentally. Challenge yourself to recall details like names, dates, or action items. This self-test reinforces your memory and helps identify gaps that need further attention.

Spaced Repetition

Revisiting information at intervals, rather than cramming it all at once, enhances long-term memory. This technique, known as spaced repetition, leverages the spacing effect—a phenomenon where information is better recalled when exposure is spaced out over time.

Creating a schedule for revisiting information is a practical way to incorporate this into your routine. Whether setting reminders on your phone or using a calendar, having a structured approach ensures you revisit key points regularly. Spaced repetition software or apps can also be beneficial, offering tailored schedules that adapt to your learning pace and retention needs. These tools guide you in revisiting information optimally, ensuring it remains accessible in your memory.

Engaging in memory games with friends or colleagues can be fun and practical to hone your active recall skills. These games challenge you to retrieve information in a dynamic setting, reinforcing your recall abilities.

Simple games like "20 Questions" or memory card matches can stimulate your mind and encourage quick recall.

Practicing recall through storytelling is another engaging exercise. Share a story or teach someone a concept, focusing on accurately recalling details. This method strengthens your memory and enhances your ability to communicate clearly and confidently. Teaching others requires a deep understanding of the material, pushing you to retrieve and organize information effectively.

As you explore these techniques, active recall will become a natural part of your conversational practice. Your effort in retrieving information pays off in more substantial, more reliable memories. Each conversation becomes an opportunity to reinforce what you've learned, turning memory retention into an engaging and rewarding process. By making active recall a habit, you unlock a powerful tool that enhances your interactions and enriches your understanding of the world.

Boosting Memory with Visualization Strategies

Visualization is a powerful tool that taps into the brain's ability to create and store vivid mental images, making it easier to remember information. Visualization engages the brain more fully by transforming abstract data into concrete images, enhancing retention and recall. The science behind this lies in how our mind processes images and relationships.

Visualization takes advantage of this natural inclination, converting words, numbers, or concepts into colorful, dynamic mental snapshots. When you visualize, you create a mental movie where each element plays a role, linking together to form a coherent, memorable scene. This technique can be a game-changer in learning and retaining complex information, turning dry facts into visual narratives.

Developing compelling visualizations requires some creativity and practice. Start by crafting detailed mental pictures for the information you want to remember. If you're trying to memorize a process, imagine each step as a scene in a movie. Use color to differentiate elements, movement to show progression, and emotion to highlight importance. For example, if you're learning about the water cycle, you might picture a vibrant blue river, the sun's warmth causing evaporation and the clouds forming in a dramatic sky. This vivid imagery makes the concept more engaging and easier to recall.

Another technique is to use mind maps or diagrams, where you sketch out the relationships between ideas. This helps organize information visually and allows you to see connections that might not be immediately obvious in a text-based format.

Scenarios where visualization enhances memory are numerous. Consider a student preparing for an exam on human anatomy. By visualizing the body as a complex network of interconnected systems, they can picture how blood flows through veins, how muscles contract, or how nerves transmit signals. This mental imagery provides a framework that helps to understand and recall during the test. Similarly, when planning a project, visualizing the sequence of tasks as a flow chart can help you remember the order and dependencies of each step. Imagery acts as a mental anchor, making it easier to retrieve information when needed.

Incorporating visualization into your daily routine can have lasting benefits for memory improvement. One way to do this is by visualizing daily tasks or goals during your morning routine. As you sip your coffee, imagine your day unfolding like a storyboard, each task a scene that leads naturally to the next. This practice helps you organize your day and primes your mind for action.

Meditation or relaxation techniques can also enhance visualization skills. During a quiet moment, allow your mind to wander through a mental scene, focusing on the sights, sounds and feelings. This exercise not only relaxes the mind but also sharpens your ability to create and retain detailed mental images.

Visualization is more than just a memory aid; creating vivid images transforms abstract ideas into something tangible and memorable. This effective and enjoyable technique encourages you to explore your imagination and creativity. As you practice visualization regularly, you'll find that your ability to recall information improves, making learning and memory retention more intuitive and effective.

Memory Palace Journey Description

Imagine you're entering a spacious, contemporary house for a memorable journey through its various rooms, each distinctly decorated and filled with unique objects to aid in your memory exercise.

The Hallway: As you open the bright red front door, you're greeted by a large ornate mirror to your right and a small, antique wooden table to your left. On the table sits a silver tray holding a set of keys and a white porcelain vase with fresh red roses.

The Living Room: Moving forward into the living room, you see a deep blue sofa facing a stone fireplace where a brass clock ticks prominently on the mantel. Adjacent to the fireplace is a tall bookshelf filled with assorted books, a model ship and a globe.

The Kitchen: Next, you enter the kitchen, where a round table covered with a checkered tablecloth stands in the center. There's a fruit bowl filled with bananas and apples on the table. Hanging above the table is a chandelier with crystal pendants. The counter holds a red coffee maker and a stack of green plates.

The Study: Heading into the study, you notice a large oak desk dominating the room, with a black leather chair pushed against it. There are several items on the desk: a laptop, a stack of colorful notebooks and a brass desk lamp. The wall above the desk features an array of family photos.

The Bedroom: Lastly, the bedroom features a king-sized bed with navy blue bedding and gold pillows. A plush grey rug lies at the foot of the bed and beside it stands a nightstand on which rests a digital alarm clock and a stack of three mystery novels.

Memory Palace Quiz

Now, test your recall of the details from each room in the memory palace:

The Hallway: What color is the front door and what items are placed on the antique table?

Living Room: Describe two items found on the mantel of the fireplace and one item from the bookshelf.

Kitchen: What are the two main colors noticed in the kitchen and what items can be found on the round table?

Study: What are the three items located on the oak desk and what decorates the wall above it?

Bedroom: What are the colors of the bedding?

10

CULTURAL SENSITIVITY IN COMMUNICATION

"Cultural diversity brings a collective strength that can benefit all."
Robert Allan

In a conference room filled with professionals from around the globe, a simple gesture—a nod, a smile, a handshake—can carry different meanings, each shaped by cultural diversity. These small actions, often taken for granted, can bridge or widen gaps, depending on our awareness and sensitivity.

Cultural diversity in communication isn't just about avoiding faux pas; it's about embracing the wealth of perspectives that different backgrounds bring. When diverse teams come together, they don't just share ideas; they create a synergy that can lead to unprecedented innovation. I've seen many creative solutions emerge when people from varied backgrounds collaborate, each bringing unique insights shaped by their experiences and cultures. This blend of perspectives fosters an environment where new ideas flourish, challenging conventional thinking and pushing boundaries.

Consider the benefits of cultural insights in problem-solving. When a team comprises individuals from different cultures, they're equipped to approach challenges from multiple angles. This diversity of thought can lead to more comprehensive solutions. It's like having a kit with various tools, each suited for a specific task. Studies have shown that a workplace that embraces cultural diversity can lead to better decision-making and a more inclusive environment where everyone feels valued[6]. This inclusivity doesn't just transform the dynamics within teams; it also opens doors to wider markets and audiences, reflecting the diversity of the world we live in.

Solving Complex Problems in a Multicultural Team

A few years ago, I was coaching a team leader of a multinational NGO. He was responsible for co-ordinating a complex project involving team members from Brazil, Sweden and India. The aim was to launch a health initiative in multiple countries. He confided in me that the team faced communication challenges and conflicts over project management styles. The Swedish members preferred a more egalitarian and direct approach, while the Brazilian and Indian members were accustomed to a more hierarchical structure and indirect communication. So here's what we did.

- **Workshops:** We ran several cross-cultural workshops to help team members understand each other's communication styles and work preferences.

- **Facilitation:** A facilitator was brought in to help mediate discussions, ensuring that all cultural perspectives were respected and understood.

- **Hybrid Approaches:** The team adopted a hybrid management approach, blending direct and indirect communication and respecting hierarchical sensitivities without compromising egalitarian values.

- **Outcome:** This culturally sensitive approach allowed the team to collaborate more effectively, leveraging the diverse strengths of its members. The health initiative was successfully launched with tailored approaches in each target country, reflecting the nuanced understanding of local contexts contributed by team members.

Be Open & Curious

To truly appreciate and understand different cultures, it's crucial to approach them with a mindset of openness and curiosity. This means actively seeking knowledge and experiences that broaden your understanding of cultures other than your own. Participating in cultural events and festivals is one way to immerse yourself in the traditions and practices of different communities. These experiences offer a firsthand glimpse into the values and customs that shape people's lives, providing a richer context for your interactions.

I find that reading literature and watching films from various cultures transports me to different worlds, offering narratives and perspectives that deepen my empathy and understanding. These stories are windows into the lives and experiences of others, allowing me to connect with them on a more profound level.

Asking respectful questions invites others to share their cultural stories and insights. For instance, instead of making assumptions about a colleague's background, you might ask, "What are some traditions you celebrate with your family?" or "How do you find this cultural practice impacts your daily life?" These questions demonstrate your interest and create a space for cultural exchange.

Integrating diverse perspectives into conversations and decision-making processes requires intentional effort and openness. One effective strategy is to foster inclusive brainstorming sessions where every voice is heard and valued. Encourage team members to share their ideas and insights, ensuring that each perspective is considered in the decision-making process. This might involve setting ground rules that promote equal participation, such as rotating speaking turns or using anonymous idea submissions to ensure everyone feels comfortable contributing.

Take a moment to reflect on a recent conversation where cultural differences were present. Consider the questions you asked and the responses you received. How did curiosity shape the interaction? Jot down a few questions you might ask in future encounters to deepen your understanding and connection. Reflect on how these questions can foster a more inclusive and culturally sensitive dialogue.

Recognizing and Respecting Cultural Norms

Cultural norms are the unwritten rules that guide behavior within a society. They shape how we greet one another, how we express respect and even how we communicate. These norms influence expectations and interactions, often without us realizing it. For instance, in Japan, bowing is a common greeting, a gesture deeply rooted in respect and tradition. Meanwhile, a handshake is the norm in Western cultures, symbolizing openness and equality. Understanding these customs goes beyond mere etiquette; it is about recognizing the values they represent. In many Asian cultures, hierarchical respect is crucial, dictating how individuals interact based on age or status. Ignoring such norms can lead to misunderstandings, affecting social and business relationships. In professional settings, recognizing these nuances can mean the difference between a successful negotiation and a missed opportunity.

When entering a new cultural setting, take time to observe social interactions. Watch how locals greet each other, note the language they use, and pay attention to their body language. This silent observation can offer invaluable insights into the standards that guide their interactions. Additionally, seeking guidance from cultural insiders or mentors can be incredibly helpful. These individuals provide context and explanations that deepen your understanding. They offer perspectives that might not be immediately visible, helping you navigate the nuances of a new culture with greater ease. By actively listening to their experiences and advice, you can better adapt to and respect the cultural norms of those around you.

Respecting cultural differences is foundational in building trust and fostering positive relationships. It demonstrates an appreciation for the values and traditions of others, creating a sense of mutual respect.

In business negotiations, for example, acknowledging and adhering to cultural norms can significantly impact outcomes. Respect for hierarchy, understanding the importance of saving face, and adapting communication styles to suit cultural expectations are just a few ways respect can enhance negotiations. Ignoring these norms, however, can lead to misunderstandings.

Imagine a meeting where a Western executive addresses a Middle Eastern counterpart by their first name without prior permission. In many Middle Eastern cultures, such personal familiarity in a formal business setting may be seen as presumptuous or disrespectful. This cultural faux pas could make the counterpart feel undervalued or disrespected, potentially compromising the relationship and obstructing successful negotiations. This small oversight can derail the conversation, creating tension and hindering collaboration.

Diplomats often undergo extensive cultural training, honing their skills to navigate diverse cultural landscapes with sensitivity and respect. This preparation allows them to communicate effectively, even when cultural norms differ drastically.

Cross-cultural friendships also thrive on respect for each other's backgrounds. Take, for instance, a friendship between an American and an Indian. By respecting each other's customs—whether it be celebrating Diwali or acknowledging the importance of Thanksgiving—the friendship deepens. These relationships are built on an understanding that transcends cultural differences, fostering an enriched and resilient connection.

In our world of interconnectedness, embracing cultural norms is more crucial than ever. It requires a willingness to step outside of comfort zones and explore the vast array of human experiences that cultures offer. By doing so, you show respect and gain a deeper appreciation for the diversity that shapes our world. This respect is not just about avoiding missteps; it's about building bridges and creating spaces where varied perspectives can flourish. As you navigate these different relationships, remember that the goal is not to perfect every interaction but to approach each with openness and a genuine desire to connect.

Adapting Communication Styles for Cultural Sensitivity

Imagine you're attending a business meeting with colleagues from different corners of the globe. As the discussion unfolds, you notice that what seems to be effective communication for one person might not work for another. This difference often stems from the varying communication styles inherent in different cultures. Understanding the need to adapt your communication style is crucial when interacting across cultures.

Some cultures, known as high context, rely heavily on implicit communication and non-verbal cues. In these settings, much is understood through context, relationships and shared experiences. Japan and many Middle Eastern countries exemplify high-context communication, where messages are often indirect and understanding the subtleties is key.

Conversely, low-context cultures, like the United States and Germany, prioritize explicit, direct communication. Clarity and detail are valued in these environments, with less reliance on the surrounding context to convey meaning. See the table at the end of this chapter.

Furthermore, the preference for direct versus indirect communication varies across cultures. Direct communication is straightforward and unambiguous, often favored in low-context cultures where honesty and clarity are paramount. In contrast, indirect communication is more nuanced, focusing on maintaining harmony and avoiding confrontation. This style is prevalent in high-context cultures, where the relationship takes precedence over bluntness. Recognizing these differences can help you navigate conversations with cultural sensitivity, adjusting your approach to align with the preferences of those you interact with.

Adapting your communication style involves practical strategies that align with cultural expectations. One technique is adjusting your tone and formality based on the cultural context. In some cultures, a formal tone is a sign of respect, particularly in professional settings. This might mean using titles and honorifics or maintaining a certain level of politeness in your language. In more relaxed cultures, informal language might be more appropriate, fostering a sense of camaraderie and openness.

Additionally, when communicating in low-context cultures, strive for clarity by using concise language. Avoid jargon or idiomatic expressions that might not translate well, ensuring your message is understood without relying on context. This approach not only enhances understanding but also demonstrates respect for the communication preferences of your audience.

Adapting communication styles can present challenges, particularly when balancing authenticity with respect for cultural differences. You might find yourself navigating the fine line between staying true to your personality and adjusting to fit the cultural norms of others. The key is maintaining clarity while adapting your style, ensuring your message is not lost in translation. This requires a delicate balance, where you honor the cultural context without sacrificing authenticity. It's important to approach these challenges with an open mind and be willing to learn and adapt as needed. This flexibility enhances your communication and fosters mutual respect and understanding.

Consider engaging in exercises that encourage adaptation to become more flexible in your communication approaches. Role-playing scenarios with diverse cultural contexts can be particularly effective. This involves practicing conversations with individuals from different backgrounds and experimenting with various communication styles to see what resonates. These exercises provide a safe space to explore and refine your approach, offering insights into how different styles impact interactions. Reflective exercises on past cross-cultural interactions can also be valuable. By analyzing previous experiences, you can identify what worked well and where adjustments might be needed. This reflection encourages continuous learning and growth, empowering you to adapt your communication style with confidence and ease.

Avoiding Cultural Missteps in Dialogue

Picture yourself at an international business meeting. You're feeling confident and ready to make a great impression. But in an instant, a seemingly harmless gesture causes the room to fall silent. You've unknowingly committed a cultural blunder. Misinterpretations of gestures and body language are among the most common oversights that derail communication. For instance, a thumbs-up might be a positive affirmation in one culture, but in another, it can be offensive. Similarly, eye contact, a sign of engagement in some societies, might be seen as disrespectful in others. These unintentional missteps can create barriers, impacting relationships and causing unnecessary tension.

Language, too, can be a minefield. Words and phrases that seem neutral to us might carry unintended meanings elsewhere. For example, colloquial expressions or idioms that translate poorly can confuse or offend. Even the tone of voice can alter the message. What sounds assertive in one language may come off as aggressive in another. These language-related pitfalls require careful navigation to prevent misunderstandings that might compromise your intentions. The consequences of such missteps can be significant, leading to damaged relationships, lost opportunities and a communication breakdown.

To avoid these cultural pitfalls, preparation is paramount. Before engaging in cross-cultural interactions, take the time to research the cultural etiquette of the people you'll be communicating with. This might involve learning about their customs, traditions and social norms. Understanding the historical and cultural context can explain why certain gestures or words are significant. Seeking feedback from cultural liaisons or colleagues familiar with the culture can also be invaluable. They can offer guidance, helping you navigate the intricacies of communication that might take time to become apparent.

In a cultural misstep, humility and the ability to apologize can make a significant difference. Acknowledging mistakes openly, without defensiveness, shows respect and a willingness to learn. A sincere apology can go a long way in repairing any damage caused by cultural blunders. It's about accepting responsibility and expressing a genuine desire to understand and improve. Consider the impact of a thoughtful apology that acknowledges the error and seeks to learn from it. Such gestures can restore harmony, demonstrating that your intentions were never to offend.

Many apologies have mended relationships and fostered greater understanding between different cultures.

In 2008, the Australian government formally apologized to the indigenous Aboriginal population for past injustices, including the forced removal of children from their families. This apology, delivered by then Prime Minister Kevin Rudd, was a landmark in Australian history and marked a step towards reconciliation and better understanding between the Indigenous communities and the broader Australian society.

In 2018, Dolce & Gabbana faced backlash for an advertising campaign perceived as stereotyping and disrespecting Chinese culture. The founders, Domenico Dolce and Stefano Gabbana issued a video apology in Mandarin, acknowledging their mistake and expressing their love and respect for Chinese culture. This apology was important in mending the relationship with Chinese consumers and demonstrating cultural sensitivity.

Continuous learning and adaptation are crucial for navigating the complexities of cross-cultural communication. Each interaction offers an opportunity for growth, allowing you to refine your understanding and approach. Embracing a mindset of cultural learning means being open to new experiences and willing to adapt. It involves celebrating small successes in cultural sensitivity and recognizing that each step forward enhances your communication ability. This learning journey is ongoing, requiring patience and a commitment to personal growth. You pave the way for more meaningful and enriching connections by approaching cultural interactions with curiosity and openness.

As we conclude this chapter, remember that cultural sensitivity is not an end point but a continuous process of learning and adapting. It's about recognizing the richness diverse perspectives bring to our lives and communication. Let this be the beginning of your exploration into the intricate world of cultural dialogue, where every conversation is an opportunity to deepen your understanding and broaden your horizons.

This table compares high-context and low-context cultures along with specific communication strategies that are effective in each. It illustrates the differences and shows how to adapt your communication approach accordingly.

Communication Strategies for Each CultureType:

High-Context Cultures: Japan, Arab, China

- **Prioritize Relationship Building:**
  Spend time building relationships before getting into business or negotiations.

- **Observe Non-verbal Cues:**
  Pay attention to body language, tone of voice, and facial expressions, as they are integral to understanding the entire message.

- **Use Indirect Language:**
  Be sensitive to the indirect communication style, using tact and reading between the lines.

- **Seek to Understand the Context:**
  Understand the background and the environment your counterparts are operating within to better interpret their communications.

Low-Context Cultures: USA, Germany, Scandanavia

- **Be Clear and Concise:**
  Communicate your ideas clearly and avoid ambiguity as these cultures value straightforwardness.

- **Focus on the Task:**
  Emphasize getting to the point and dealing with tasks directly.

- **Use Direct Questions:**
  Feel free to ask direct questions to clarify points and make sure mutual understanding is achieved.

- **Provide Detailed Explanations:**
  Do not rely on shared background or knowledge; explain with specifics and details as needed.

11

SPECIAL CONSIDERATIONS FOR INTROVERTS

"Quiet people have the loudest minds." Stephen Hawkings

Leveraging Introverted Strengths in Conversations

Bill Gates is often described as an introvert. Despite being one of the richest individuals in the world and a leading figure in technology and philanthropy, Gates has frequently shared in interviews and his writings that he is naturally introverted. He is known for his deep focus and concentration, a common trait among introverts. This ability allowed him to spend hours coding and solving complex problems during the early days of Microsoft, driving innovation and setting the stage for the technology revolution.

Gates is not known for being outspoken or charismatic in the traditional, extroverted sense. Instead, he communicates thoughtfully and deliberately. He has used his platform to advocate for global health and education reforms, influencing policy and public opinion through well-reasoned arguments and detailed presentations. Instead of relying on charisma, Gates led Microsoft with a focus on strategic planning and execution. His reflective and analytical leadership style helped Microsoft innovate and remain a leader in competitive tech spaces.

He has also used his introverted nature in public advocacy, often sharing detailed research and data to make compelling arguments for his causes.

He regularly thoughtfully engages with leaders and experts, facilitating discussions that lead to actionable insights and solutions.

I share this with you because Bill Gates exemplifies how introverts can leverage their natural tendencies towards deep thought, concentration, and careful planning to effect positive change on a global scale. His work has not only transformed the technology landscape but also significantly contributed to improving health and education outcomes worldwide.

Through my work, I have learned that introverts have an innate ability to listen deeply, which fosters genuine understanding and connection. While extroverts might enthusiastically dominate a conversation, introverts excel in creating space for others to express themselves. This ability to listen attentively allows you to pick up on subtle cues and emotions, offering insights that others might overlook. Your thoughtful nature means that when you do speak, your words carry weight and depth. By embracing these qualities, you can transform conversations, making them more meaningful and impactful.

Introverts often take time to consider their words carefully. This introspection results in well-considered opinions and questions that add depth to discussions. Before entering a conversation, some find preparing topics or questions of interest helpful. This preparation boosts confidence and ensures that your contributions are insightful and relevant.

Introverts need to consider strategies that highlight their contributions to ensure their voice is heard and appreciated in group settings. Volunteering to lead or organize small group discussions can provide a platform to share your ideas in a controlled environment. Your natural leadership and listening skills can shine in these settings as you guide the conversation with empathy and focus. Additionally, writing follow-up emails is a powerful tool for introverts. When thoughts go unvoiced in meetings, an articulate email can capture your insights and ensure they're acknowledged and valued. This approach allows you to contribute meaningfully without the pressure of on-the-spot speaking.

One-on-one conversations are where introverts often truly excel. In these intimate settings, you have the opportunity to engage deeply with individuals, free from the distractions of larger groups. Small meetings can often be more productive than large gatherings.

Here are some tips to enhance one-on-one interactions:

- **Choose the right setting**:
  Opt for quiet, comfortable environments where you can focus without distractions. A cozy café or a serene park can be ideal.

- **Prepare thoughtful questions**:
  Before the meeting, consider questions that invite deeper dialogue. This preparation will help guide the conversation and ensure it remains engaging.

- **Be present**:
  During the conversation, practice active listening. Pay attention to verbal and non-verbal cues, and respond thoughtfully, reinforcing your interest and understanding.

- **Reflect and follow up**:
  After the meeting, take a moment to reflect on the conversation. Consider sending a follow-up message expressing gratitude and summarizing key points discussed. This gesture reinforces your connection and leaves a lasting impression.

Preparing for Social Engagements with Intention

Walking into a social event can feel like stepping onto a stage, lights glaring, and the audience waiting. For introverts, this can be daunting. To navigate these situations with confidence, setting clear objectives can really help. Before attending an event, take a moment to identify your specific networking goals. Are you aiming to meet a certain number of new contacts, or is there a particular individual you'd like to connect with?

These objectives provide focus and direction, turning what might feel like a chaotic whirlwind into a series of achievable tasks. This intention acts as your compass, guiding your interactions and ensuring each conversation feels purposeful rather than perfunctory.

Beyond setting goals, preparing your mindset and emotions is crucial. Visualization exercises can be particularly effective here. Picture yourself at the event, engaging in successful conversations, feeling at ease and connected. This mental rehearsal can ease anxiety, replacing fear with familiarity. Similarly, affirmations can bolster your confidence. Simple phrases like "I am capable of meaningful conversations" or "I bring value to every interaction" can shift your mindset, reducing self-doubt. By affirming your strengths, you step into the event with a sense of empowerment, ready to embrace new encounters.

Pre-event research and planning are often overlooked but are powerful strategies. Knowing who will be attending or speaking can be a game-changer. You can identify common interests or professional overlaps by researching attendees and providing natural conversation starters. Planning conversation topics related to the event theme can further enhance your preparedness. These small acts of research create a sense of familiarity, transforming the unknown into the known and allowing you to approach conversations with curiosity and confidence.

Personal rituals can serve as grounding anchors in the moments leading up to an event. Establish a routine that calms your mind and centers your focus. As mentioned in previous chapters, deep breathing exercises can be incredibly effective; they slow your heart rate and help you remain present. As you breathe in, visualize positive energy filling your body, and as you exhale, imagine stress and anxiety leaving your body. This simple practice can have a profound impact on your state of mind. Listening to calming music or podcasts en-route to the event can also set a positive tone. Choose content that inspires or soothes you, creating a mental space where you feel relaxed and open to new experiences.

Creating Personal Conversation Comfort Zones

For many introverts, walking into a room that's buzzing with chatter and laughter can feel like stepping into a foreign land, where the noise and energy levels are overwhelming. To navigate these spaces with ease, consider the concept of conversation comfort zones—environments that feel familiar and reassuring, allowing you to engage more naturally. Choosing venues that are comforting can make a world of difference, these settings provide a sense of control, enabling you to focus on the conversation rather than the chaos around you. Physical spaces that allow for quieter interactions are particularly beneficial, as they reduce sensory overload and create a more intimate atmosphere. In these environments, you can connect more deeply without the distraction of background noise or bustling crowds.

Establishing conversational boundaries within these comfort zones is equally important. It's about knowing your limits and respecting them to protect your energy. If you feel overwhelmed, it's perfectly acceptable to excuse yourself politely. A simple "I need a moment to recharge" can be both respectful and practical. Scheduling breaks during long events is another strategy to help maintain your energy levels. Stepping outside for a few minutes of fresh air or finding a quiet space, to regroup can provide the solitude needed to refresh and return with renewed focus. By setting these boundaries, you honor your needs, ensuring that each social interaction is enjoyable and sustainable. You will be surprised to discover that most people will respect your honesty and the opportunity to recharge their own social battery.

The presence of trusted allies in your comfort zones can offer invaluable support. Attending events with a friend or colleague who understands your preferences can alleviate much of the pressure. They can help navigate conversations, introduce you to new people, or provide familiarity in an unfamiliar setting. Having someone by your side who knows when to step in or when to step back can make social engagements feel less daunting. Partnering with someone who shares your social rhythm can transform even the most intimidating environments into welcoming spaces.

Personalizing your comfort zones to fit your preferences can enhance your social experiences. Bringing personal items that provide comfort—like a favorite pen or notebook—can offer reassurance. These items serve as reference points, grounding you when interactions become too much. Positioning yourself in quieter areas of a venue can also help. Whether choosing a table away from the main crowd or sitting near an exit, these minor adjustments can create a buffer, allowing you to engage at your own pace. Tailoring your environment in these ways makes you feel more at ease and empowers you to participate fully and authentically in conversations.

People have told me that these strategies have helped transform social engagements from draining obligations into opportunities for genuine interaction.

Strategies for Sustainable Social Energy

Recognizing the signs of social fatigue is the first step in managing your energy. When you start to feel drained, it often manifests as a sense of irritability or an overwhelming urge to withdraw. These are signals from your body and mind that it's time for a break. Ignoring them can lead to burnout, making future interactions even more challenging. Balancing social activities with periods of solitude is essential. Just as athletes need rest days to recover and build strength, introverts need downtime to recharge. This balance lets you approach social engagements with renewed vigor and enthusiasm rather than dread.

The role of prioritization in managing social energy cannot be overstated. Choosing social engagements that align with your personal goals and values is vital. Not every invitation needs a "yes." Select events that offer personal or professional growth opportunities. These are the interactions that will nourish you, providing more than just surface-level connections.

Conversely, learn to decline invitations that don't resonate with your interests. It's about quality, not quantity. By focusing your energy on interactions that matter, you ensure that you're investing your time and resources wisely. This selective approach allows you to maintain your energy reserves for the moments that count.

Self-reflection is a powerful tool in understanding your energy patterns. I encourage you to keep a journal and track your high and low energy periods, providing insights into your social rhythms. Reflect on past engagements to determine when you felt most energized and when you didn't. Was it the environment, the people, or perhaps the time of day? Identifying these factors can guide you in planning future interactions, allowing you to choose the best times and settings for socializing. This awareness empowers you to tailor your social calendar to fit your energy needs, ensuring you remain vibrant and engaged in your interactions.

Managing your energy effectively will not only improve your communication skills but enhance your overall well-being. Engaging meaningfully without feeling depleted is a gift that keeps giving, enriching your personal and professional relationships. As you continue this journey, remember that your energy is valuable. Treat it with the care and respect it deserves, and it will serve you well.

Social Personality Quiz: Are You an Introvert or an Extrovert?

Answer each question truthfully based on how you typically feel or behave in social situations. At the end, count the number of A's, B's, and C's to see if you're more of an introvert or an extrovert.

When you go to a party with lots of new people, you usually:

A) Stick to your close friends and avoid initiating conversations with strangers.

B) Sometimes mix between sticking with friends and meeting new people.

C) Enjoy meeting new people and often start conversations with strangers.

How do you feel after spending a few hours surrounded by a lot of people?

A) Drained, and you need time alone to recharge.

B) It depends on the context and the people involved.

C) Energized and ready for more social interaction.

If you had to choose, what kind of vacation would you prefer?

A) A quiet retreat in a secluded place with a few close friends or family members.

B) A balanced vacation with some days spent in solitude and other days exploring busy tourist spots.

C) A bustling city trip with lots of activities and social opportunities.

When it comes to making new friends, you:

A) Find it quite challenging and prefer to have a few close friends.

B) Can sometimes find it easy, but other times you're hesitant.

C) Find it easy and enjoyable to expand your social circle.

At work or in class, when you have a big project, you prefer to:

A) Work alone, as it's easier to concentrate and function effectively.

B) Work alone or with others, depending on the nature of the project.

C) Work in a team, as the interaction stimulates your creativity.

During conversations, you:

A) Tend to listen more and speak less.

B) Balance listening and talking, depending on who you're with.

C) Tend to dominate the conversation and share your thoughts freely.

How do you usually feel about talking on the phone or video calls?

A) Avoid it if possible, preferring texts or emails instead.

B) Don't mind it sometimes, but it's not always your favorite.

C) Enjoy it and often spend a long time chatting away.

You're more likely to spend your free evening:

A) Reading a book or engaging in a hobby at home alone.

B) Maybe catching up with a friend or two or just relaxing at home.

C) Going out to social events or inviting friends over.

How do you usually handle conflict in social or work situations?

A) Prefer to deal with it internally or avoid confrontation.

B) Address it if necessary, but it's not your comfort zone.

C) Tackle it head-on, discussing issues openly with all parties involved.

What is your approach to social media?

A) Limited use, mainly to keep in touch with close friends and family.

B) You use it moderately, depending on your mood and purpose.

C) Very active, enjoy engaging with many people and making new connections.

Results:

Mostly A's: Introvert —You likely find social interactions with strangers or large groups draining and prefer more intimate gatherings or alone time.

Mostly B's: Ambivert —You exhibit traits of both introverts and extroverts, depending on the situation. You can enjoy social interaction but also value your alone time.

Mostly C's: Extrovert —You thrive in social situations and feel energized by interacting with others, including strangers.

This quiz offers a general look into where you might fall on the introversion-extroversion spectrum in social contexts. Remember, personality can be fluid, and people may exhibit different traits in different situations.

12

Advanced Psychological Insights

"Seek first to understand, then to be understood." St Francis of Assisi

Do you sometimes feel judged as soon as you walk into a room of strangers? Do you find yourself judging others before you've even started to talk to them? Most of us do. It's part of human nature. A series of experiments[7] by Princeton psychologists Janine Willis and Alexander Todorov show that we form an impression of a stranger from their face, often within milliseconds, and this first impression tends to influence all future interactions.

This phenomenon is known as the primacy effect, where the information we first encounter about someone heavily impacts our ongoing perceptions. It's why those first few moments matter so profoundly.

First Impressions

First impressions hinge on a complex interplay of visual cues and body language. Your posture, facial expressions, and even the tilt of your head can communicate volumes without uttering a sound. As mentioned in the chapter about body language, a confident stance and a warm smile can convey approachability, while crossed arms and averted eyes might suggest aloofness or discomfort. These non-verbal signals are potent, as they tap into our primal instincts, influencing how others perceive us. In professional settings, attire and grooming add another layer to these impressions. The clothes you choose and how you present yourself can speak to your personality competence and attention to detail, subtly guiding the opinions others form about you. A friend of mine who advocates for women's empowerment, uses her wardrobe to echo that message. She always wears pink tops or jackets, dyes her hair pink, and wears spectacles with pink frames. What are you conveying through your appearance?

Crafting a positive first impression involves more than what you wear; it's about the energy you project. It's about finding that sweet spot between confidence and warmth. Your language, both verbal and non-verbal, plays a crucial role.

Choosing words that reflect positivity and maintaining an approachable demeanor can make you seem more inviting. These elements, when harmonized, create a memorable first impression that can open doors and foster positive connections. Despite our best efforts, sometimes first impressions falter. Perhaps you were distracted or nervous, and the interaction didn't unfold as you hoped. I remember a client of mine, Ethan, telling me he was excited yet nervous about attending a high-profile networking event in his industry. It was his first big opportunity to make connections that could advance his career. He spent the week before the event brushing up on industry news, preparing an elevator pitch and picking a professional outfit.

On the evening of the event, Ethan arrived at the venue, a sleek hotel, he checked in, grabbed a name badge and stepped into the grand ballroom filled with professionals exchanging business cards. The atmosphere was charged with opportunity, and Ethan felt a surge of confidence. However, as he approached a group of potential contacts, his phone vibrated intensely in his pocket. It was an urgent work call that couldn't be ignored, so he stepped outside to respond, thinking it would only take a moment.

Unfortunately, sorting out the issue took longer than expected, and by the time he returned the group had dispersed.

Attempting to regroup, Ethan told me that he approached another cluster of attendees. He introduced himself with a smile and reached out for a handshake. As he did, he accidentally knocked the other person's drink. The spill was minor, but it was enough to fluster Ethan and divert the conversation toward apologies and cleanup rather than business and opportunities. Despite the rocky start, Ethan laughed off the mishap, which helped break the ice. The rest of the evening went smoother, with Ethan making a few good connections, although not as many as he had hoped. He left the event with mixed feelings—grateful for the contacts he made but aware that his first impressions might not have been as impactful as intended due to distractions and a bit of bad luck.

The good news is that negative first impressions, while sticky, are not set in stone. Acknowledging any missteps openly and sincerely can be a decisive first step in repairing them. Demonstrating consistent positive behavior over time can gradually reshape perceptions. Actions speak louder than words, and by consistently showing up in a positive light, you can gradually overwrite initial judgments.

First Impression Exercises

Engage in role-playing with a friend or colleague where you practice introductions. Focus on refining your body language, tone, and choice of words to create a welcoming atmosphere. Observe how these changes impact your friend's perception and gather feedback. Additionally, observe others in social settings or through video analysis. Note the elements contributing to strong first impressions and consider how you might incorporate similar techniques into your interactions. This practice will help hone your skills, making those pivotal first moments more impactful.

Understanding the art of first impressions equips you with the tools to gracefully navigate social and professional environments. By harnessing the power of visual cues, body language, and genuine self-presentation, you can create the impressions you wish to leave on others.

Using Persuasion Techniques Ethically

I remember the first time I truly understood the power of persuasion. During a community meeting, a local leader spoke passionately to create change. He didn't manipulate the audience or twist the truth. Instead, he laid out his vision with transparency and honesty, respecting the intelligence and autonomy of those he addressed. This approach is the cornerstone of ethical persuasion: building trust through sincerity and shared goals rather than coercion or deceit. Moral persuasion is about aligning your intentions with the needs and values of your audience, ensuring mutual benefit and respect.

Persuasion becomes ethical when it is rooted in transparency. This means being upfront about your intentions and providing truthful information. It's about engaging others with respect, valuing their perspectives, and recognizing their right to make informed decisions. Ethical persuasion also involves crafting logical arguments supported by evidence, creating a foundation of credibility and trust. When you present data or anecdotes, ensure they are accurate and relevant, reinforcing the integrity of your message. Highlighting shared values and goals can further strengthen your persuasive efforts. By aligning your objectives with those of your audience, you create a sense of partnership and common purpose, making your message more compelling.

The impact of ethical persuasion on relationships can be profound. When you persuade with integrity, you lay the groundwork for long-term partnerships built on trust and cooperation. Consider a negotiation scenario where both parties enter with a clear understanding of their respective goals and constraints. They foster a collaborative atmosphere that enhances mutual respect and trust by maintaining openness and seeking win-win outcomes. This approach resolves immediate issues and strengthens the relationship, paving the way for future cooperation.

In team settings, persuasive communication can enhance collaboration by encouraging open dialogue and shared decision-making, ultimately leading to more effective and innovative outcomes.

There are countless examples of ethical persuasion in practice that demonstrate its positive impact. I recall a case where a company I worked with sought to merge with a smaller firm. Rather than using aggressive tactics, the larger company presented a vision for the merger that emphasized the benefits for both parties, such as increased market reach and shared resources. By focusing on transparency and mutual gain, they secured a fair and beneficial deal, setting the stage for a successful partnership.

Nelson Mandela, once a political prisoner for 27 years under the apartheid regime, became the first Black President of South Africa in 1994. His leadership was pivotal during the fragile transition from an apartheid state to a democracy. Mandela's approach to leadership and reconciliation was grounded in ethical persuasion, focusing on unity, forgiveness, and inclusivity. One of his most striking acts was his support for the South African national rugby team, the Springboks, during the 1995 Rugby World Cup. Previously, the Springboks had been a symbol of white oppression. However, Mandela embraced the team and encouraged all South Africans to do the same, which helped bridge racial divides and foster a sense of national unity. This act was not just symbolic but a deliberate, strategic effort to bring a divided country together and heal the wounds of apartheid. Mandela's leadership and his ethical approach to persuasion helped to stabilize a volatile political landscape and lay the foundation for the peaceful coexistence of diverse racial groups in South Africa. Mandela's example demonstrates how ethical persuasion can be used effectively to promote peace and reconciliation, highlighting its positive impact on a national and even global scale.

Incorporating the principles of ethical persuasion into your daily interactions can transform how you communicate and connect with others. By focusing on transparency, respect, and shared goals, you enhance your ability to persuade and build stronger, more meaningful relationships. Whether in professional settings, community initiatives, or personal interactions, ethical persuasion is a powerful tool for fostering trust, cooperation, and positive change.

Understanding Group Dynamics in Conversations

Group dynamics stand out in human interaction as a vibrant, complex pattern. Unlike one-on-one conversations, group settings introduce many social roles and hierarchies. Each participant brings a unique voice, yet they often navigate unspoken rules that govern the interaction. Social roles can dictate who speaks the most and whose opinions are given the most weight. Formal or informal hierarchies can influence the flow of conversation, often determining who leads and who follows. These dynamics are crucial to understanding, affecting how ideas are shared, and decisions are made. The size of the group also plays a significant role. In a smaller group, each voice might have more space to be heard, while in a larger gathering, some might find themselves lost in the crowd. This can impact communication flow, creating a need for strategies that ensure everyone has a chance to participate.

Navigating group conversations effectively requires awareness and adaptability. Techniques for facilitating inclusive dialogue are key. Encouraging everyone to contribute can be as simple as inviting quieter participants to share their thoughts. This might involve directly asking them for their opinions or creating an environment where they feel comfortable speaking up. As mentioned in chapter six, managing dominant voices is another challenge. While some individuals naturally take charge, their dominance can stifle others. One way to balance this is by setting ground rules at the start of the discussion, such as limiting how long one person can speak or rotating the speaking order. This ensures that all voices are heard, promoting a more balanced and equitable conversation. Encouraging quieter participants to voice their opinions can also be facilitated by breaking the group into smaller units or using technology like chat functions for anonymous input.

Groupthink and conformity pose significant challenges in group settings. Groupthink occurs when the desire for harmony or conformity results in irrational or dysfunctional decision-making. It can suppress dissenting viewpoints and stifle creativity. To counter this, it's important to foster an environment where diverse opinions are encouraged and valued. Encouraging critical thinking involves asking probing questions and challenging assumptions. Facilitators can play a crucial role by actively seeking alternative perspectives and highlighting their importance to the group. Creating a culture where dissent is respected requires patience and a commitment to openness. It might mean explicitly stating that all ideas are welcome and that disagreement is a natural part of the process. This can prevent the silencing of minority opinions and help avoid the pitfalls of groupthink.

Practicing Group Communication Skills

Consider participating in group debates focusing on balanced contributions to refine your group communication skills. This involves setting a topic and dividing it into smaller groups, where each person is responsible for presenting a point of view. Role-playing scenarios can also be beneficial. Practice leading group discussions by taking turns facilitating and managing the conversation. This exercise helps develop skills in guiding dialogue, encouraging participation, and managing group dynamics. As you engage in these practices, pay close attention to the flow of conversation and the balance of voices. Reflect on your experiences and consider what strategies worked well and where improvements could be made.

Understanding and navigating group dynamics is not just about managing the conversation; it's about fostering an environment where all participants feel valued and heard. By employing strategies that promote inclusivity and critical thinking, you can enhance your ability to engage effectively in group settings. These skills are valuable in professional contexts and enrich personal interactions, allowing for more meaningful and productive exchanges.

The Role of Cognitive Biases in Communication

Think about the moment you form an opinion of someone based on a single interaction. This is the power of cognitive biases at play. Cognitive biases are systematic patterns of deviation from norm or rationality in judgment, affecting how we perceive and interact with others. These biases can warp our understanding, leading us to make judgments that may not always be fair or accurate.

Take confirmation bias, for instance, where we tend to seek information that confirms our pre-existing beliefs, ignoring evidence to the contrary. This bias can create echo chambers, reinforcing our views without challenging them.

Similarly, the halo effect idealizes someone based on one positive trait, often overlooking flaws or negative behaviors. These biases profoundly impact our decision-making and judgment, influencing our interactions in ways we might not consciously be aware of. Imagine a workplace scenario where a manager consistently favors one employee, believing them to be more competent based on an initial impression. This halo effect can lead to unequal opportunities and resentment among team members, impacting morale and productivity. Addressing this bias requires conscious effort and reflection, such as implementing fair evaluation criteria and seeking input from multiple sources.

Recognizing and mitigating these biases requires intentional effort. One effective strategy is reflective questioning, which involves critically examining your assumptions. Ask yourself why you hold a particular belief and consider what evidence supports or contradicts it. This practice encourages a more balanced perspective, helping to dismantle biases before they take root.

Seeking diverse perspectives is another powerful method for countering biases. Exposing yourself to different viewpoints broadens your understanding and challenges the reinforcement circles that biases create. Engaging in discussions with people from varied backgrounds can provide fresh insights, breaking down the barriers that biases build.

In conflict resolution, awareness of biases plays a crucial role. Acknowledging biases can pave the way for more effective communication and resolution of misunderstandings. When entering mediation or negotiation, it's important to approach the situation with an open mind, recognizing your own biases and how they might color your perceptions. Techniques such as active listening and empathy can help bridge the gap between differing perspectives, fostering a more collaborative atmosphere.

Encouraging open dialogue about biases within team settings can also lead to healthier communication. Creating a safe space where biases can be discussed without judgment promotes transparency and mutual respect. This openness allows for a more honest exchange of ideas, ultimately leading to more effective and harmonious interactions.

Personal anecdotes also highlight the subtle ways biases influence our interactions. Reflect on a time when you might have misjudged someone based on first impressions or allowed confirmation bias to cloud your judgment. Recognizing these moments is the first step toward more mindful communication.

As we close this chapter, the influence of cognitive biases in communication becomes clear. We can foster more meaningful and equitable interactions by understanding, recognizing, and addressing these biases. This awareness enhances personal relationships and impacts professional environments, paving the way for a more inclusive and understanding world. As we move forward, we will explore how these insights into human behavior can be applied to strengthen your communication skills, transforming how you connect with others.

13

SUSTAINING LONG-TERM GROWTH AND CONNECTION

"If you can learn to master the art of communication, you can achieve anything you want in life." Brian Tracy

I recently overheard a group of individuals sharing their dreams and ambitions for the future. I listened to them plotting their next big move. As a coach, I know that everyone is driven by something—a dream, a purpose. These aspirations propel us forward, give us direction and motivation.

When it comes to improving your communication skills, setting clear goals can be transformative, turning vague desires into tangible milestones. Without clear goals, we risk drifting and losing sight of where we want to go. Communication goals serve as signposts, helping us confidently navigate the complexities of social and professional interactions.

I encourage you to set a short-term goal like improving your ability to engage in small talk at networking events. Defining this objective creates a specific focus, allowing for targeted practice and growth. Over time, this small goal lays the groundwork for long-term dreams, such as becoming a confident public speaker.

I've written a book about public speaking that includes many practical exercises. If you'd like to check it out scan the QR code at the back of this book.

Each short-term objective achieved, builds momentum, leading to bigger achievements. Long-term goals, like enhancing your overall communication style, provide a vision of your ultimate potential. Together, these goals form a roadmap, guiding you toward a more fulfilling and connected life.

Identifying specific, measurable goals requires thoughtful reflection. The SMART criteria offers a structured approach based on logical conscious decisions: goals should be **S**pecific, **M**easurable, **A**chievable, **R**elevant, and **T**ime-bound. For instance, instead of vaguely aiming to "improve communication skills," a SMART goal might be "to enhance listening skills by attending three workshops over the next eight weeks." This clarity makes goals more attainable and provides a clear path to follow.

However, as a coach, I know the unconscious mind can hinder SMART goals. If you don't believe the goal is achievable, you will struggle to attain it. It is important to consider the subconscious influence when setting goals. This means including emotions and internal drive when setting goals. If you read SMART backward, you will see it spells the word TRAMS. I use this acronym with clients when goal setting to go a bit deeper. TRAMS goals focus on: **T**owards, **R**elationships, **A**ttitude, **M**eaningful, **S**imple. Let me explain.

We begin by looking forward **T**owards what we want, not focusing on what we don't want, or living in the past. We rarely achieve anything on our own. **R**elationships are an essential ingredient in all goal-setting exercises. It is necessary to have a team of supporters and teachers to help you along the way. **A**ttitude is everything when aiming to master something new. The right attitude can help overcome any obstacle. Subconscious goals need to be **M**eaningful and **M**emorable; otherwise, we may give up too quickly or when the going gets tough. And all goals should be kept **S**imple, we tend to overcomplicate goal setting, and that can lead to overwhelm and result in a lack of goal getting.

Using the TRAMS theme, I help clients visualize their journey to achieving their goals. I ask them the following questions:

Who's driving the tram? Are you in the drivers seat taking control, or sitting up the back looking out the window?
Do you have a map of where you're going?
Do you have a schedule and are you committed to it?
Who's on the tram with you? Are they encouraging you or holding you back?
What signs will you follow along the way?
What will you do when struggling uphill?
What does your destination look like?
How will you know when you've arrived?
How will you celebrate when you get there?

When setting goals, consider different areas of your life. Professionally, you might aim to refine your presentation skills to captivate an audience. Socially, perhaps you want to expand your network by attending one event monthly. Enhancing empathy in your interactions could be a worthy pursuit. By diversifying your goals, you ensure well-rounded growth.

Track Your Progress

Tracking progress is integral to the goal-setting process. A communication journal can be invaluable, allowing you to record experiences, insights, and reflections. By documenting your journey, you gain perspective on how far you've come and what lies ahead.

Digital tools and apps can also assist in setting reminders and milestones, keeping you accountable and motivated. These tools serve as gentle nudges, ensuring you stay on track. Regularly reviewing your progress fosters a sense of accomplishment and allows you to celebrate small victories, reinforcing your commitment to growth.

Goal reflection and adjustment are crucial as you evolve. Life is dynamic, and circumstances change, requiring flexibility in your approach. By reflecting on past achievements, you gain insight into what works and needs adjustment. This process of reflection allows you to refine your goals, ensuring they remain aligned with your current needs and aspirations. Changing circumstances might prompt you to pivot or redefine your objectives. Feedback from trusted peers can also offer valuable perspectives, guiding you toward meaningful adjustments. Embracing this fluidity ensures that your goals continue to inspire and challenge you, propelling you toward a future filled with connection and growth.

Creating a Feedback Loop for Self-Improvement

A feedback loop in communication is an ongoing process of receiving, interpreting, and integrating feedback into daily interactions. Think of feedback as a diagnostic tool that highlights your strengths and identifies areas for growth. It's like a compass that helps you navigate the complex terrain of communication skills. Whether it's a nod of approval or a subtle suggestion for improvement, each piece of feedback holds potential insights. In various contexts, effective feedback methods vary. In a professional setting, structured performance reviews provide formal feedback. Yet, informal settings, like a casual chat over coffee, can offer valuable insights too, often through candid conversations with trusted colleagues or friends.

Seeking constructive feedback requires a proactive approach. It's not just about passively waiting for comments to come your way; it's about actively inviting them. Start by asking specific questions that elicit detailed responses. Instead of a broad, "How did I do?" frame your inquiry around particular aspects, like, "How can I improve my presentation skills?" This specificity encourages precise feedback, targeting areas where you seek to grow. Approach people whose opinions you respect—those who have observed your communication style. A mentor or a seasoned colleague can offer a perspective that blends experience with empathy, guiding you through constructive criticism. Their insights can illuminate blind spots and inspire new strategies for improvement.

Once you receive feedback, the challenge lies in processing and applying it constructively. It's easy to become defensive or dismissive, especially when faced with criticism. However, viewing feedback as a tool for growth can shift this perspective. Begin by analyzing the feedback for recurring themes and patterns. If multiple sources mention the same issue, it's likely an area that warrants attention. Use this analysis to create an action plan. Break down larger goals into manageable steps, focusing on one aspect at a time. For instance, if active listening is a recurring theme, you might set a goal to practice it in your next three meetings. By addressing each area incrementally, you turn feedback into a plan for refining your communication skills.

Maintaining an open mindset toward feedback is crucial. It involves letting go of ego and embracing humility. Remember, feedback is not an attack on your character but an opportunity to learn and evolve. Practicing gratitude when receiving feedback can transform the experience. Thank those who offer their insights, acknowledging the effort they put into helping you grow. This gratitude fosters a positive feedback culture, where people feel valued and are more likely to provide constructive input in the future. By cultivating this mindset, you create an environment where learning thrives, and you continuously refine your communication skills.

Fostering Long-Term Relationships with Authenticity

I mentioned the importance of authenticity in communication in chapter one and I want to talk about it again here because I believe it is the backbone of meaningful relationships, serving as the bedrock upon which trust, and connection are built. Genuine interactions are the key to creating bonds that withstand the test of time. When you approach others with sincerity, you invite them into a space where they can also be true to themselves. This mutual exchange fosters deeper connections, making both parties feel valued and understood. Authenticity lends resilience to relationships, allowing them to weather challenges and adapt to changing circumstances. Interactions become more profound without the veneer of pretense, and bonds grow deeper. Authentic behaviors, like expressing genuine concern and showing empathy, naturally strengthen these connections.

Being authentic means sharing your true self with all your strengths and vulnerabilities. This openness invites others to do the same, creating a foundation of mutual respect and understanding. Sharing personal stories and experiences builds rapport and transforms conversations from surface-level exchanges into meaningful dialogues. Practicing honesty and transparency in communication is vital. When you speak your truth, you signal trustworthiness, encouraging others to reciprocate. This transparency fosters an environment where open dialogue thrives, and differences are navigated with respect and empathy.

Despite its importance, maintaining authenticity is challenging. Social expectations and pressures often demand conformity, urging you to present a curated version of yourself. This pressure can be overwhelming, disconnecting your true self and the persona you project. To overcome this, remind yourself of the value authenticity brings. Reflect on what matters most and align your actions with those values. This alignment is a powerful antidote to external pressures. Addressing conflicts or misunderstandings with integrity is another hurdle. Authenticity in disagreements means approaching them with honesty and a willingness to listen. It involves acknowledging and learning from mistakes rather than avoiding difficult conversations. The following story of two colleagues who, despite initially clashing, forged a solid professional partnership through authenticity, is a perfect example. They learned to appreciate each other's strengths and openly discussed their differences. By embracing vulnerability and addressing conflicts head-on, they built a relationship based on mutual respect.

Story of Authenticity in Disagreements

Angela is a meticulous project manager who thrives on systems and clear deadlines. Liam is a visionary creative strategist whose ideas flow best in unstructured environments. Angela walked into her first team meeting, a notebook tucked under her arm, her list of objectives neatly outlined. The project—a high-stakes client pitch—was ambitious and under a tight deadline. As she clicked her pen and launched into an agenda, Liam leaned back in his chair, arms behind his head, a faint smirk on his face.

"Timelines are great, Angela," he interrupted, "but creativity doesn't run on a stopwatch."

Angela paused, trying to keep her voice calm. "We need structure, Liam. Without it, we'll miss the client deadline."

Liam shrugged. "I think what we need is room to think outside the box. Not box ourselves in."

The tension was palpable. Over the next few weeks, their working relationship went from strained to outright combative. Angela sent detailed follow-up emails; Liam ignored them. Liam presented incomplete ideas; Angela dismissed them. One day, after Liam turned in a half-finished concept for review, Angela lost her patience.

"This isn't acceptable, Liam!" she snapped in front of the team. "We don't have time to clean up half-baked ideas."

Liam bristled. "Maybe if you trusted me instead of treating me like an intern, I'd have the space to do my job."

The room fell silent. Both left the meeting fuming.

Later that day, their manager, Rose, pulled them into her office.

"Sit," Rose said, shutting the door. "Look, I don't expect you two to be best friends, but I need you to figure this out. Angela, Liam's ideas drive the heart of this pitch. Liam, Angela's structure makes sure we deliver it on time. If you keep working against each other, you will fail this team. So, figure it out!"

Rose's words stung—but they were true. After an awkward silence, Angela glanced at Liam. "Can we talk off the record?" Liam nodded.

"Look, I get it. I'm intense," she admitted. "I like control because, without it, I believe everything will fall apart. I've worked hard to get where I am, and I can't afford mistakes."

Liam stirred his coffee thoughtfully. "I get that. But when you micromanage, it feels like you're saying my ideas don't matter."

"That's not true," Angela said softly. "You are talented. Your concepts are brilliant—I just don't know how to fit them into a process."

Liam looked up. "And I need a process. I just don't want one that suffocates me. What if we figure out a balance?"

"What do you mean?" Angela asked.

Liam grabbed a napkin and began sketching. "You build a framework—deadlines, milestones—but leave space for me to brainstorm without hovering."

Angela nodded. "And if I need progress updates, you'll share where you're at—even if it's messy?"

"Deal."

This example illustrates how authenticity can transform potential adversaries into allies. Similarly, friendships often deepen when individuals are willing to bare their insecurities. A friend who shares their struggles invites you to do the same, forming a bond fortified by shared experiences. These relationships become sanctuaries where you can be your true self, free from judgment or pretense.

Authentic relationships thrive because they are anchored in reality. They are not built on fleeting impressions or superficial charm. Instead, they are nurtured by genuine interactions that celebrate individuality. When you embrace authenticity, you create a space where others feel seen and heard, fostering an environment of acceptance and trust. This openness encourages ongoing growth, as both parties feel safe to explore and evolve within the relationship. Authenticity is not about perfection; it's about embracing imperfections and finding beauty in them. It's about being honest, even when it's uncomfortable, and choosing connection over convenience. In a world that often prioritizes image over substance, authenticity is a refreshing reminder of what truly matters: the depth and richness of human connection.

Embracing Lifelong Learning in Communication Skills

In a rapidly changing world, the ability to adapt and grow is more important than ever. Communication, much like any other skill, requires continuous learning and evolution. It's not enough to rest on past achievements; staying open to new ideas and trends is vital for personal and professional growth. Lifelong learning keeps you adaptable and ready to meet the challenges of modern communication. It enables you to navigate diverse interactions, from virtual meetings to face-to-face conversations, with ease and confidence. By evolving your communication skills, you enrich your relationships and expand your horizons, opening doors to opportunities you might never have imagined.

People who embrace lifelong learning often actively seek knowledge, not just for its own sake but to improve how they connect with others. Think of a colleague who always brings fresh insights into team discussions or a friend who effortlessly engages people from different walks of life. These individuals exemplify the power of continuous learning. They show us that communication is not static; it's dynamic and ever-changing. By keeping their skills sharp, they inspire those around them and foster environments that thrive on collaboration and innovation. They remind us that learning doesn't stop at a certain age or stage; it's a lifelong pursuit.

Integrating learning into daily life can be a manageable task. It can be woven seamlessly into your routine, making it enjoyable and rewarding. Attending workshops or seminars is one way to gain new insights and perspectives. These events offer a platform to explore emerging trends and engage with experts in the field. But learning isn't confined to formal settings. Books, podcasts, and online courses provide a wealth of knowledge at your fingertips, allowing you to learn at your own pace. Engaging with diverse perspectives through literature or conversations broadens your understanding and enhances your communication repertoire.

Curiosity and exploration are the driving forces behind lifelong learning. They urge you to step outside your comfort zone and experiment with new communication methods and technologies. Try a new platform, like a digital collaboration tool, or converse with people from varied backgrounds. Each experience is a chance to learn, adapt, and grow. Curiosity keeps your mind agile and ready to embrace change and innovation. It challenges you to ask questions, seek answers, and explore possibilities you might not have considered before. This openness to exploration fuels your growth, propelling you toward new horizons.

To truly embrace lifelong learning, making it a core aspect of your personal and professional life is essential. Set aside regular time for skill development, treating it as a priority rather than an afterthought. Reflect on your progress, celebrate milestones, and identify areas for further growth. Setting new learning goals keeps you motivated and focused, ensuring that your communication skills continue to evolve. By committing to continuous development, you cultivate a mindset that thrives on improvement and adaptability. This commitment enhances your skills and enriches your interactions, making each conversation more meaningful and impactful.

ANNE MCKEOWN

Lifelong learning in communication is a journey without a destination. It's about the growth process, the continuous pursuit of knowledge and improvement. As you embrace this journey, you'll find that your communication skills become more refined, your connections deeper, and your understanding broader. Each step you take adds to the richness of your interactions, enhancing your personal and professional life. With each new insight and skill, you become more equipped to navigate the complexities of communication, turning challenges into opportunities for connection and growth.

14

FINAL WORD

"Communication leads to community, understanding, intimacy and mutual valuing." Rolo May

As we reach the end of this journey together, I hope you feel a sense of empowerment in your communication abilities. The core message of this book is simple yet profound: effective communication is a skill you can learn and refine. It can transform personal and professional relationships, opening doors to deeper connections and more fulfilling interactions.

Throughout these pages, we have explored various aspects of communication, from understanding your unique style to navigating the intricacies of non-verbal cues. We've delved into the roots of social anxiety and discovered strategies to overcome it. You've learned to start conversations seamlessly and transform small talk into meaningful dialogue. We've also examined the importance of empathy, active listening, and maintaining a balance between speaking and listening.

The key takeaways from this book are designed to guide you in your everyday interactions. Remember the importance of authenticity—showing your true self builds trust and fosters genuine connections. Embrace the growth mindset; see each conversation as an opportunity to learn and improve. Apply active listening techniques and pay attention to verbal and non-verbal signals. Recognize the power of empathy in bridging gaps and creating understanding.

Now, it's time to take action. I encourage you to implement the strategies you've learned. Practice them daily, whether at work, with friends, or social gatherings. Be mindful of your communication style and strive to adapt it to different contexts. Challenge yourself to step out of your comfort zone and engage with new people. Each interaction is a chance to refine your skills and build your confidence.

Communication is a lifelong journey. It's not about reaching a destination but about continuous improvement. Embrace this journey with an open heart and a willingness to learn. The transformative impact on your life will be profound. As you grow in your communication abilities, you'll find that you can easily navigate complex social environments. You'll build strong relationships and open up new personal and professional growth opportunities.

I want to express my deepest gratitude for allowing me to guide you. Your willingness to engage with this book shows a commitment to personal development. If you're looking to take your learning further, or perhaps you're interested in personal coaching tailored to your specific needs and goals, I can help you. Scan the QR code below to get in touch.

15

MAKE A DIFFERENCE WITH YOUR REVIEW AND UNLOCK THE POWER OF CONNECTION

"Kind words don't cost much. Yet they accomplish much." Blaise Pascal

In everyday conversations, we're surrounded by moments of small talk, deep discussions, and connections that shape our lives. But there's something even more powerful that binds this world together: the joy of sharing. Just as a good story can captivate, so too can your voice leave a lasting impact.

Remember when you felt unsure about striking up a conversation or feared you wouldn't hold someone's interest? There's someone out there who feels just like that—eager to build relationships and make an impact, but unsure where to begin.

My aim with *How To Talk to Anyone: From Small Talk to Big Impact* is simple: to make the art of confident conversation accessible to all. And the only way to truly accomplish this? By reaching out to everyone.

Most people judge a book by its cover, but even more judge it by its reviews.

So, for the timid talker, the nervous networker, or the curious reader you've never met, I ask:

Could you please spare a moment to leave a review for this book?

Your review, which takes no more than a minute, could...

inspire someone to start a conversation that may change their life
provide a valuable tool for educators teaching communication skills
bring people closer together in both professional and personal spheres
empower another individual to make their own big impact with small talk.

Ready to make that difference? Just scan the appropriate QR code on the following page.

If the magic of sharing resonates with you, then you truly understand the spirit of effective communication. Welcome to the conversation. You're one of us.

With immense gratitude,

Your fellow conversationalist,

Anne McKeown

PS - There's an old saying: when you share a skill, the skill grows stronger in you. If you think this book can inspire another conversation artist, pass it along. They'll thank you, and you might just make a new friend!

USA Amazon Review Link

UK Amazon Review Link

Australia Amazon Review Link

16

REFERENCES

1. Genetic Risk Variants for Social Anxiety – PubMed
https://pmc.ncbi.nlm.nih.gov/articles/PMC5325045/

2. The Impact of Social Media on Social Anxiety
https://nationalsocialanxietycenter.com/2016/12/20/the-impact-of-social-media-on-social-anxiety/

3. Carol Dweck, Mindset. Changing the way you think to fulfil your potential
https://www.google.com.au/books/edition/Mindset_Updated

4. Mehrabian, A. (1968). Inference of attitudes from the posture, orientation, and distance of a communicator. *Journal of Consulting and Clinical Psychology, 32(3), 296–308. https://doi.org/10.1037/h0025906*

5. Jeffrey D. Karpicke and Henry L. Roediger III, titled "The Critical Importance of Retrieval for Learning," published in the journal Science in February 2008
https://www.science.org/doi/abs/10.1126/science.1152408

6. Elsa Haagensen Karlsen and Mohammed Nazar, titled "How Cultural Diversity Affects Business Communication and Collaboration" July 2024
https://www.sciencedirect.com/science/article/pii/S1877050924014406

7. Janine Willis and Alexander Todorov, titled "First impressions: making up your mind after 100 minutes exposure to a face," July 2006 *https://pubmed.ncbi.nlm.nih.gov/16866745/*

Public Speaking

From Stage Fright to Spotlight

Calm your fear and anxiety, captivate the audience and command any room with confidence, even if you've never been on stage before!

A. McKeown

1

THE POWER OF PUBLIC SPEAKING

"Words have incredible power, they can make people's hearts soar."
M Grothe

Public Speaking is the greatest fear for 77% of the population.[1] It can be terrifying to have the spotlight on you. Just the thought of it makes most people feel vulnerable, judged and inadequate. So why would anyone put themselves through that? Why would I write a book encouraging you to do that?

Because public speaking is liberating!

Public speaking offers an opportunity to open hearts and minds, highlight biases, educate, inspire, and motivate change. The personal and professional growth that takes place when you step out of your comfort zone and put yourself forward to share your ideas and knowledge is unparalleled. Public speaking can be fun when viewed through a positive lens. It is also gratifying when you get it right and receive favorable feedback. Public speaking is powerful, and it is a privilege.

My sincere hope for you, the reader, is that by the time you've finished this book, you will be excited about delivering speeches and presentations

---

1. Furmark T, Tillfors M, Everz P, Marteinsdottir I, Gefvert O, Fredrikson M. Social phobia in the general population: prevalence and sociodemographic profile. *Soc Psychiatry Epidemiol.* 1999;**34**(8):416–424.

of every kind. You will use anxiety as a positive stress, squash all limiting beliefs, craft great stories with ease, take command of any stage with confidence, share what you have learned with others, and most importantly, have fun!

This is a step-by-step guide where each chapter builds on the previous one, so I encourage you to read it chronologically. Some experienced speakers may prefer to dip in and out of chapters, depending on the resources they are looking for. You may notice some topics or suggestions repeated in a few chapters. For example, 'seeking feedback from peers and mentors' is useful and relevant when working on your natural strengths, core message, unique voice, and delivery style; all of these topics are individual chapters. I have endeavored to put a different slant on any repeated key lessons or suggestions. I know from experience that repetition is beneficial when learning something new.

My journey to public speaking mastery has spanned over 25 years of coaching individuals and teams from all walks of life. I've worked with large corporations, small businesses, government departments and local storytellers. Drawing from disciplines like Neuro Linguistic Programming, Positive Psychology, and Chaplaincy, I've developed a holistic approach that addresses the roots of our fears while providing practical strategies to build real confidence and captivating presentations and speeches.

In this book, you'll embark on a transformative path from a nervous novice to a masterful speaker who can engage any audience. We'll explore techniques and the psychology behind public speaking anxiety. We'll look at how to retrain your conscious and unconscious mind so they work in your favor. You'll gain insights into leveraging your personality and adapting to diverse cultural contexts.

Whether you're planning a business pitch, preparing a wedding speech, or just looking to write and share an inspiring story, this book is for you. Questionnaires and checklists are included to help you every step of the way. So, let's get started...

2

CONQUERING YOUR FEAR OF PUBLIC SPEAKING

"Everything you want is on the other side of fear."
J Canfield

Are you terrified of being asked to stand up and give a presentation? Does the mere thought of being in front of an audience, all eyes fixed upon you, send shivers down your spine and make your palms sweat?

If you answered yes, you're not alone. Fear of public speaking, otherwise known as glossophobia, is one of the most common human phobias. But there's good news: with the right strategies and mindset, you can conquer your fears and unlock your full potential as a confident, engaging speaker.

In this chapter, we'll dive into the physiological and psychological origins of public speaking anxiety, differentiate between irrational fears and realistic outcomes, and explore how the brain reacts to the prospect of speaking in front of others. You'll be armed with powerful strategies to diminish fear's hold over you, learn preparation rituals to minimize nervous symptoms, and discover techniques to foster audience engagement and reduce perceived judgment.

By the end of this chapter, you'll have the tools and knowledge needed to face your fears head-on.

The Science of Fear

To conquer your fear of public speaking, it's essential to understand its roots. When faced with speaking in front of an audience, your body's sympathetic nervous system kicks into high gear, triggering the fight, flight or freeze response. This evolutionary mechanism, designed to protect you from perceived threats, releases adrenaline and cortisol, leading to physical symptoms like sweating, shaking, and a racing heartbeat.

However, the origins of public speaking anxiety go beyond mere physiology. Psychologically, the fear often stems from a deep-seated need for approval and acceptance. The prospect of judgment, criticism, or rejection from an audience can be incredibly daunting, triggering feelings of self-doubt and inadequacy. This fear is further compounded by the spotlight effect, a cognitive bias that leads us to believe that others are paying more attention to us than they are.

At its core, stage fright is rooted in fear of the unknown and fear of failure, both of which trigger our body's default stress responses. This fear is not just about speaking in front of an audience but is deeply tied to our sense of self and our desire to be viewed favorably by others. It's the dread that a single mistake could undermine our credibility or embarrass us in front of our peers. This intense anxiety can be debilitating, but understanding that this fear is a natural human response is the first step toward managing it. Knowledge about the psychological triggers of stage fright, such as feeling out of control, being the center of attention, and fearing negative evaluation, can demystify this fear and reduce its power over your psyche.

Irrational Fears vs. Realistic Outcomes

One critical step in overcoming public speaking anxiety is to differentiate between irrational fears and realistic outcomes. Our minds tend to conjure up worst-case scenarios, such as forgetting our speech, being laughed at, or fainting on stage. However, these catastrophic outcomes are rarely, if ever, realized.

In reality, audiences are generally forgiving and understanding. Most people are glad it's you on the stage and not them. They want you to succeed and are not there to judge or criticize you. Minor mistakes, like stumbling over a word or losing your place, are often barely noticed by others and are quickly forgotten. By putting your worries into perspective and recognizing the unlikelihood of your feared outcomes, you can begin to chip away at the power fear holds over you.

Retraining Your Brain

The good news is that our brains are remarkably adaptable. Through neuroplasticity, we can rewire our neural pathways to change how we respond to the prospect of public speaking. Exposure therapy is a powerful technique for retraining your brain, which involves gradually confronting your fear in a controlled, safe environment.

Start by visualizing yourself successfully delivering a speech to a supportive audience. Mentally rehearse your successful performance, picturing yourself speaking confidently, clearly, and passionately. Engage all your senses, imagining the room, the faces of interested listeners, and the sound of your strong voice amid applause. Feel confidence pulse through your body as you lift your chin and straighten your shoulders. As you become more comfortable with this mental rehearsal, gradually expose yourself to increasingly challenging speaking situations, such as practicing in front of a mirror, recording yourself, or speaking to a small group of trusted friends.

Cognitive restructuring is another effective tool for rewiring your brain. This involves identifying and challenging the negative thoughts and beliefs that fuel your anxiety. When you think, "I'm going to make a fool of myself," or "I'm not good enough," take a step back and question the validity of these thoughts.

Use the acronym T.H.I.N.K. to ask yourself, is what I'm thinking and saying to myself: **T**rue? **H**elpful? **I**nspiring? **N**ecessary? **K**ind?

If the answer to any of these questions is "no," then stop that train of negative thought immediately and replace it with positive, realistic beliefs such as "I am well-prepared and have valuable insights to share" or "The audience is keen to hear what I have to say and wants me to succeed."

Techniques for Reducing Anxiety

Physical relaxation techniques, such as progressive muscle relaxation or gentle stretching, can help calm your body and mind before speaking. Try the following exercises.

> **Physical Relaxation Techniques**
>
> **Neck Stretches**
> - Gently tilt your head towards your shoulder and hold for 8-10 seconds. Repeat on the other side. Slowly roll your head in a full circle twice, then reverse the direction.
>
> **Shoulder Rolls**
> - Lift your shoulders towards your ears and then roll them back, creating large circles. Do 5 rolls backward, then 5 rolls forward.
>
> **Arm Stretches**
> - Extend one arm across your chest, use the other arm to pull it closer, and hold for 10 seconds. Switch arms and repeat.
>
> **Wrist Flexes**
> - Extend your arm, palm up, and gently pull back on the fingers of your extended hand with your other hand. Hold for 5 seconds. Flip your arm so the palm is facing down and gently press down on the back of the hand. Hold for 5 seconds. Repeat with the other arm.

Torso Twists
- Sit or stand with your feet hip-width apart. Gently twist your torso to the right, using your hands to deepen the stretch. Hold for 10 seconds, then twist to the left and hold for another 10 seconds.

Leg Stretches
- While sitting, extend one leg outward and reach toward your toes, holding for 10-15 seconds. Switch legs and repeat.

Deep Breathing
- Close your eyes, place a hand on your abdomen, and slowly inhale through your nose, feeling your stomach rise. Exhale slowly through your mouth, pushing out as much air as you can while contracting your abdominal muscles. Repeat 5 times.

Perform these stretches in a quiet, comfortable space. Focus on your breathing throughout the stretches to enhance relaxation. Don't push into pain; stretches should feel relieving.

Breathing techniques are among the most effective ways to control the physical symptoms of anxiety. Deep belly breathing is particularly beneficial, as it involves breathing deeply and slowly through the abdomen rather than shallowly through the chest. This method counteracts the rapid, shallow breaths that often accompany anxiety, helps lower the heart rate, and promotes a sense of calm.

The breathing technique I use is called box breathing. Try it now by following these simple steps.

Box Breathing Technique

Inhale

- Action: Breathe in slowly through your nose.
  Count: 4 seconds.
  Visual Cue: Imagine drawing the first side of a box in your mind.

Hold

- Action: Keep the air inside.
  Count: 4 seconds.
  Visual Cue: Visualize drawing the second side of the box.

Exhale

- Action: Slowly breathe out through your mouth.
  Count: 4 seconds.
  Visual Cue: Picture drawing the third side of the box.

Hold Again

- Action: Do not inhale immediately.
  Count: 4 seconds.
  Visual Cue: Complete the box by drawing the fourth side.

Repeat: Continue this pattern for several minutes until you feel more relaxed.

Anchoring is a powerful technique for strengthening the mind-body connection. An anchor is a physical stimulus you associate with a desired emotional state, like confidence or calm. By consistently pairing your anchor with the desired state during practice, you create a conditioned response you can trigger when speaking. For example, you can use your special speaker shoes as an anchor. Let me explain. Wearing slippers at home signals to the mind and body that it's time to relax. Putting on your runners indicates it's time to work your body and increase your heart rate. Women may wear high-heeled sandals when out socializing, associating them with an evening of dancing and drinking. In the same way, as soon as your feet slip into your nominated speaker shoes, your mind and body know it's time to enter a state of self-assured readiness, and you instantly take on the persona of a capable, confident public speaker.

Discover Your Anchor: A Personal Exercise

By identifying your own personal anchor, you can create a reliable pathway to reach your peak state whenever you need to speak publicly.

1 Reflect on Comfort and Confidence
Think about a time when you felt incredibly confident and at ease.
What were you doing?
What objects were around you?
What actions were you taking?

2 Choose Your Anchor
Select an object or action from your reflection that you can easily replicate or carry with you. This could be anything from a piece of jewelry to a specific gesture.

3 Write It Down
Write down your chosen anchor.
Describe why this object or action makes you feel confident and how you plan to use it before or during your public speaking engagements.

Set aside time to develop a pre-talk ritual that works for you. By consistently performing your pre-talk routine, you retrain your brain to associate the routine with readiness and confidence, reducing the intensity of nervous symptoms. The connection between mental preparation and physical symptom reduction is powerful. When you feel mentally prepared and confident, your body follows suit, releasing tension and allowing you to present easily.

Pre-Talk Ritual for Public Speaking

Visualization
- **Purpose:** Mentally rehearse your success to create a positive mindset.
- **Method:** Close your eyes for a few minutes and imagine yourself delivering a flawless presentation. Visualize the audience engaging with your content, smiling, and nodding in agreement.

Mindful Meditation
- **Purpose:** Reduce stress and center your thoughts.
- **Method:** Spend 5-10 minutes in meditation. Focus solely on your breathing and let go of distracting thoughts. This practice can ground your emotions and sharpen your focus.

Vocal Warm-ups
- **Purpose:** Prepare your voice for public speaking.
- **Method:** Perform a series of vocal exercises such as humming, lip trills, and tongue twisters. This will help clear your throat and ensure your voice is clear and strong.

Physical Exercise
- **Purpose:** Release tension and increase energy levels.
- **Method:** Engage in light physical activity such as jumping jacks, a quick walk, or stretching. This stimulates blood flow and enhances oxygen supply to your brain.

Review Key Points
- **Purpose:** Solidify your material and boost confidence.
- **Method:** Go over your notes or cue cards and rehearse your opening and closing statements. Familiarity with your material will reduce anxiety and improve delivery.

Set Intentions
- **Purpose:** Align your goals for the presentation.
- **Method:** Write down or mentally note what you wish to achieve with your talk. Focusing on your intentions can help you steer the presentation effectively.

Engage with Early Arrivers
- **Purpose:** Reduce feelings of isolation and build rapport.
- **Method:** If possible, mingle with some of the audience members who arrive early. This can make the environment feel more familiar and less daunting.

Engagement is a potent way to reduce anxiety and perceived judgment and foster a positive connection with your audience. When you actively involve your listeners in your presentation, you shift the focus from yourself to the shared experience, diminishing the intensity of your self-consciousness.

Take the spotlight off yourself and focus on your audience. Choose to serve them and include some of the following techniques to foster engagement.

Engagement Techniques

Ask Questions
- **Description:** Begin with a thought-provoking question to spark curiosity and encourage audience interaction. Tailor questions to the topic and the interests of your audience to maintain relevance. **Example:** "By a show of hands, how many of you have experienced...?"

Share Personal Stories
- **Description:** Share anecdotes and personal experiences to build rapport and add authenticity to your message. Stories can make complex ideas more relatable and memorable. **Example:** "Let me tell you about a time when I was in your shoes..."

Use Humor
- **Description:** Lighten the atmosphere and connect with the audience through appropriate humor. Jokes or amusing remarks can help break the ice and make the content more digestible. **Example:** "Why don't scientists trust atoms anymore? Because they make up everything!"

Maintain Eye Contact
- **Description:** Make eye contact with different members of the audience throughout your presentation. This creates a sense of intimacy and can significantly reduce the feeling of speaking to a crowd. **Example:** "As I look around the room, I see faces of people who are here to make a difference."

Preparation is one of the most effective ways to minimize nervous symptoms before speaking. The more familiar you are with your material, the more confident and at ease you'll feel when delivering it. Dive deep into your topic, gather information, organize your thoughts into a clear, logical structure, and practice, practice, practice.

Real-Life Examples

Throughout history, many renowned speakers have faced moments of audience judgment or skepticism, only to fall back on their thorough preparation and turn those challenges into opportunities for positive engagement. Consider the following examples:

In 1963, Martin Luther King Jr. delivered his iconic "I Have a Dream" speech to over 250,000 people at the Lincoln Memorial. Initially met with some resistance and skepticism, King's powerful oratory and visionary message soon won over the audience, inspiring a nation and galvanizing the Civil Rights Movement.

In his 2005 Stanford commencement speech, Apple co-founder Steve Jobs faced an audience of graduates eager for success tips and career advice. Instead, Jobs shared three deeply personal stories of love, loss, and perseverance. By revealing his vulnerabilities and life lessons, Jobs created a powerful, lasting impact on his listeners, transcending preconceived notions or judgments.

A less famous example from my experience as a coach involved a corporate trainer who addressed an initially skeptical audience by inviting them to share their reservations about the new company policy she was there to explain. She disarmed the audience's initial judgment by addressing these concerns directly and integrating their feedback into her presentation. She turned them into active participants in a meaningful dialogue about the policy's implementation.

As these examples illustrate, even in the face of initial audience judgment or skepticism, speakers who approach their listeners with authenticity, vulnerability, and a genuine desire to connect can transform those perceptions into robust, positive engagement.

Remember, your audience is not there to judge you but to learn from you and be inspired by your insights. By providing value, fostering engagement, and approaching your listeners with openness and authenticity, you create a positive, supportive environment that diminishes the power of fear and allows your unique voice to shine through.

The Power of Positive Self-Talk

French Psychologist Émile Coué discovered that his patients recovered more quickly if they repeated optimistic autosuggestions frequently.[1] Over time, the term optimistic autosuggestions has been replaced with positive affirmations, but the idea is the same. Thorough academic research of the power of affirmations began in the late 80s when social psychologist Claude Steele presented Self Affirmation Theory.[2] Positive self-talk and affirmations are among the most effective tools for overcoming stage fright and self-doubt. The way we speak to ourselves has a profound impact on our thoughts, emotions, and actions. By consciously engaging in positive self-talk, we can reshape our mindset and boost our confidence.

I encourage you to develop a set of affirmations that resonate with you and align with your goals as a public speaker.

The following examples are some of my favorites.

---

1. Coué, E. (1922c), "Self Mastery Through Conscious Autosuggestion", pp. 5–35 in Emile Coué, *Self Mastery Through Conscious Autosuggestion*, New York, NY: American Library Service.

2. Steele, C. M. (1988). The psychology of self-affirmation: Sustaining the integrity of the self. Advances in experimental social psychology, 21, 261-302

"I am a confident and capable speaker."
"My message is valuable and deserves to be heard."
"I embrace challenges as opportunities for growth."
"I trust in my preparation and ability to connect with my audience."

Repeat these affirmations regularly, especially in the days leading up to your presentation. Write them down, post them in visible locations, or record yourself saying them and listen to the recording daily. By consistently reinforcing positive self-talk, you gradually rewire your brain to embrace a more confident and self-assured mindset. In moments of self-doubt or anxiety, catch yourself engaging in negative self-talk and actively replace those thoughts with your affirmations. For example, if you think, "I'm going to forget what I want to say," immediately counter that thought with, "I am well-prepared and will deliver my message with clarity and confidence."

Building Resilience and Embracing Failure

Fear of failure is one of the most significant barriers to conquering stage fright. However, it's essential to recognize that failure is inevitable in the growth process. Every successful speaker has experienced setbacks, stumbles, and less-than-perfect presentations. The key is to view these experiences not as defeats but as valuable lessons and opportunities for improvement.

Cultivate a growth mindset by embracing failure as a stepping stone to success. When things don't go as planned, take the time to reflect on what you can learn from the experience. Ask yourself questions like:

What worked well in my presentation?

What areas could I improve upon next time?

How can I use this experience to strengthen my speaking skills?

By approaching failure with curiosity and a willingness to learn, you build resilience and develop the mental fortitude to bounce back from setbacks. Remember that every challenge you face is an opportunity to grow, refine your craft, and become a more effective communicator.

Self-Care and Stress Management

Conquering stage fright and anxiety is not just about the moments you spend on stage; it's also about the way you care for yourself off stage. Engaging in regular self-care practices and effective stress management techniques can significantly impact your ability to manage public speaking anxiety. Prioritize physical self-care by:

1. Getting enough sleep: Aim for 7-9 hours of quality sleep each night to ensure your mind and body are well-rested and prepared for the demands of public speaking.

2. Eating a balanced diet: Fuel your body with nutrient-rich foods that provide sustained energy and support cognitive function.

3. Exercising regularly: Engage in physical activities you enjoy. Exercise helps reduce stress, improves mood, and boosts overall well-being.

Attend to your mental and emotional well-being by:

1. Practicing mindfulness and meditation: Incorporate mindfulness techniques, such as deep breathing and present-moment awareness, to help calm your mind and reduce anxiety.

2. Engaging in hobbies and activities you enjoy: Make time for pursuits that bring you joy and provide a sense of fulfillment outside of public speaking.

3. Surrounding yourself with supportive people: Build a network of friends, family, and colleagues who encourage and uplift you, and don't hesitate to seek support when needed.

Develop effective stress management strategies, such as:

1. Time management and organization: Create a structured plan for your speaking engagements, break tasks down into manageable steps, and allocate sufficient time for preparation.

2. Boundary setting: Learn to say "no" to commitments that overwhelm you or detract from your primary goals as a speaker.

3. Seeking professional support: If your stage fright or anxiety feels overwhelming, consider working with a therapist or coach who specializes in helping individuals overcome public speaking fears.

By prioritizing self-care and implementing effective stress management techniques, you create a strong foundation for managing public speaking anxiety and showing up as your best self when it's time to take the stage.

Mentorship and Community in Overcoming Fear

Conquering stage fright and developing as a speaker is not a journey you must undertake alone. Seeking mentorship and building a supportive community of fellow speakers can be invaluable in overcoming fear and reaching your full potential. Consider reaching out to experienced speakers whose work you admire and respect. Many successful speakers are generous with their time and wisdom and are happy to guide those just starting. A mentor can provide valuable insights, offer constructive feedback, and share strategies for managing stage fright and honing your craft.

In addition to mentorship, surrounding yourself with a community of supportive peers can make all the difference in your growth as a speaker. Attend workshops, conferences, and networking events to connect with other speakers who share your passion and goals. These connections can lead to valuable friendships, collaborations, and learning opportunities from one another's experiences. Create a safe space within your community to share fears, celebrate successes, and offer mutual encouragement. Knowing that you're not alone in your journey and having a network of individuals who understand the challenges and triumphs of public speaking can provide a powerful source of motivation and resilience in the face of fear.

Embracing the Journey

Conquering stage fright and unleashing your potential as a speaker is an ongoing journey of growth, self-discovery, and resilience. As you implement the strategies and mindset shifts explored in this chapter, remember to celebrate your progress and embrace the process. Every small victory, whether delivering a presentation with less anxiety or receiving positive feedback from an audience member, is a testament to your dedication and growth. Acknowledge these wins and use them as fuel to keep moving forward.

Remember that conquering fear is not a one-time event but a continuous practice. There will be moments of doubt and setbacks along the way, but these experiences are all part of the journey. By viewing challenges as opportunities for learning and growth, you cultivate the resilience and adaptability needed to thrive as a speaker.

I encourage you to embrace the journey, trust your preparation, and let your passion for your message guide you.

3

FINDING YOUR DISTINCT PUBLIC SPEAKING VOICE

"The best speeches come from the heart and reflect your passion."
R Robinson

The art of public speaking is about more than fitting into a predefined mold or adhering to a rigid set of rules. It's about discovering the distinct voice within you – a voice shaped by your personality, experiences, and perspectives. The path to becoming a genuinely impactful and unforgettable speaker is paved with self-discovery and the courage to embrace your authentic self. When we speak from a place of authenticity, anchored in our core values and beliefs, we create a profound connection with our audience beyond mere words.

In this chapter, we will embark on a transformative journey of self-exploration, equipped with strategies to help you discover your unique speaking style and harness the power of genuineness to captivate and inspire your listeners. We'll explore the significance of understanding your purpose and tailoring your delivery to align seamlessly with your natural strengths and abilities.

It's time to find your authentic voice and speak with unwavering confidence, firm conviction, and the ability to leave an impact on your audience.

Authenticity: Why Being Yourself Matters

Authenticity has become a rare and valuable commodity in a world saturated with information and competing voices. Audiences crave speakers who are genuine, relatable, and authentic. When you speak from a place of authenticity, you create a sense of trust and connection with your listeners that goes beyond the mere transmission of information.

Authenticity in public speaking is more than honesty or transparency; it's about aligning your words, delivery, and presence with your core values and beliefs. It's about speaking from the heart, sharing your unique experiences and insights, and allowing your personality to shine. When you embrace your authentic self on stage, you permit your audience to do the same, fostering a deeper engagement and rapport.

The benefits of authentic speaking are numerous. First and foremost, authenticity builds trust. When your audience perceives you as genuine and sincere, they are more likely to believe in your message and be open to your ideas. This trust is the foundation upon which all effective communication is built. Authenticity allows you to connect with your audience on a human level. Sharing your own stories, struggles, and triumphs creates a bridge of empathy and understanding. Your listeners see themselves in your experiences and feel a sense of kinship. This emotional connection is what makes your message memorable.

Authenticity is one of the main things that can set you apart from other speakers. In a sea of cookie-cutter presentations and generic messages, a speaker who is unashamedly themselves stands out. Your unique voice, perspective, and style become your competitive advantage, making you memorable and sought-after in your field.

Speaking from a place of authenticity is liberating. When you embrace your true self, you free yourself from the pressure to be perfect or to fit someone else's mold. You can speak confidently, knowing you are being true to yourself and your message. This freedom translates into a more natural, engaging, and impactful performance on stage.

Knowing Your Purpose

First, clarify your purpose to find your authentic voice as a speaker. What is the core message you want to convey to your audience? What change do you hope to inspire, or what action do you want to motivate? By identifying your central theme or objective, you create a guiding light that illuminates your content, delivery, and overall approach.

Start by reflecting on your experiences, passions, and areas of expertise. What topics ignite your curiosity and enthusiasm? What lessons have you learned that could benefit others? What unique perspective do you bring to the conversation? As you explore these questions, look for emerging patterns and themes and use them to craft a clear, compelling core message. For example, if you're passionate about environmental sustainability and have experience implementing green initiatives in your workplace, your core message might be the business case for sustainability. You could share success stories, best practices, and actionable strategies that inspire other leaders to embrace eco-friendly practices in their organizations.

If you've overcome significant challenges in your personal or professional life, your core message might be about resilience and perseverance. You could share your story of overcoming adversity and offer insights and strategies to bounce back from setbacks and achieve success despite the odds.

The key is to identify a message that resonates deeply with you and that you feel compelled to share with others. Your words can move and inspire your audience when you speak with genuine passion and conviction.

Embracing Your Natural Strengths

Each speaker has unique strengths and abilities that shape their delivery style. Some speakers are gifted storytellers; others excel at breaking complex ideas into simple, relatable concepts. To find your authentic voice, identify your natural strengths and tailor your delivery style to align with your congruent self.

One way to identify your natural strengths is to reflect on a time you felt most comfortable and confident speaking in front of others. What were you talking about? How did you structure your message? What kind of feedback did you receive from your audience? For example, if you feel most comfortable sharing personal anecdotes and weaving them into your larger message, storytelling may be one of your natural strengths. You can leverage this strength by incorporating more stories into your presentations and honing your storytelling skills. Or, if you have a knack for breaking down complex ideas into simple, easy-to-understand concepts, your strength may lie in your ability to educate and inform. You can leverage this strength by presenting information clearly and in a structured way, using analogies, examples, and visual aids to make your content accessible and engaging.

Another way to identify your natural strengths is to seek feedback from others. Ask colleagues, friends, or mentors who have seen you speak to share their observations about your style and approach. What do they see as your unique talents and abilities? What do they find most compelling or memorable about your presentations? For instance, if you consistently receive feedback that your passion and enthusiasm are contagious, your strength may lie in your ability to inspire and motivate others. You can capitalize on this strength by focusing on topics that ignite your passion and bringing a high level of energy and conviction to your delivery.

Once you've identified your natural strengths, look for ways to tailor your delivery style to align with them. If humor comes naturally to you, consider incorporating more light-hearted anecdotes or witty observations into your presentations. If you have a talent for painting vivid word pictures, use descriptive language and sensory details to bring your ideas to life.

The key is to embrace what makes you unique and let your authentic personality shine through in your speaking. When you do, your words will have a more significant impact, and your presence on stage will be more powerful and engaging.

Balance Authenticity and Professionalism

While authenticity is crucial, it's equally important to maintain professionalism. Express your true self through a filter of professionalism that respects the audience and the context. Be aware of the appropriate language, humor, and anecdotes for the setting while staying true to yourself.

In situations where your authentic self may not align with the audience's expectations or the event's context, focus on finding common ground. Identify the aspects of your message that resonate with the audience's needs and values and emphasize those points. Adapt your delivery style to suit the context while maintaining the core of your authentic self. For example, if you're a more casual, humorous speaker addressing a formal corporate audience, you might tone down the jokes but keep your warm, relatable demeanor. By striking this balance, you can remain true to yourself while connecting with your audience.

Another way to navigate this balance is to be transparent about your intentions and style. If you know that your approach may be unconventional or unexpected given the context, acknowledge that upfront. You might say, "I know my style is a bit different from what you may be used to, but I promise that my message is relevant and valuable to your work." This transparency can help build trust and rapport with your audience, even if your authentic style doesn't perfectly match their expectations. It shows you respect their needs and perspectives while being true to yourself.

Remember that authenticity doesn't mean oversharing or crossing professional boundaries. While sharing personal stories and experiences is valuable, be mindful of the level of detail and relevance to your more significant message. Avoid sharing anything that might make your audience uncomfortable, or that could undermine your credibility as a speaker. Ultimately, balancing authenticity and professionalism is about being intentional and strategic. It's about finding ways to let your true self shine through while still being respectful and mindful of your audience and the context in which you're speaking.

Letting Go of the Script

Relying too heavily on scripts can hinder your ability to connect with your audience. While it might feel safer to have every word planned, this approach can make your delivery feel stiff and inauthentic. Instead, focus on internalizing your content, understanding it deeply, and speaking from that place of knowledge and conviction.

One way to let go of the script is to practice your presentation multiple times, not to memorize every word, but to deeply understand your key points and the flow of your argument. As you practice, pay attention to the parts of your presentation that feel most natural and authentic. Notice where you tend to ad-lib or go off-script and consider how to incorporate more of that spontaneity into your delivery.

Another strategy is to create a simple outline or roadmap for your presentation rather than a word-for-word script. This approach lets you stay on track and ensure you hit all your key points while leaving room for flexibility.

One technique I use is to create an Acronym for my topic. For example, I use the Acronym I.M.P.A.C.T to talk about the Art of Public Speaking. Each letter reminds me of the subject matter and keeps me on track:

I is for Introduction.
M is for the core Message.
P is for Presentation skills.
A is for Audience engagement.
C is for Confidence.
T is for Technoloy and media tools.

As you become more comfortable with your material, challenge yourself to speak spontaneously for longer. Start with a few minutes of unscripted speaking and gradually build up to more extended periods. This practice will help you develop greater confidence and flexibility as a speaker.

It's also important to remember that letting go of the script doesn't mean abandoning preparation altogether. The more deeply you know your material, the more freedom you have to be authentic and responsive in the moment. By investing time in researching, organizing, and practicing your content, you give yourself the foundation to speak from a place of knowledge and conviction.

Practice and Feedback

Discovering your unique speaking style is an ongoing journey of experimentation and refinement. Seek out opportunities to practice and gather feedback from trusted peers or mentors. Remember, finding your voice is about progress, not perfection. One of the most effective ways to practice is to seek out low-stakes speaking opportunities, such as local Toastmasters clubs, community organizations, or volunteer groups. These environments provide a supportive and encouraging space to try new techniques, hone your skills, and get real-time feedback from your audience. As you practice, experiment with different approaches and styles. Try incorporating more storytelling into one presentation and more data and evidence into another. Play with your vocal variety, pacing, and physical presence on stage. Notice what feels most natural and resonates most with your audience.

Another valuable tool for finding your voice is recording yourself. Use your smartphone or a camera to capture video of your presentations, and then watch them back with a critical eye. Notice your strengths and areas for improvement and look for patterns in your style and approach.

As you review your recordings, ask yourself questions like:

What moments felt most authentic and engaging?

Where did I seem to lose my audience's attention or interest?

How can I make my content or delivery more impactful?

What unique strengths or perspectives do I bring to my speaking?

Be brave and ask colleagues, friends, or mentors who have seen you speak to share their honest observations and insights. Be open to positive and constructive feedback and use it to inform your growth and development as a speaker.

Finally, remember that finding your voice is an ongoing process. As you evolve and grow as a person and a professional, your speaking style will also likely evolve. Be open to this continuous learning and improvement journey, and trust that your authentic voice will emerge more fully with each new experience and opportunity.

Discovering Your Natural Delivery Style: A Speaker's Quiz

1. When preparing for a presentation, I prefer to:

a) Write out a detailed script and rehearse it extensively

b) Create a general outline and trust my ability to improvise

c) Visualize myself delivering the speech and focus on the key messages

2. I feel most energized and engaged when:

a) Interacting directly with the audience and fielding their questions

b) Sharing personal stories and anecdotes that illustrate my points

c) Presenting complex information in a clear, structured manner

3. My natural speaking pace is:

a) Fast and dynamic, with a sense of urgency and excitement

b) Measured and deliberate, with thoughtful pauses for emphasis

c) Adaptable, varying depending on the content and audience

4. When it comes to using humor in my presentations, I:

a) Actively seek opportunities to incorporate jokes and witty observations

b) Use humor sparingly and only when it naturally fits the context

c) Prefer to maintain a more serious, professional tone throughout

5. I feel most authentic and confident when:

a) Inspiring and motivating the audience to take action

b) Educating and informing the audience about a topic I have a passion for

c) Connecting emotionally with the audience through shared experiences

6. When faced with a challenging or skeptical audience, I tend to:

a) Directly address their concerns and engage in open dialogue

b) Focus on delivering my message with conviction and clarity

c) Adapt my approach and find common ground to build rapport

7. My preferred way of incorporating visuals into my presentations is:

a) Using bold, high-impact images and graphics to capture attention

b) Creating simple, clean slides that reinforce critical points without distracting

c) Minimizing visuals and relying primarily on my words and presence

8. When telling a story during a presentation, I aim to:

a) Entertain the audience and leave them with a memorable anecdote

b) Illustrate a lesson or insight that ties back to my core message

c) Create an emotional connection and tap into the audience's empathy

9. I believe the most important aspect of vocal delivery is:

a) Projecting confidence and authority through a robust and clear voice

b) Using vocal variety and inflection to engage and maintain interest

c) Speaking at a pace that allows for understanding and retention

10. When it comes to body language and movement on stage, I:

a) Use expansive gestures and dynamic movement to command attention

b) Prefer a more restrained, controlled approach to convey professionalism

c) Focus on maintaining an approachable presence and open facial expressions

11. I feel most in my element when:

a) Improvising and thinking on my feet during a presentation

b) Delivering a carefully crafted, well-rehearsed speech

c) Engaging in interactive exercises or demonstrations with the audience

12. My ultimate goal as a speaker is to:

a) Inspire the audience to see things in a new way and act

b) Provide practical, actionable insights that the audience can apply immediately

c) Create a memorable, engaging experience that resonates on an emotional level

Interpretation of Quiz Results:

If you scored primarily a's, Your strengths lie in engaging and interacting with the audience. You may thrive in improvisational settings and enjoy using humor and storytelling to create a memorable experience. To improve, focus on structuring your content effectively and practicing a more controlled pace.

Example: If you're naturally inclined to use humor, make sure your jokes are entertaining and relevant to your message. Practicing your timing and delivery can ensure that your humor enhances, rather than detracts from, your content. You might also work on developing a clear roadmap for your presentations to ensure that your engaging style is balanced with a well-structured and purposeful message.

If you scored primarily b's, Your strengths lie in delivering clear, well-structured presentations that educate and inform. You may excel at breaking down complex topics and maintaining a professional presence. To improve, inject more personality and emotion into your presentations, using storytelling and vocal variety to engage your audience.

Example: If you're presenting technical information, consider opening with a personal anecdote that illustrates the human impact of your topic. This can help you connect with your audience more emotionally, making your content more relatable and memorable. You might also experiment with using more vocal variety, such as changing your tone, volume, or pace to emphasize critical points or create a sense of drama and interest.

If you scored primarily c's, Your strengths lie in connecting emotionally with the audience and creating a warm, approachable presence. You may excel at using personal stories and genuine expressions to build rapport. To improve, focus on developing a more structured approach to your content, using clear, vital messages and simple visuals.

Example: If you rely heavily on personal stories, ensure each has a clear purpose and ties back to your main message. Practicing with a well-defined outline can help you balance emotional connection and practical, actionable insights. You might also work on incorporating more data, evidence, or examples to support your key points and give your message greater credibility and impact.

Embracing the Power of Your Unique Voice

Your voice is a powerful tool for connection, persuasion, and transformation. By staying true to yourself, speaking from the heart, and consistently refining your craft, you'll find your authentic voice and unlock your full potential as a speaker and leader. Remember, your unique perspective, experiences, and style set you apart and make you valuable as a speaker. Embrace what makes you different, and trust that your authentic voice is precisely what your audience needs to hear.

Be patient and kind with yourself as you continue on your public speaking journey. Celebrate your successes, learn from mishaps, and keep pushing yourself to grow and evolve. The more you practice and speak from a place of authenticity, the more powerful and impactful your voice will become. Take a deep breath, step onto the stage, speak your truth, and watch as your words ignite the hearts and minds of those who have the privilege of listening.

Your voice is your power – use it wisely.

4

CRAFTING COMPELLING CONTENT

"Speech content is crafted to persuade, convert and compel."
R Emerson

Crafting compelling content is the foundation of delivering a presentation that informs, persuades, and inspires. In this chapter, we will look at ways to make your presentation engaging by developing a captivating hook, defining your core message, structuring your speech effectively, and using repetition techniques to emphasize your key points and leave a lasting impression.

Structuring for Success

A compelling presentation relies on a clear and effective structure to support its content and ideas. With a well-defined framework, your audience can quickly understand your message. A classic presentation structure follows the "Tell them what you're going to tell them, tell them, then tell them what you told them" Approach, which involves:

1. Opening with a clear introduction that previews your core message and main points.
2. Delivering the body of your presentation, exploring each of your main points in depth.
3. Concluding with a summary of your key takeaways and a call to action for your audience.

Engaging Introductions

Your introduction is your opportunity to capture your audience's attention, establish your credibility, and provide a preview of the content you will be presenting. A strong introduction should:

1. Begin with an attention-grabbing statement: start with a surprising statistic, a thought-provoking question, or a powerful story that immediately captures your audience's interest. For example, "The average person spends 90,000 hours at work, over a third of our waking lives. How can we make that time more meaningful, fulfilling, and impactful?"

2. Establish credibility: share a brief anecdote or qualification demonstrating your expertise and authority on the topic. For instance, "As a career coach who has worked with thousands of professionals over the past decade, I have witnessed the transformative power of finding purpose and passion in your work."

3. Preview your core message and main points: give your audience an overview of what they can expect from your presentation, highlighting your key takeaways. For example, "Today, I will share three strategies for crafting a career that aligns with your values, leverages your strengths, and positively impacts the world around you."

The next step is to create a presentation that genuinely resonates with your listeners, which starts with defining your core message and building your content around it with clarity and engagement.

Defining Your Core Message

Every excellent presentation has a clear, concise, and compelling core message. This is the single idea that you want your audience to remember and take away from your speech. Your core message is the foundation of your content creation process, supporting every story, statistic, and argument you include in your presentation.

To define your core message, ask yourself: What is the one thing I want my audience to know, feel, or do as a result of hearing my speech? This could be a call to action, a shift in perspective, or a key takeaway that will help them personally or professionally. For example, suppose you're giving a presentation on the importance of innovation in the workplace. In that case, your core message might be: "Fostering a culture of innovation is crucial for staying competitive in today's fast-paced business landscape, and it starts with empowering employees to think creatively and take calculated risks."

This core message accomplishes several key things:

1. It clearly states the central idea of your presentation: the importance of innovation in the workplace.

2. It highlights the stakes: staying competitive in a rapidly changing business environment.

3. It offers a specific call to action: empowering employees to think creatively and take calculated risks.

4. It suggests the solution is achievable: anyone can foster innovation by starting with small, concrete steps.

A great example is Brene Brown's TED Talk "The Power of Vulnerability." Her core message is that vulnerability is not a weakness but a source of courage, connection, and innovation. This clear, counterintuitive message challenges her audience's assumptions and invites them to rethink their approach to vulnerability.

By crafting a clear, compelling core message, you provide your audience with a roadmap for your presentation and a key takeaway that they can apply to their work and lives.

Ensuring Your Message is Understood

Clarity is essential for making your message stick in your audience's minds. When your ideas are presented in a clear, concise, and easy-to-follow manner, your listeners are more likely to understand, remember, and act on them.

To achieve clarity in your content, focus on:

1. Using simple, jargon-free language that your audience can easily understand.

2. Breaking down complex ideas into smaller, more digestible chunks.

3. Providing examples and analogies to illustrate your points.

4. Repeating key ideas and themes throughout your presentation.

One specific example is Simon Sinek's use of clarity in his TED Talk "How Great Leaders Inspire Action." In this presentation, he:

1. Uses simple language to introduce the concept of the Golden Circle and its three components (Why, How, What).

2. Breaks down the complex idea of leadership and motivation into the simple framework of the Golden Circle.

3. Provides examples of companies like Apple and the Wright brothers to illustrate how starting with "Why" can lead to innovation and success.

4. Throughout the presentation, he repeats the phrase, "People don't buy what you do; they buy why you do it," reinforcing his core message.

By employing these clarity techniques, Sinek has become one of our time's most popular and influential speakers. His TED Talk garnered over 50 million views, and his ideas were widely adopted across industries and sectors.

Making Intricate Topics Accessible

When dealing with complex topics that your audience might need to become more familiar with, it is essential to strike the right balance between complexity and simplicity. While delving into intricate details can showcase your expertise, it can overwhelm your listeners if not handled carefully.

The power of simplicity lies in its ability to make your information more accessible and memorable for your audience. By distilling your content to its most essential elements, you make it easier for your listeners to grasp and retain your key points long after the presentation.

To simplify complex topics effectively:

1. Determine what your audience needs to know versus what is just supplementary information. Focus on the most critical information to convey the big picture and achieve your presentation's goals.

2. Adopt a step-by-step approach. Begin by outlining your topic's main components, then gradually unpack each one logically. This helps your audience follow along and understand the progression of your ideas.

3. Use analogies and examples to make abstract concepts more relatable. Choose comparisons that are relevant and easily understood by your specific audience.

4. Incorporate interactive elements directly related to the simplified concepts you're discussing. This helps make the abstract ideas more concrete and demonstrates how they apply in real-world situations.

It's important to note that simplifying your presentation means eliminating only some essential details. It's about strategically refining your message to focus on the most critical information, breaking down complex ideas into manageable parts, and using tools like analogies to make the content more accessible and engaging. When you strike the right balance between simplicity and substance, your audience will leave feeling like they truly grasp the subject matter and will have a positive impression of your ability to communicate complex ideas in an effective and relatable way.

Making Your Points Memorable

The "Rule of Three" is a well-established principle in various fields, including writing, public speaking, and psychology. Organizing your presentation around three main points makes your message more compelling and memorable for your audience.

When structuring your content, consider how you can break down your core message into three key points or arguments. Each point should be distinct yet interconnected, building upon the previous one to create a cohesive and compelling narrative. For example, if your core message is about the importance of self-care, your three main points might be:

1. The physical benefits of self-care: improved health, energy, and resilience.

2. The mental and emotional benefits of self-care: reduced stress, increased happiness and better relationships.

3. Practical strategies for incorporating self-care into daily life: setting boundaries, prioritizing sleep, and engaging in hobbies.

In his product launch presentation, Elon Musk introduced Tesla's Powerwall battery system by focusing on three key benefits: cost savings, energy independence, and environmental sustainability. This simple, memorable structure helped emphasize the product's value proposition and potential impact.

Reinforcing Your Core Message

As mentioned above, repetition is a necessary and powerful tool for reinforcing your ideas and ensuring that your message sticks. When you repeat your core message throughout your presentation, you signal to your audience that this is the most crucial takeaway they should remember. The key is to find creative ways to weave your core message into your content without sounding dull and repetitive. This can be done through:

1. Reiterating your core message at critical points in your presentation (e.g., in your introduction, transitions, and conclusion).

2. Using different language, examples, or stories to illustrate your core message in new ways.

3. Incorporating rhetorical devices like anaphora (repeating a word or phrase at the beginning of successive clauses), "Every day, we face a choice. Every day, we decide who we want to be. Every day, we have the power to make a difference." Or epistrophe (repeating a word or phrase at the end of successive clauses) to emphasize your message. "In times of hardship, we must persevere. In moments of doubt, we must persevere. When faced with seemingly insurmountable obstacles, we must persevere."

By strategically repeating your core message throughout your presentation, you ensure that your audience walks away with a clear understanding of your central idea and its importance.

Leaving a Lasting Impression

The conclusion of your presentation deserves just as much thought and preparation as the opening. Your closing remarks reinforce your core message and directly impact your audience's ability to retain and act upon what you've shared. An impactful conclusion does more than signal that you're done speaking. It ties all the preceding information together in a cohesive, memorable way. Your audience's minds will be pulled in many directions after your talk, so having a robust, well-constructed close can mean the difference between your message getting lost or sticking with people.

A powerful conclusion should:

1. Summarize your key takeaways: recap the main points of your presentation, reinforcing your core message.

    For example, "Crafting a fulfilling career requires self-reflection, strategic planning, and a willingness to take risks. By identifying your values, leveraging your strengths, and pursuing meaningful opportunities, you can create a professional path that aligns with who you are and what you stand for."

2. Leave your audience with a call to action: give your listeners concrete steps to apply your ideas to their lives or work.

    For instance, "Take some time next week to reflect on your values, passions, and strengths. Write them down, share them with a trusted friend or mentor, and start brainstorming ways to incorporate them into your career. Remember, small steps can lead to big changes over time."

3. End with a memorable statement or story: close your presentation with a thought-provoking quote, a robust statistic, or a personal anecdote that ties back to your core message.

For example, "As the poet Rumi once said, 'Let yourself be silently drawn by the strange pull of what you love. It will not lead you astray.' Trust that pull, and let it guide you toward a career that lights you up. Thank you."

By crafting a powerful conclusion summarizing your key points, inspiring action, and leaving a lasting impact, you ensure that your message resonates with your audience long after your presentation ends.

Storyboarding for Crafting Content

Visualizing the flow and structure of your presentation using a storyboard can be incredibly helpful as you begin to craft your content. A storyboard is a graphic organizer that allows you to plan your content slide by slide or section by section.

To create a storyboard, start by breaking down your presentation into its key components:

Introduction
Main Point 1
Main Point 2
Main Point 3
Conclusion

For each component, outline the key ideas, examples, and visuals you want to include. This could involve writing bullet points, creating rough sketches, or using sticky notes to rearrange and refine your content.

Storyboarding allows you to see your presentation as a cohesive whole, ensuring that each element builds upon the last and supports your core message. It also helps you identify gaps or redundancies in your content to streamline and optimize your presentation for maximum impact.

As you storyboard, keep the following tips in mind:

1. Focus on your core message: ensure every storyboard element supports your central idea.

2. Prioritize clarity and simplicity: use clear, concise language and visuals that support your message without overwhelming your audience.

3. Incorporate variety: alternate between different types of content (e.g., stories, statistics, examples) to keep your audience engaged.

4. Build opportunities for interaction: consider where you might include questions, polls, or activities to involve your audience in the learning process.

Storyboarding is also a powerful tool for unleashing your creative potential in public speaking. Each frame of your storyboard allows you to experiment with different narrative techniques, such as storytelling, analogies, or demonstrations. It's not just about planning what you will say but how you will say it.

Storyboarding can be particularly helpful when you need help or more inspiration. Sketching out your presentation visually can help kick your brain into high gear, engaging different cognitive muscles and helping you make new connections and spark fresh ideas.

Storyboards provide a unique and efficient way to gather and incorporate valuable insights before finalizing your speech. Sharing your storyboard with colleagues or mentors gives them a clear overview of your planned presentation and invites constructive feedback on your talk's structure, content, and flow. This feedback can then be directly applied to the storyboard, allowing you to rearrange, add, or remove elements as needed. This process ensures that your final presentation is as strong, coherent, and impactful as possible.

Overcoming Challenges in Content Creation

Crafting compelling content is rarely straightforward. Even experienced speakers can face challenges such as writer's block, dealing with complex topics, or adapting content for different audiences. Let's explore these common challenges and look at some practical strategies for overcoming them.

Writer's block is a common challenge that can strike at any stage of the content creation process. When you find yourself struggling to generate ideas or put your thoughts into words, try these strategies:

1. Freewriting: set a timer for 10-15 minutes and write continuously without stopping to edit or censor yourself. This can help you bypass your inner critic and get your creative juices flowing.

2. Mind mapping: start with your core message or topic in the center of a blank page, then branch out with related ideas, examples, and stories. This visual brainstorming technique can help you generate new ideas and see connections between different aspects of your topic.

3. Change your environment: sometimes, a change of scenery can help break through writer's block. Try working in a different room, walking, or writing at different times to shake up your routine and stimulate new ideas.

By being proactive and flexible in your approach to content creation, you can overcome common challenges and craft presentations that resonate with any audience. The key is to stay focused on your core message while adapting your content and delivery to your listeners' specific needs and interests. Remember, crafting compelling content is a skill that can be learned and refined over time. The more you practice, the more you'll develop your unique style. Every presentation is an opportunity to educate and entertain your audience. With the right tools and techniques, you have the power to create content that not only communicates your ideas but also sparks meaningful change in the lives of your listeners.

Crafting Compelling Content: A Checklist for Speakers

1. Define your core message:

- Identify the central idea or takeaway you want your audience to remember
- Ensure your core message is clear, concise, and compelling
- Align all your content to support and reinforce this core message

2. Analyze your audience:

- Research your audience's demographics, psychographics, and prior knowledge
- Identify their expectations, needs, and potential objections
- Gather information through surveys, interviews, focus groups, and social media

3. Structure your presentation:

- Use the "Tell them what you're going to tell them, tell them, then tell them what you told them" Approach
- Craft an engaging introduction that captures attention and previews your main points
- Organize your content into clear, logical sections that flow smoothly from one to next
- Create a powerful conclusion that summarizes your key points, inspires action, and leaves a lasting impact

4. Employ the "Power of Three":

- Break down your core message into three main points or arguments
- Ensure each point is distinct yet interconnected and supportive of your central idea
- Use this structure to make your content more memorable and impactful

5. Prioritize clarity and simplicity:

- Use clear, concise language that your audience can easily understand
- Break down complex ideas into smaller, more digestible chunks
- Provide examples, analogies, and visuals to illustrate your points
- Focus on the information that is most critical for achieving your presentation's goals

6. Incorporate storytelling and examples:

- Use stories, case studies & examples to engage and make your ideas more relatable
- Choose examples that are relevant and demonstrate your points in action
- Use different types of content (stories, statistics, examples) to maintain engagement

7. Leverage repetition:

- Repeat your core message throughout your presentation to reinforce its importance
- Use different words, examples, or stories to illustrate your core message in new ways
- Incorporate rhetorical devices like anaphora or epistrophe to emphasize your message

8. Storyboard your presentation:

- Visualize the flow and structure of your presentation using a storyboard
- Use the storyboard to identify gaps, redundancies, or opportunities for improvement
- Seek feedback on your storyboard from colleagues or mentors to refine your content
- Break down your presentation into critical components and outline the main ideas, examples, and visuals

9. Tailor your content to your audience:

- Highlight the aspects of your topic that are most relevant and beneficial to audience
- Address potential objections and provide evidence to support your perspective
- Use the insights from your audience analysis to adapt your language, tone, and delivery style

10. Overcome common challenges:

- Employ analogies, visuals, and examples to break down complex topics
- Be proactive and flexible in adapting your content to different audiences and contexts
- Use strategies like free writing, mind mapping, or changing your environment to overcome writer's block

By following this checklist and incorporating these critical strategies into your content creation process, you'll be well-equipped to craft presentations that educate, engage, and inspire your audience to take action.

So get excited and get started.

5

MASTERING THE ART OF STORYTELLING

"The most powerful person is the storyteller."
S Jobs

Storytelling is a fundamental strategy for creating connection and resonance in public speaking that statistical data alone cannot achieve. The power of storytelling lies in its universal appeal. Humans have told stories since ancient times, finding a shared language transcending individual experiences and technical jargon. As a speaker, you engage your audience intellectually, emotionally, and psychologically using narrative form.

Stories are more than entertainment; they are a fundamental way humans communicate and make sense of the world. A well-told story can illuminate complex ideas, bring abstract concepts to life, and stir emotions that facts alone cannot. When you share a story, you invite your audience to experience reality through your perspective, making the abstract tangible. This connection is invaluable in public speaking, especially when the goal is to persuade, motivate, or inspire.

To understand the impact of storytelling in public speaking, let's look at a couple of real-world examples.

Barack Obama successfully used this technique to engage and inspire audiences during his 2008 presidential campaign. In his speech, "A More Perfect Union," he delivered a groundbreaking message about race relations in America. He used storytelling to address the controversial remarks made by his former pastor, Reverend Jeremiah Wright. He shared his personal story of being born to a black father and a white mother, growing up in a multiracial family, and witnessing both the triumphs and struggles of the African American community.

By weaving his narrative into the larger story of race in America, Obama created a powerful and nuanced speech that addressed a divisive issue with empathy, honesty, and hope.

Oprah Winfrey is regarded as an exceptional public speaker who frequently uses storytelling to captivate her audience and effectively convey her messages. One notable example is her 2018 Golden Globes speech, where she accepted the Cecil B. DeMille Award for lifetime achievement.

In her speech, Oprah shared personal stories highlighting the importance of speaking truth to power and standing up against injustice. She began by recounting her childhood memory of watching Sidney Poitier become the first black man to win an Oscar in 1964. This story set the stage for her to discuss the significance of representation and its impact on her as a young girl. She then transitioned to the story of Recy Taylor, a young African American woman who was raped by six white men in 1944. Despite the challenges, Taylor fought for justice, and her story served as an inspiring example of courage and resilience in the face of adversity.

Through these stories, Oprah emotionally connected with her audience. She used vivid imagery and descriptive language to paint a picture in the minds of her listeners, allowing them to empathize with the characters in her stories.

Oprah's storytelling technique also reinforced her central theme of speaking truth to power. By sharing real-life examples, she demonstrated the impact that individuals can have when they stand up for what is right, even in the face of seemingly insurmountable challenges.

Writing Your Story

Writing your story requires more than a compelling narrative; it demands authenticity and relevance to your core message. As mentioned in the previous chapter, you first must identify the key message or lesson you want your audience to take away. Once clear, think back to experiences in your own life that align with this message. Integrate stories at points in your presentation where you must underscore a particular argument or when the audience needs a break from technical content. Additionally, stories can be used as powerful openers or closers, captivating interest immediately or leaving a lasting impression.

When selecting stories to include in your presentation, consider the following criteria:

1. Relevance: the story should directly relate to your core message and help illustrate or reinforce your key points. Ask yourself, "Does this story contribute to the overall purpose of my presentation, or is it just an interesting anecdote?" Leave it out if the story doesn't support your main arguments or themes.

2. Authenticity: choose genuine stories that reflect your own experiences, values, and beliefs. Audiences can sense when a story feels contrived or inauthentic, which can undermine your credibility as a speaker. When sharing personal stories, be honest about your struggles, failures, and triumphs. This vulnerability can help create a stronger connection with your audience.

3. Emotional impact: select stories that evoke emotions and create a connection with your audience. Stories that elicit joy, surprise, empathy, or inspiration are more likely to be remembered and acted upon. Consider the emotional journey you want to take your audience on and choose stories that support that arc.

4. Conciseness: keep your stories concise and focused, avoiding

unnecessary details that can distract from your main message. Aim for stories that can be told in 2-3 minutes or less. If a story is too long or complex, consider breaking it up into more minor anecdotes or focusing on the most essential elements.

When crafting your stories, it's also essential to consider the structure and delivery. A good story should have a clear beginning, middle, and end, a compelling hook that draws the audience in, and a satisfying resolution that ties back to your main message. Use vivid, sensory language to help your audience visualize the events and emotions of the story, and vary your tone, pacing, and volume to create a dynamic and engaging delivery.

Structuring Your Presentation Like a Story

Every compelling story follows a fundamental structure that captivates audiences and keeps them engaged. This structure is a powerful tool in public speaking, especially when sharing complex information. As mentioned before, a good structure involves the following:

1. A clear beginning: set the stage and introduce the central theme. This is where you introduce the characters, establish the setting, and present the central conflict or question that will drive your story forward.

2. A middle: develop the core of your narrative through arguments or points that build upon each other. This is where the story unfolds, with rising action, obstacles, and revelations that keep the audience engaged.

3. An end: provide a resolution. This is where the story reaches its climax, and the central conflict is resolved, leaving the audience with a sense of satisfaction and closure.

Creating a Narrative Arc

The emotional connection that stories forge sets them apart from other forms of communication. While the brain's analytical areas process facts, stories activate parts of the brain involved in experiencing emotions and sensations. To enhance this connection, focus on the emotional arc of your story:

1. How do the characters in your story feel? What are their hopes, fears, and motivations? By making your characters relatable and their emotions palpable, you invite your audience to empathize and become invested in their journey.

2. What challenges do they face, and how do they overcome them? Every good story involves some conflict or obstacle that the characters must navigate. By highlighting the difficulties your characters face and how they rise to meet those challenges, you create a sense of tension and release that keeps your audience engaged.

3. How does their journey mirror the emotions you want your audience to feel? Consider the emotional trajectory you want your audience to experience throughout your presentation. Do you want them to feel inspired, empowered, or curious? Use your story to guide them through those emotional states, creating a shared experience that resonates.

The narrative arc of your presentation should guide your audience through an emotional and intellectual journey. Begin with an introduction that poses a question or presents a challenge that grabs interest. This could be a provocative statement, a surprising statistic, or a relatable anecdote that establishes the stakes and draws your audience in.

As you move into the body of your presentation, escalate the "action" by introducing new information, increasing the stakes, or revealing significant facts that build towards a climax. Use storytelling techniques like cliffhangers, plot twists, and dramatic reveals to keep your audience on the edge of their seats, wondering what will happen next.

Following this, your conclusion should serve as the resolution, answering the initial questions posed or summarizing the journey in a satisfying and complete way. Use callback humor (a comedic technique where a joke or reference made earlier in a performance or conversation is brought back unexpectedly later on, often in a new context. This creates humor through repetition and surprise.)

Here's an example I might use: "Many speakers worry about forgetting their material. One common advice is to imagine the audience in their underwear to feel less intimidated. However, this can backfire if you start giggling at the thought of your CEO in boxer shorts with heart patterns." Then, later in my presentation, when discussing visual aids, I may say: "When preparing slides, remember that less is more. You want your audience focused on your words, not squinting at a cluttered screen. After all, you're not trying to distract them from imagining you in your underwear – that's supposed to be your trick, remember?"

Incorporate a Full Circle Ending. This is a storytelling technique where the conclusion of a narrative returns to an element, theme, or idea introduced at the beginning. This creates a sense of completeness and symmetry, often leaving the audience with a satisfying feeling of closure. Here's an example of a Full Circle Ending for a speech about overcoming challenges in the workplace:

Opening: "Ladies and gentlemen, when I entered my first job 20 years ago, I was carrying a briefcase my father had given me. He said, 'This briefcase is empty now, but by the time you retire, it should be full of experience, wisdom, and stories.'" [The speaker then discusses various challenges faced in their career and the lessons learned from each.] Closing: "As I stand here today, I realize that briefcase my father gave me isn't just full – it's overflowing. Every challenge we face in our professional lives is an opportunity to add something valuable to our briefcases. So, I encourage you to embrace the difficulties, learn from the setbacks, and fill your briefcase. Because at the end of the day, it's not about what you carry – it's about the wisdom you've gained along the way."

Full-circle endings or powerful quotes are great ways to create a sense of closure and reinforce your main message.

Include Conflict and Resolution

Introducing conflict or challenge in your story provides tension that can pique and sustain interest. The conflict could be a market challenge your company faces, a common misconception about your field, or a problem your product or service can solve. By presenting this conflict and guiding your audience through the steps toward resolution, you mimic the emotional satisfaction of a story, resolving its plot. The resolution should provide a clear answer or solution, ideally tied to the action you want your audience to take. For example, if you're presenting a new marketing strategy, you might introduce the conflict by discussing the declining effectiveness of traditional advertising methods. You could share statistics about ad fatigue, banner blindness, and the rise of ad-blocking software, painting a picture of the challenges marketers face in reaching their target audiences.

As you move into the body of your presentation, you could introduce your new marketing strategy as the solution to this conflict. Use case studies, examples, and data to show how your approach addresses your outlined problems and delivers better results than traditional methods. Build a sense of excitement and possibility around your solution, helping your audience envision a future where this conflict is resolved.

In your conclusion, you could offer a clear call to action that ties your solution to your audience's needs and goals. For example, you might invite them to attend a workshop, sign up for a free trial, or collaborate with your team to implement the new strategy in their organization. Providing a clear path forward and a sense of resolution leaves your audience empowered and motivated to take action.

Personal Stories vs. Universal Themes

Balancing personal stories with universal themes can significantly enhance the relatability of your presentation. Personal stories allow your audience to see real-world applications of your points and make your presentation more engaging. However, tying these examples to universal themes—such as success, innovation, perseverance, or collaboration—elevates your narrative, connecting individual stories to broader, more relatable contexts. This blend makes your presentation more impactful and ensures it resonates with a diverse audience. For example, if you're giving a presentation about leadership, you might share a personal story about a difficult decision you made as a manager. You may have to choose between two equally qualified candidates for a promotion or navigate a tense conflict between team members. By sharing the specifics of your own experience, you give your audience a window into the realities of leadership and the challenges that come with it.

On the other hand, you could tie your story to universal themes like integrity, fairness, or empathy to make it more broadly applicable. You could discuss how your decision-making process was guided by a commitment to doing what was right, even when it was difficult. Or you could highlight how your ability to see the situation from multiple perspectives and consider the needs of all parties involved helped you find a resolution that worked for everyone. Connecting your personal story to these universal themes makes it more relatable to audience members who may not have had the same experience but can still identify with the underlying principles and emotions. You also elevate your story from a simple anecdote to a powerful illustration of larger truths about leadership, teamwork, and human nature.

Balancing specificity and universality is essential when incorporating personal stories into your presentations. Share enough detail to make your story vivid and engaging, but also take the time to draw out the broader lessons and themes that make it relevant to your audience. Doing so creates an authentic and inclusive narrative, inviting your audience to see themselves in your experiences and apply your insights to their lives and work.

Framework for Inspirational Speeches

The Hero's Journey is a robust narrative framework that has shaped stories from ancient myths to modern cinema. It was recognized and coined by literature professor Joseph Campbell, who noticed all stories and myths followed a distinct pattern and he broke it down into twelve sections. Its universal appeal lies in the journey of a hero who ventures from the ordinary into the extraordinary, faces challenges, secures victory, and returns transformed. This framework is incredibly effective in public speaking, especially when crafting speeches that aim to inspire and motivate.

Understanding the Hero's Journey in the context of public speaking involves recognizing each part of the journey and how it can mirror the path you want your audience to embark upon:

1. The Ordinary World: the hero's everyday life before the adventure begins. In a presentation, this is where you introduce the status quo that your audience is familiar with. You might discuss your audience's challenges or limitations in their current situation, setting the stage for the journey ahead.

2. The Call to Adventure: the hero is presented with a problem, challenge, or opportunity. In your presentation, this is where you introduce the central theme or idea that will be the focus of your talk. You might present a new perspective, a groundbreaking solution, or a call to action that challenges your audience to step out of their comfort zone.

3. Refusal of the Call: the hero hesitates to accept the challenge due to fear, insecurity, or inadequacy. In your presentation, acknowledge the doubts or concerns that your audience might have about embarking on this journey. Address their fears and provide reassurance that the journey is worth taking.

4. Meeting the Mentor: the hero encounters a mentor who provides guidance, training, or gifts to help them overcome their fears and accept the call. In your presentation, you can position yourself as the mentor, offering expertise, insights, and support to guide your audience through the challenges ahead.

5. Crossing the Threshold: the hero commits to the adventure and enters the particular world. In your presentation, this is where you invite your audience to fully engage with your ideas and take the first steps towards change. You might offer a specific tool, strategy, or mindset shift that helps them cross the threshold into a new way of thinking or being.

6. Tests, Allies, and Enemies: the hero faces challenges, makes allies, and confronts enemies. In your presentation, discuss the obstacles and setbacks that your audience might face on their journey. Share examples of how others have navigated similar challenges and the lessons they learned. Highlight the importance of building a support network and surrounding oneself with positive influences.

7. Approach to the Inmost Cave: the hero approaches the central ordeal of the adventure. In your presentation, build suspense and anticipation for the main point or revelation that will be the turning point of your talk. Foreshadow the challenges and rewards that await your audience as they near the heart of their journey.

8. The Ordeal: the hero faces the most significant challenge and experiences "death" (literal or metaphorical). In your presentation, this is where you confront the most critical obstacle or fear that holds your audience back. You might share a personal story of facing a similar challenge and its transformative impact on your life. Emphasize the importance of perseverance and growth from pushing through difficult times.

9. Reward: the hero survives and gains the reward (knowledge, treasure, or insight). In your presentation, celebrate the breakthroughs and victories that your audience will experience as they overcome their challenges. Share the benefits and opportunities that await them on the other side of their journey.

10. The Road Back: the hero returns to the ordinary world. In your presentation, acknowledge that the journey is not over and that there will be ongoing challenges and opportunities for growth. Encourage your audience to integrate their newfound knowledge and insights into their daily lives and to continue pushing forward.

11. Resurrection: the hero faces a final test where the knowledge or treasure gained is put to use. In your presentation, offer a final call to action or challenge that allows your audience to apply what they've learned. Encourage them to take concrete steps towards their goals and force positive change in their lives and communities.

12. Return with the Elixir: the hero returns to the ordinary world with a reward or knowledge that can benefit others. In your presentation, emphasize the ripple effect your audience's journey will have on those around them. Inspire them to share their insights and experiences with others and to be catalysts for transformation in their spheres of influence.

By structuring your presentation around the Hero's Journey framework, you create a powerful narrative that resonates with your audience profoundly and emotionally.

Identifying with the Audience

Position your audience as the story's hero to make your speech impactful. Speak directly to their experiences, challenges, and aspirations. Use second-person narrative or direct questions to make your speech more engaging and personal. This technique increases engagement and encourages personal reflection, creating a deeper emotional connection with your message. For example, instead of saying, "Many people struggle with public speaking anxiety," you could say, "Have you ever felt your heart race and your palms sweat at the thought of giving a presentation? You're not alone." By using "you" language and inviting your audience to reflect on their own experiences, you create a sense of empathy and connection that makes your message feel more relevant and applicable.

Similarly, instead of saying, "Effective leaders need to communicate their vision clearly," you could say, "Imagine yourself as a leader, inspiring your team to achieve greatness. How will you communicate your vision to motivate and empower them?" By placing your audience in the protagonist role and inviting them to envision themselves in the situation you're describing, you make your message more engaging and memorable.

Throughout your presentation, look for opportunities to highlight how your audience can relate to the hero's journey. Emphasize the universal themes and emotions your story touches on, such as the desire for growth, the fear of failure, or the satisfaction of overcoming obstacles. Use inclusive language that makes your audience feel seen and understood, such as "we" instead of "I."

By positioning your audience as the story's hero and speaking directly to their experiences and aspirations, you create a powerful sense of identification that makes your message more impactful and inspiring. Your audience will feel like you are speaking directly to them, understanding their challenges, and rooting for their success. They will be more likely to see themselves in your story and feel motivated to take action based on your message.

Balancing Emotion and Logic

To achieve a balance between emotional and logical appeals, it's essential to understand that emotions can significantly influence how information is perceived and retained. Emotional appeals connect with the audience on a human level, making your message more relatable and memorable. However, these appeals must be grounded in logical facts to maintain credibility and substance. Begin by identifying the core message of your presentation and the logical data that supports it, then weave in emotional elements that complement this data. For example, if you're giving a presentation about the importance of employee well-being in the workplace, you could start with some statistics about the impact of stress and burnout on productivity, absenteeism, and turnover. These logical data points establish the scope and severity of the problem, appealing to your audience's rational side.

To make your message more emotionally resonant, you could follow up the data with a personal story about an employee who struggled with work-life balance and the toll it took on their health and happiness. By putting a human face on the issue and describing the emotional impact of poor well-being, you create a sense of empathy and connection that makes your message feel more urgent and relevant.

Similarly, if you're giving a presentation about the benefits of a new product or service, you could start with some logical data points about its features, performance, and ROI. These appeals to reason and evidence help to establish the credibility and value of your offering. To make your message more emotionally compelling, you could share a customer success story that highlights the real-world impact of your product or service. By describing how your offering helped a specific customer overcome a challenge or achieve a goal, you create a sense of aspiration and possibility that makes your message more inspiring and memorable.

The key to balancing emotional and logical appeals is to use them in a complementary and mutually reinforcing way. Logical appeals provide the foundation and credibility for your message, while emotional appeals make it more relatable and inspiring. By weaving these two types of appeals together throughout your presentation, you create a more well-rounded and persuasive argument that engages your audience's head and heart.

Common Pitfalls to Avoid

While storytelling is a powerful tool in public speaking, there are some common pitfalls to avoid:

1. Overusing Personal Anecdotes: while personal stories can be engaging, too many can make your presentation feel self-indulgent or disconnected from your main message.

2. Failing to Tie Stories to the Core Message: every story you include should have a clear purpose and contribute to your overall message.

3. Neglecting the Emotional Arc: avoid flat or disjointed stories that fail to create an emotional connection or provide a clear takeaway.

4. Overlooking the Importance of Practice: storytelling requires practice and refinement to be effective.

5. Relying Too Heavily on Storytelling: stories are powerful, but they should be balanced with other presentation elements, such as data, evidence, and logical arguments.

6. Failing to Consider the Audience: not all stories will resonate with all audiences.

7. Overcomplicating the Story: a good story should be clear, concise, and easy to follow.

8. Neglecting the Power of Visuals: stories are often more powerful when accompanied by visual aids that help bring the narrative to life.

By being aware of and avoiding these common pitfalls, you can effectively incorporate storytelling into your presentations to enhance your credibility, engage your audience, and drive your message home.

Storytelling is a transformative skill for you as a public speaker. As you can see, it offers a powerful way to connect with audiences on multiple levels. It is more than mere entertainment; it is a universal language that brings complex ideas to life and creates deep emotional resonance. You can create informative, profoundly engaging, and memorable presentations by skillfully blending emotional appeals with logical arguments. Ultimately, the art of storytelling is about more than just relaying information; it's about creating a shared experience that moves, inspires, and motivates.

Storytelling is an essential tool that should be in every public speaker's kit.

6

BODY LANGUAGE AND NONVERBAL COMMUNICATION

"The most important thing in communication is to hear what isn't being said." P Drucker

Mastering the art of body language in public speaking is like learning to play a complex musical instrument. It requires understanding the basics, continuous practice, and, most importantly, a keen sense of awareness and adaptability. Appreciating the subtle yet powerful nonverbal language cues can transform your ability to persuade, command respect, and convey confidence in public speaking.

This chapter is dedicated to unraveling the complexities of body language and promoting you to a communicator who speaks not only with words but with every nuance of your being.

Understanding Nonverbal Signals

Body language is a form of nonverbal communication that includes facial expressions, gestures, posture, and physical distance.

At the core of mastering body language is understanding that your body speaks a language as intricate as any spoken dialect. Nonverbal cues can affirm or contradict what's being said, reveal emotions not explicitly expressed, and enhance or undermine the perceived sincerity of your message. For instance, crossing your arms while delivering a message intended to welcome feedback can subconsciously signal defensiveness, deterring the engagement you seek.

Your words alone are just a fraction of what your audience is absorbing. How you carry yourself, your facial expressions, and your physical presence can reinforce or undermine the verbal content you're delivering.

Your body language should complement and reinforce your verbal message, not contradict it. Congruence between what you're saying and how you're saying it is vital for building trust and credibility with your audience. For example, suppose you verbally express enthusiasm or passion about a topic. In that case, your body language should reflect that energy through open gestures, an animated presence, and facial expressions that convey genuine excitement. Conversely, if you deliver a somber or severe message, your body language should match that tone with a more subdued, grounded demeanor.

Nonverbal signals can broadly be categorized into positive and negative cues, each capable of creating vastly different reactions from your audience. Positive body language includes maintaining an open posture, nodding, smiling, and using hand gestures that indicate openness and inclusiveness. These cues make you, the speaker, appear approachable, engaged, and confident. Conversely, negative body language, such as avoiding eye contact, fidgeting, or maintaining a closed posture (like crossed arms or legs), can make a speaker seem untrustworthy, disinterested, or even nervous.

Facial Expressions

Facial expressions are one of the most important aspects of nonverbal communication, as they convey various emotions and attitudes. Key facial expressions to be aware of include:

1. Smiling: a genuine smile can help create a positive, approachable demeanor and build rapport with the audience.

2. Frowning: depending on the context, frowning can convey disapproval, concern, or concentration.

3. Raised eyebrows: raised eyebrows can indicate surprise, interest, or skepticism.

4. Narrowed eyes: narrowed eyes can suggest suspicion, anger, or intense focus.

To use facial expressions effectively, maintain a natural, congruent expression that aligns with your verbal message and stay relaxed.

Practicing Awareness

Developing an awareness of your body language is an essential first step. Begin by observing how you communicate in business settings and everyday interactions. Consider questions like:

How do you react when faced with questions? Do you look puzzled or confronted?

What does your posture say about your level of interest in a conversation? Are you leaning in to listen or sitting back looking at your watch?

A practical exercise to enhance awareness is to ask someone to watch you and give honest feedback or record yourself presenting and look for inconsistencies between your verbal and nonverbal cues. For example, are you saying "yes" while shaking your head from side to side? Such mismatches can confuse your audience and detract from your message's credibility. Gradually, you will start to notice patterns and can correct them.

Using Gestures to Enhance Your Message

Gestures are potent tools for emphasizing your message. When used deliberately, they can significantly strengthen the delivery of your message, making it more memorable and engaging for your audience. However, it's essential to avoid excessive, aimless gesturing, which can be distracting and undermine your professionalism. Gestures should feel natural and purposeful, almost like visual punctuation for your words.

One effective strategy is to practice incorporating gestures that directly illustrate or emphasize key points in your speech—for example, using hand motions to represent size, height, or numerical values when stating facts and figures or opening your arms wide when expressing an overarching concept or idea. Keep all gestures authentic; they must feel natural and confident, not forced or overdone.

Different types of gestures can convey different meanings and emotional undertones. They can be categorized into descriptive, emotive, suggestive, and prompting gestures:

1. Descriptive gestures describe or mimic physical details about an object or action, such as the size or shape of something.

2. Emotive gestures express feelings like joy or frustration.

3. Suggestive gestures subtly hint at or suggest an idea, often used to provoke thought or highlight implications.

4. Prompting gestures are intended to elicit a response from the audience, such as raising your hand to signal them to stop or think.

Understanding these varieties and their associated meanings allows you to use gestures more effectively to complement your verbal messages. For instance, when trying to convey the importance of a concept, you might clench your fist to communicate intensity and conviction visually.

When speaking to diverse or international audiences, it's crucial to consider how cultural differences can influence the interpretation of your gestures. What might be a positive gesture in one culture could be offensive or confusing in another. For example, the thumbs-up gesture is considered affirmative in many Western cultures but can be offensive in parts of the Middle East and South America. Similarly, pointing one finger is often rude in Asian and African cultures, where pointing with an open hand is preferable. If you need more clarification, observe the gestures used by local speakers and adapt accordingly.

Eye Contact and Building Trust

Eye contact is a fundamental component of communication that can bridge the gap between speaker and listener, fostering a connection of trust and understanding. The eyes, often described as the windows to the soul, can convey honesty, confidence, and empathy—qualities essential for effective communication.

In public speaking, consistent eye contact helps hold the audience's attention and convey confidence in the subject matter. It also plays a critical role in making your delivery appear sincere and genuine, bolstering the audience's trust in you and your message. When you look someone in the eyes, you say, "I am open to communication, and I value this interaction." This nonverbal cue is crucial in making your audience feel acknowledged and respected.

Effective eye contact goes beyond merely 'looking' at your audience. It involves intentionally connecting with your listeners through your gaze, which should be inviting and informative. Eye contact can guide your audience through your presentation, emphasizing key points and facilitating a better understanding of your message. When executed well, it helps to create an atmosphere of inclusivity and engagement, making each audience member feel as though you are speaking directly to them, thus enhancing the overall impact of your speech.

Understanding the balance between too much and too little eye contact is essential. Excessive eye contact can be perceived as intimidating or aggressive, which may cause discomfort or disengage your audience. On the other hand, insufficient eye contact can be interpreted as a lack of confidence, interest, or sincerity, potentially undermining your credibility and the trust you wish to establish.

Finding the right balance involves maintaining eye contact long enough to connect with the audience, typically around three to five seconds per person or group, before shifting your gaze naturally to others in the audience. This balance is about the duration and the distribution of your eye contact across the audience.

Ensure that your eye contact is evenly distributed to include everyone in the conversation, regardless of their position. Neglecting certain areas or individuals can lead to feelings of exclusion and reduce your audience's overall engagement. Consider implementing one of the following strategic techniques:

1. The 'lighthouse' technique: sweep your gaze across the audience in a slow, steady motion, like a lighthouse beam. This technique ensures that your attention reaches everyone, creating a sense of engagement and connection throughout the room.

2. The 'triangular gazing' method: this involves making eye contact with three different people in various parts of the audience at random intervals. This method can make your gaze feel more natural and spontaneous while covering a broad range of the audience space.

Practice focusing on the eyes of your audience members during rehearsals or when speaking to smaller groups. This practice will help you become more comfortable maintaining eye contact in less formal settings, building your confidence and proficiency over time. It is also helpful to simulate eye contact when practicing alone by using placeholders like chairs or objects to represent different audience members, training yourself to make natural transitions between focal points.

Overcoming Eye Contact Anxiety

For many, maintaining eye contact during a presentation can evoke anxiety stemming from the vulnerability of being in the spotlight.

To overcome this anxiety, start by understanding that eye contact is a skill that improves with practice and exposure. Begin in low-pressure situations, such as conversations with friends or during team meetings, and gradually work your way up to larger, more formal settings.

This gradual exposure can help desensitize your apprehensions, making eye contact feel more natural and less daunting.

Another technique is to focus on the friendly faces in the audience—the individuals who nod, smile, or otherwise positively engage with your presentation. Focusing on these receptive audience members can boost your confidence and reduce anxiety, making maintaining eye contact with the rest of the room easier.

Remember that your audience generally wants you to succeed, and their gaze often reflects interest and encouragement rather than judgment.

The Power of Pausing

Strategic pauses in public speaking are not mere breaks in sound; they are purposeful tools that help to emphasize points, give the audience time to absorb information, and create an element of suspense or anticipation. Imagine delivering a powerful statement and then pausing—this silence allows your words to resonate, giving the audience time to reflect on their significance. This technique can transform a good speech into an unforgettable one by punctuating your message with moments that invite the audience into more profound thought or heightened emotion.

The timing and length of pauses are crucial for achieving the desired effect without disrupting the flow of your speech. Generally, a pause can range from a half-second to up to four seconds, depending on its purpose. Shorter pauses are effective for slight emphasis and allow the audience to catch up with quick shifts in the topic. Longer pauses help draw attention to significant transitions or conclusions within your speech. They can also be instrumental when you switch from one section of your presentation to another, signaling a shift in focus or introducing a new concept.

To master pauses, consider the rhythm of your speech and the nature of your content. For instance, after introducing a controversial or surprising statistic, a longer pause can allow the magnitude of the information to sink in. Conversely, when listing several points quickly, shorter pauses can help maintain the momentum of the speech while still marking each item.

The key is to balance pauses with the natural cadence of your speech, ensuring they enhance rather than disrupt your delivery.

Practicing the use of pauses can dramatically improve the effectiveness of your speech. Identify spots in your remarks where a pause could enhance understanding or emphasize a point. During rehearsals, experiment with different lengths of pauses to see how they affect the delivery and reception of your message.

Recording your practice sessions can be beneficial. Playback allows you to objectively assess the timing and impact of your pauses and make adjustments as needed. Over time, you will develop a sense of when and how to use pauses most effectively to complement your speaking style and message.

Another helpful practice is reading passages from books or speeches aloud, paying attention to punctuation like commas, periods, and paragraph breaks, and using them as cues for natural pauses. This exercise can help you get accustomed to the rhythmic use of pauses in language.

You can also practice with a partner or coach who can provide feedback on the timing and effectiveness of your pauses, offering insights you might not notice on your own.

Embracing the Sound of Silence

Overcoming the fear of silence is essential for using pauses effectively. Many speakers fear that moments of silence may be perceived as awkward or a sign of forgetfulness. However, when used deliberately, silence is a powerful tool that shows confidence and control.

To overcome this fear, start by incorporating brief pauses into your speeches, gradually increasing their duration as you become more comfortable with the silence. Remind yourself that these pauses are not empty spaces but opportunities for your message to be absorbed and understood more deeply by your audience.

By understanding the strategic use of pauses, you enhance the clarity and impact of your presentations and demonstrate professionalism and confidence that sets you apart as a speaker. As you continue to integrate effective pauses into your speeches, remember that silence, like speech, is a form of communication that, when used wisely, can transform the pace and perception of your public speaking endeavors.

Mastering the Use of Space on Stage

When you step onto a stage, you're not just delivering a speech but commanding a space. Your movement and positioning within that space can significantly influence how your message is perceived and received.

Spatial awareness in public speaking involves understanding how the physical space you occupy can either enhance or detract from the impact of your message. It's about arranging your movements to complement your words, creating a blend of verbal and visual communication that captivates your audience.

The concept of spatial awareness extends beyond simply not bumping into furniture or avoiding awkward stances. It encompasses strategically using your presence in the room to command attention and convey confidence. For instance, moving toward the audience can make your delivery feel more intimate and engaged, particularly when making key points. Conversely, stepping back can allow the audience to reflect or absorb the gravity of what you've just said.

This dynamic approach to using space can make your presentation feel like a well-choreographed performance rather than a static lecture, keeping the audience visually and mentally engaged.

Every step you take on stage should serve a purpose. Purposeful movement is about making your physical actions deliberate in your message delivery. For example, if you're discussing a journey or progression, physically moving from one side of the stage to the other can visually represent this concept, making it more tangible for your audience. Similarly, stepping forward when sharing personal anecdotes can create a feeling of closeness and authenticity. The key is to ensure that your movements align with and enhance your verbal message rather than seeming random or distracting.

Plan your space usage in advance to integrate purposeful movement into your presentations. Consider the key points of your presentation and how movement could underscore these moments. During rehearsals, mark the spots on the stage where you plan to stand or move during different speech segments. This preparation helps you move confidently and fluidly, avoiding unnecessary or awkward transitions that can disrupt your delivery flow.

Developing a commanding stage presence is an essential part of effective public speaking. It's about projecting confidence and authority through your posture, movements, and how you occupy the space. A vital stage presence reassures the audience of your expertise and credibility, making your message more persuasive.

To cultivate a powerful stage presence, start by practicing your posture. Stand straight, with shoulders back and head held high, projecting confidence and readiness. Practice your movements to ensure they are smooth and purposeful. Use video recordings to critique your performance and make adjustments where necessary. If you can, practice in the venue where you will speak. Familiarity with the exact space can boost your confidence and help you tailor your movements and positioning to the specific stage and audience layout.

The Impact of Dress and Appearance

When you step onto the stage, the first thing your audience perceives, even before you utter a word, is your appearance. This initial visual impression can significantly influence how your message is received and establish or erode your credibility within seconds.

'Dressing for success' in public speaking is not about superficial aesthetics but strategically using your wardrobe to complement your message. It involves choosing attire that enhances your comfort and confidence and aligns with your audience's expectations and norms.

Understanding the subtle dynamics of audience expectations regarding professional appearance is crucial. For instance, dressing in a sharply tailored suit might be appropriate for a corporate finance conference, where traditional business attire can convey professionalism and competence. Conversely, suppose you are addressing a tech start-up event. In that case, a more casual blazer and jeans might be more relatable, aligning with that audience's innovative and laid-back culture. The key is to research and understand your audience's professional norms beforehand. This preparatory step ensures that your appearance supports your speech, reinforcing your key messages rather than distracting from them.

I talk more about this topic in Chapter 12 under the banner of building your brand.

I've created a short checklist to help you remember the most critical points of non-verbal communication when presenting.

Body Language Checklist for Public Speakers

1. Open body language: avoid crossing arms or creating barriers between you and the audience to appear more approachable and confident.

2. Posture: stand tall with shoulders back and chin up to project confidence and command attention.

3. Stance: keep your feet shoulder-width apart for a stable, grounded appearance.

4. Facial expressions: ensure your facial expressions match your message and convey appropriate emotions.

5. Hand gestures: use purposeful, open gestures to emphasize points and appear more engaging.

6. Pause: use strategic pauses to emphasize points, allow audience reflection, and control pacing.

7. Silence: remember to see silence as an opportunity for your message to be absorbed and understood more deeply by your audience.

8. Proximity: be aware of your distance from the audience and adjust for intimacy or authority as needed.

9. Stage movement: move purposefully on stage to maintain audience engagement and emphasize key points.

10. Dress For Success: make sure your outfit aligns with the expectations of your audience.

As you practice these techniques, your confidence and connection with audiences will strengthen, and your overall effectiveness as a speaker will grow. Remember that mastering these skills is a journey of self-discovery and continuous improvement that takes time.

Every great speaker you admire has honed these skills through practice and persistence. You, too, have the power to command the stage, so step forward with confidence, knowing that with each presentation, you're not just speaking – you're communicating with your entire being.

Let your body language amplify your voice in ways words alone never could.

7

VOCAL TECHNIQUES FOR MAXIMUM IMPACT

"Your voice is your calling card." S Rye

When used effectively, the human voice is a powerful instrument that can captivate, persuade, and inspire an audience. As a public speaker, your vocal delivery is crucial in engaging listeners and conveying your message. However, many speakers fall into the trap of delivering their speeches in a monotonous, flat tone that fails to capture the attention or emotions of their audience. This is where vocal variety comes in – the art of using changes in pitch, volume, pace, and tone to add depth, meaning, and interest to your words.

This chapter explores the importance of vocal variety in public speaking, and I share practical exercises and techniques to help you develop your vocal skills. We will also look at the speeches of renowned speakers to understand how they use vocal variety to enhance their delivery. In addition, I share strategies for incorporating vocal variety into your presentations, ensuring you keep your audience engaged and attentive throughout your speech.

The Power of Vocal Variety

Imagine listening to a speaker maintaining the same volume, pitch, and pace throughout their presentation. No matter how compelling their message or how well-crafted their words are, the lack of vocal variety will likely leave you feeling bored, disengaged, or even frustrated.

On the other hand, a speaker who skillfully employs vocal variety can transform even the most complex or dry topics into a captivating and memorable experience for their audience.

Vocal variety serves several vital functions in public speaking:

1. Maintaining audience attention: by varying your vocal delivery, you create a dynamic and engaging experience that keeps your listeners focused and interested in your message. Monotony is the enemy of attention, and vocal variety is the antidote.

2. Conveying emotions and meaning: your voice can convey a wide range of emotions, from passion and excitement to sincerity and concern. By aligning your vocal delivery with the emotional content of your words, you can create a deeper connection with your audience and enhance the impact of your message.

3. Emphasizing key points: strategic changes in volume, pitch, or pace can help highlight the essential ideas in your speech, ensuring that your audience gets all the crucial takeaways. This is particularly important when delivering complex or information-dense content.

4. Creating a conversational tone: incorporating vocal variety can help you sound more natural, conversational, and relatable to your audience, even in formal speaking contexts. This conversational approach can break down barriers between the speaker and the audience, fostering a sense of connection and trust.

Developing Your Vocal Variety

Like any skill, developing vocal variety takes practice and intentional effort. Here are some exercises and techniques you can use to expand your vocal range and expressiveness:

Diaphragmatic breathing: proper breathing is the foundation of a robust and flexible voice. Practice taking deep breaths from your diaphragm, filling your lungs, and exhaling slowly and evenly. This will help you project your voice without straining and give you greater control over your vocal delivery. Inadequate breathing can lead to a weak, strained, or monotonous voice, quickly losing your audience's attention. A speaker who takes shallow breaths from the chest causes their voice to sound thin and weak.

In contrast, a speaker who breathes deeply from their diaphragm allows their voice to resonate with fullness and power, making a significant difference in vocal impact. To practice diaphragmatic breathing, place one hand on your chest and the other on your belly. Breathe deeply through your nose, focusing on expanding your belly rather than your chest. Exhale slowly through your mouth, feeling your belly contract. Repeat this process several times, ensuring your chest remains relatively still while your belly rises and falls.

Exploring volume: volume refers to the loudness or softness of your voice. Varying your volume can help emphasize important points, create contrast, and maintain your audience's attention. A louder volume can convey excitement, passion, or urgency, while a softer volume can suggest intimacy, sincerity, or confidentiality. Practice speaking at different volumes, from a whisper to a loud projected voice. Be sure to maintain good breath support and avoid shouting or straining your voice.

A great exercise is to choose a simple phrase, such as "I have something important to say," and repeat it at different volume levels, from a whisper to a normal speaking voice to a loud, projected voice. Notice how the volume change affects the words' perceived meaning and impact. When incorporating volume changes into your speeches, be strategic and intentional. Use louder volumes sparingly, reserving them for your presentation's most critical or exciting points. This contrast will make those moments stand out and grab your audience's attention. Conversely, a softer volume can draw your listeners in, creating a sense of intimacy and encouraging them to focus more intently on your words.

Playing with pitch: pitch refers to the highness or lowness of your voice. Varying your pitch can help emphasize key points, create differences, and maintain your audience's attention. A higher pitch can convey excitement or urgency, while a lower pitch can suggest authority or seriousness. A speaker may use a higher pitch when sharing a surprising or exciting statistic, drawing their audience's attention to the significance of the information. Conversely, they may lower their pitch to convey gravity and importance when delivering a serious or somber message.

To increase your pitch range, try speaking or singing a phrase starting at your lowest comfortable pitch and gradually ascending to your highest comfortable pitch, then back down again. You can also practice sliding your voice up and down in a siren-like motion to help loosen and stretch your vocal cords. You can create a more dynamic and engaging delivery by strategically varying your pitch throughout your speech.

Pacing for impact: the pace at which you speak can significantly impact the effectiveness of your message. Speaking too quickly can overwhelm your audience and make it difficult for them to process your ideas. On the other hand, speaking too slowly can cause your listeners to lose interest or become impatient.

To practice pacing, try reading a passage from a book or article at different speeds, from very slow to very fast. Notice how the change in pace affects the meaning and emotional impact of the words. Aim for a conversational pace that allows your audience to follow and comprehend your message while maintaining momentum easily. Consider your message's complexity and emotional content when incorporating pacing changes into your speeches. When introducing a new or elaborate idea, slow down your pace to give your audience time to absorb and process the information. When sharing a humorous anecdote or an exciting story, slightly increase your pace to build energy and engagement. Remember to use pauses strategically to emphasize critical points, allow for audience reactions, or create dramatic tension. A well-timed pause can be just as powerful as a well-chosen word.

Varying your vocal tone: vocal tone refers to your voice's emotional quality and character, such as warmth, enthusiasm, or sincerity. Varying your tone can help convey the appropriate emotion, build a connection with your audience, and enhance the impact of your message.

To practice vocal tone, try delivering the exact phrase or sentence with different emotional inflections, such as happiness, sadness, anger, or surprise. Notice how the tone change affects the words' assumed meaning and impact. You can also practice mimicking the vocal tones of various speakers or characters to expand your range and flexibility. Be authentic and congruent with your message when incorporating vocal tone changes into your speeches. If you're sharing a personal story, use a warm, sincere tone to build a connection with your audience. If you deliver a call to action, use an enthusiastic, passionate tone to inspire and motivate your listeners.

Articulation in Speech

In addition to vocal variety, articulation is another critical component of effective vocal delivery. Articulation refers to the clarity and precision with which you pronounce words and phrases, ensuring your audience quickly understands your message. Poor articulation can result in mumbled, slurred, or rushed speech, which can be difficult for your audience to follow and comprehend. This can lead to frustration, disengagement, and even misinterpreting your message.

To improve your articulation, practice the following techniques:

1. Enunciation: focus on pronouncing each syllable and word clearly and distinctly, particularly at the beginning and end of words. Pay special attention to consonant sounds, which can often become muddled or dropped in casual speech.

2. Tongue twisters: practice saying tongue twisters, such as "She sells seashells by the seashore" or "Peter Piper picked a peck of pickled peppers." These exercises can help improve the agility and precision of your tongue and lips, leading to more accurate articulation.

3. Slow down: aim for a slightly slower pace than your average conversational speed when speaking. This will give you more time to articulate each word and phrase clearly without rushing or mumbling. Remember, a slower pace can also convey a sense of authority and importance. But too slow can be tedious—it's a fine line, but not as tricky as it sounds. Record your rehearsals, and you'll immediately hear the difference.

Choosing Words that Resonate

Your chosen words can significantly impact how your audience receives and understands your message. When selecting the language for your speeches, consider the following:

1. Clarity and simplicity: use clear, concise language that is easily understood by your audience. Avoid jargon, technical terms, or overly complex vocabulary unless it is essential to your message and your audience is familiar with the terminology.

2. Vivid and descriptive language: use language that paints a picture in your audience's minds, engaging their senses and emotions. Incorporate metaphors, similes, and other descriptive techniques to make your message more memorable and impactful.

3. Inclusive language: be mindful of your audience's diversity and choose inclusive and respectful language of different backgrounds, experiences, and perspectives. Avoid language that is biased, stereotypical, or offensive.

4. Rhetorical devices: use rhetorical devices like repetition, alliteration, and parallel structure (see examples below) to make your language more engaging and memorable. These tools can help emphasize key points, create a sense of rhythm and flow, and make your message more persuasive.

Soundbites: Powerful Little Statements

Soundbites are concise, memorable phrases that encapsulate the essence of your message. These powerful statements are often quoted and shared long after your speech has ended, helping to extend the impact and reach of your ideas.

To craft compelling soundbites, consider the following tips:

1. Keep it concise: aim for short, punchy phrases that are easy to remember and repeat. Ideally, a soundbite should be 10-15 words.

2. Make it memorable: use descriptive language to evoke a sensory experience and vivid mental image in the listener's mind. Include metaphors to create deeper meaning, or use rhetorical techniques to make your soundbite stand out.

3. Tie it to your core message: ensure that your soundbite encapsulates your speech's key theme or takeaway, reinforcing the

main point you want your audience to remember.

4. Use parallel structure: craft your soundbite using parallel structure. For example, John F Kennedy said, "Ask not what your country can do for you; ask what you can do for your country." This technique creates a sense of balance and symmetry, making the phrase more memorable and impactful.

Analyzing Renowned Speakers

One of the best ways to learn about effective vocal delivery is to study the speeches of renowned speakers known for their powerful and engaging communication skills. By analyzing their use of vocal variety, articulation, language, and soundbites, you can gain valuable insights and inspiration for your speaking practice.

Michelle Obama: the former First Lady is a powerful speaker who uses vocal variety to convey authority, empathy, and conviction. Her speech at the 2020 Democratic National Convention showcased her ability to use pitch, pace, and tone changes to deliver a personal and political message. I encourage you to watch it and notice how she varies her pitch to emphasize key points and convey emotions.

For example, when she says, "You know I hate politics," her pitch lowers, signaling a sense of seriousness and personal conviction. She strategically slows down her pace when she wants to emphasize a point, such as when she says, "But let me be as honest and clear as I possibly can," drawing the audience's attention to her forthcoming message. Michelle Obama maintains a warm, conversational tone throughout her speech, creating a sense of connection with her audience. However, when discussing the gravity of the current political situation, her tone shifts to one of urgency and concern, underlining the importance of her message.

Greta Thunberg: the young climate activist has become known for her direct, impassioned speeches that call for urgent action on climate change. Her speech at the 2019 UN Climate Action Summit demonstrated her use of vocal variety to convey frustration, determination, and moral clarity. She uses volume to describe the intensity of her emotions and the urgency of her message. When she says, "How dare you," her volume increases, expressing her anger and frustration with world leaders' inaction on climate change.

Thunberg's pace is deliberate and measured, allowing her words to sink in and create a sense of gravity. She pauses strategically after powerful statements, such as "We are at the beginning of a mass extinction, and all you can talk about is money and fairy tales of eternal economic growth." Her tone is direct, unapologetic, and, at times, accusatory. This tone effectively conveys her sense of urgency and moral outrage, captivating her audience and demanding their attention.

Winston Churchill: known for his powerful oratory during World War II, Winston Churchill used various vocal techniques to inspire and motivate the British people. He varied his pitch and volume to emphasize critical points, used strategic pauses to create dramatic tension, and employed a rich, vibrant vocal tone to convey the gravity of the situation.

In his "We Shall Fight on the Beaches" speech, Churchill uses a wide range of pitch to convey the emotional weight of his words. When he says the words, "We shall fight on the beaches," his pitch lowers, creating a sense of determination and resolve. He varies his volume throughout the speech to emphasize key points and maintain engagement. He begins softly, drawing his audience in, and then gradually increases his volume to convey the crescendo of his message. Churchill's articulation is crisp and precise, ensuring that every word is clearly understood. This clarity adds to the power and impact of his message.

Martin Luther King Jr: King's "I Have a Dream" speech is a masterclass in vocal delivery. He used a powerful, rhythmic cadence to engage his audience, varied his pitch and volume to create a sense of urgency and passion, and employed repetition and parallel structure to make his message more memorable and impactful.

His tone is passionate, inspiring, and hopeful. He conveys a sense of moral authority and conviction that resonates with his audience and compels them to act. King strategically increases his volume to emphasize critical points and emotionally charged moments, such as when he says, "From every mountainside, let freedom ring," creating a powerful crescendo that stirs his audience.

While studying and learning from renowned speakers is essential, it is important to mention here that you shouldn't aim to copy someone else's style. Instead, incorporate vocal techniques that feel natural and authentic to your personality and communication style. View vocal variety as an opportunity to develop your speaking signature.

Incorporating Vocal Variety into Your Speeches

Now that you understand the importance of vocal variety and have explored techniques for developing your vocal skills, it's time to incorporate these principles into your speeches. Here are some strategies to help you integrate vocal variety into your preparation and delivery:

1. Script your vocal delivery: when crafting your speech, consider the words you'll say and how you'll say them. Make notes in your script to remind yourself of specific vocal techniques you want to use, such as pauses, volume changes, or tonal shifts.

2. Practice with intention: as you rehearse your speech, focus on incorporating vocal variety deliberately and intentionally. Experiment with different techniques and find what feels authentic and natural to your speaking style.

3. Record and review: record yourself delivering your speech and listen back critically. Identify areas where you can incorporate more vocal variety or improve your articulation and pacing. Adjust and continue practicing until you feel confident and comfortable with your delivery.

4. Seek feedback: ask a trusted colleague, friend, or mentor to listen to your speech and provide constructive feedback on your vocal delivery. They may notice patterns or areas for improvement that you've overlooked.

5. Warm up your voice: just as athletes warm up their muscles before a game, speakers should warm up their voices before a presentation. Spend a few minutes doing vocal exercises like humming, lip trills, or tongue twisters to loosen your vocal cords and prepare your voice for optimal performance. I've prepared a list of my favorite tongue twisters below.

Tongue Twisters for Speakers

1. "A blue-backed blackbird blew big bubbles." Concentrate on pronouncing each word separately.

2. "A monk's monkey mounted a monastery wall and munched melon and macaroni." Focus on the M sounds.

3. "Six sleek sharks swam swiftly in a spiral, chasing the shimmering schools of silvery sardines." This tongue twister relies heavily on rhythm; try to keep the flow smooth.

4. "Irish wristwatch. Swiss wristwatch." This one is a real challenge! Practice saying Irish and Swiss separately before combining them.

5. "A big black bug bit a big black bear, made the big black bear bleed blood." Focus on Bs and aim for clarity with each word.

6. "Knapsack straps. Knapsack straps. Knapsack straps." The difficulty is in the 'SK' sound at the end of 'knapsack' and the beginning of 'straps.' Practice them separately first.

7. "How many cookies could a good cook cook if a good cook could cook cookies?" Pay attention to the 'ook' sound.

8. "Supercalifragilisticexpialidocious." This single-word tongue twister is challenging to master. Break it down into more minor syllables and pronounce them individually before putting it all together.

Vocal variety is a powerful tool every public speaker should perfect to engage, persuade, and inspire their audience. By understanding the importance of pitch, volume, pace, tone, and articulation, plus practicing techniques to develop your vocal skills, you can unlock the full potential of your voice and become a more dynamic, confident, and effective communicator.

Remember, developing vocal variety is an ongoing process that requires intentional practice and self-reflection. By analyzing the speeches of renowned speakers, seeking feedback from others, and continually refining your vocal delivery, you can cultivate an authentic, engaging, and impactful speaking style.

So, the next time you step onto a stage or stand before an audience, tap into the power of your voice. Use it to paint vivid pictures, evoke powerful emotions, and leave a lasting impact on your listeners. Your words can change minds, inspire action, and transform lives.

Let your voice be the instrument that brings your message to life.

8

THE ART OF AUDIENCE ENGAGEMENT

"To sway an audience you must watch them as you speak." C K Wright

Public speaking is not always a smooth sailing experience. Even the most seasoned speakers encounter challenging situations that can disrupt the flow of their presentation and test their ability to maintain composure. These challenges can come in various forms, such as tough questions from the audience, interruptions during the speech, or dealing with complex listeners who may need to be more engaged.

Navigating these situations with poise and confidence is crucial for any public speaker. It requires thorough preparation, quick thinking, and adapting to the unexpected. This chapter explores strategies and techniques for handling these challenges, ensuring you can deliver your message effectively and maintain a positive rapport with all audience members.

Building Rapport

Before diving into specific strategies for dealing with challenging situations, it's essential to understand the importance of audience engagement and analysis. Engaging your audience is not just about delivering your content; it's about creating a meaningful connection with your listeners and understanding their needs, expectations, and potential reactions.

Building rapport with your audience is the foundation of effective communication. It involves creating a sense of trust, understanding, and shared purpose between you and your listeners. When you establish a genuine connection with your audience, they are more likely to be receptive to your message, even if you encounter challenges. To build rapport, demonstrate appreciation for your audience's presence and time. Acknowledge their effort in attending your presentation and emphasize the topic's importance for everyone involved. This shows respect and sets a positive tone for the rest of your speech.

Another great rapport-building tool is mirroring your audience's mood and energy level. This doesn't mean mimicking their behavior but rather attuning yourself to the general atmosphere in the room. If the audience seems severe and focused, adopt a similarly serious tone. Feel free to incorporate some light-hearted moments into your delivery if they appear more relaxed and open to humor. By matching your audience's energy, you will create a sense of alignment and connection.

Active listening is a crucial component of building rapport with your audience. Consider their questions and comments during Q&A sessions or when interacting with them. Respond thoughtfully and directly, showing that you value their input and are engaged in a genuine dialogue. This level of attentiveness demonstrates your respect for your audience and helps foster a more open and collaborative atmosphere.

Empathy plays a vital role in establishing an authentic connection. Put yourself in your audience's shoes and try to understand their perspectives, concerns, and aspirations related to your topic. Expressing empathy by acknowledging shared challenges or highlighting common goals creates a deeper resonance with your listeners. This emotional connection builds trust and encourages a more receptive and engaged audience.

Audience Analysis

Understanding your audience deeply is crucial to engaging them and navigating potential challenges effectively. I highly recommend conducting an audience analysis, including demographics and psychographics.

Demographics refer to the statistical characteristics of your audience, such as age, gender, education level, cultural background, and professional roles. Understanding these factors allows you to tailor your language, examples, and references to better resonate with your listeners. For instance, if you're addressing a predominantly younger audience, you might incorporate more contemporary cultural references and technological examples. On the other hand, if your audience consists mainly of experienced professionals, use more industry-specific terminology and draw upon historical examples relevant to their field. To gather demographic information, consider using pre-event surveys or researching the typical attendees of similar events.

While demographics provide a broad outline of your audience, psychographics delve deeper into their attitudes, values, interests, and motivations. Understanding your audience's psychographic profile allows you to connect with them more personally and emotionally. For example, if your audience values sustainability and environmental responsibility, you can emphasize the eco-friendly aspects of your topic and highlight how your ideas align with their values. Similarly, suppose your listeners are motivated by professional development and career advancement; you can focus on the practical applications of your message and how it can help them achieve their goals.

In addition to understanding your audience's demographics and psychographics, it's important to anticipate their needs and expectations. What do they hope to gain from your presentation? What questions or concerns might they have? By proactively addressing these issues, you demonstrate your preparedness and commitment to providing value to them.

Adapting on the Fly

Despite thorough preparation and audience analysis, there may be times when you need to adapt your presentation in real time based on audience feedback and reactions. This ability to be flexible and responsive is a hallmark of effective public speaking.

Pay close attention to your audience's verbal and nonverbal cues during your presentation. Are they nodding in agreement, or do they seem confused? Are they leaning forward with interest, or are they disengaged and distracted? These cues can help you gauge how well your message is being received and whether you need to make any adjustments.

If you notice signs of confusion or disengagement, consider the following strategies:

1. Pause and clarify: if you sense that a particular point may have been unclear, take a moment to rephrase or provide additional examples to help your audience better understand.

2. Engage in dialogue: encourage your audience to ask questions or share their thoughts. This can help you identify areas where you may need to provide more information or address specific concerns.

3. Adjust your pacing: if your audience seems overwhelmed or struggling to keep up, slow down your delivery and allow more time for them to process the information. Conversely, if they seem disengaged, you may need to pick up the pace or incorporate more dynamic elements into your presentation.

4. Be open to feedback: after your presentation, actively seek feedback from your audience. Ask them what they found most valuable, what could have been improved, and what additional questions they may have. This feedback can help you refine your approach for future presentations.

By developing the ability to adapt on the fly, you demonstrate your commitment to your audience's needs and your flexibility as a speaker. This responsiveness helps build trust and credibility, making your audience more likely to engage with your message and remember your key points.

Interactive Techniques

In addition to building rapport and understanding your audience, you can use various techniques to keep your listeners engaged throughout your presentation. These strategies help maintain interest, foster interaction, and ensure your message resonates with them.

Incorporating interactive elements into your presentation can transform passive listeners into active participants. By encouraging your audience to engage with your content, you create a more dynamic and memorable experience. Here are some interactive techniques to consider:

1. Live polling or surveys: use online tools or mobile apps to gather real-time feedback and opinions from your audience. This can help you gauge their understanding, preferences, or reactions to specific points during your presentation.

2. Small group discussions: divide your audience into smaller groups and assign each group a topic or question to discuss. This will encourage active participation and allow your listeners to process and apply your content in a more intimate setting.

3. Hands-on activities or demonstrations: if applicable to your topic, consider incorporating hands-on activities or demonstrations that allow your audience to experience your content firsthand. This can help reinforce your message and create a more memorable learning experience. When planning interactive elements, consider the size and composition of your audience, the time available, and the venue's logistics. Ensure the activities

are relevant to your content and contribute to your objectives. Provide clear instructions and be prepared to facilitate the interactions effectively.

4. Q&A sessions: allocate time for your audience to ask questions and share their thoughts. This not only promotes engagement but also helps you identify areas where you may need to provide clarification or additional information.

Don't shy away from Q&A sessions. Many speakers worry that they might not know all the answers to every question. That's ok. You are human; you're not an encyclopedia (although you should be familiar with your topic). Most people will appreciate your honesty. You can also turn the tables and pose thought-provoking questions throughout your presentation. Doing this lets you take the spotlight off yourself and invite your listeners to participate in learning and exploring your topic more deeply.

Here are a few good strategies for using questions effectively:

1. Open-ended questions: ask questions that require more than a simple "yes" or "no" answer. Open-ended questions encourage your audience to think more critically and share their insights and experiences.
Example: "What do you think is the biggest challenge facing our industry today and how can we address it?"

2. Rhetorical questions: use rhetorical questions to emphasize critical points or challenge your audience's assumptions. These questions can help create a sense of intrigue and encourage your listeners to consider your topic from new perspectives.
Example: "Can we really afford to ignore the implications of artificial intelligence on job markets?"

3. Follow-up questions: after an audience member asks a question, consider asking a follow-up question to clarify their point or

encourage them to elaborate. This shows that you are interested in their input and can lead to more discussion.

Example: "Thanks for your input. How do you think businesses should adapt their training programs to better prepare employees for integrating AI in the workplace?"

When asking questions, allow adequate time for your audience to respond. Embrace the silence that may follow a question, as it gives your listeners a chance to process and formulate their thoughts. If participation is low, consider rephrasing the question or providing an example to stimulate discussion.

Handling Tough Questions

No matter how well-prepared you are, there may be times when you face tough questions from your audience. These questions may challenge your ideas, point out potential weaknesses in your argument, or catch you off guard. How you handle these situations can significantly impact your credibility and the overall success of your presentation.

One of the best ways to handle tough questions is to anticipate them in advance. Before your presentation, take some time to brainstorm potential questions or concerns your audience may have. Consider the following strategies:

1. Put yourself in your audience's shoes: what questions or objections might they have based on their background, experience, or perspective?

2. Review previous feedback: re-read feedback from previous presentations on similar topics. This can give you insight into common concerns or areas of confusion.

3. Conduct thorough research on your topic: be aware of controversies or differing opinions around the topic you are

presenting. This will help you identify potential challenges and prepare thoughtful responses.

4. Ask others: share your presentation with colleagues or friends and ask them to pose challenging questions. This can help refine your responses and build your confidence.

Consider the tone or attitude behind each challenging question. Some may be asked out of genuine curiosity or a natural desire for more information, while others may be aggressive or skeptical. Preparing for a range of question types can help you feel more equipped to handle whatever comes your way.

Maintaining Composure

When faced with a tricky question, it's essential to maintain your composure and project confidence. Remember, your audience is looking to you as the expert, and how you respond can significantly influence their perception of your credibility and authority.

Here are some tips for maintaining composure and confidence:

1. Take a deep breath: pause before responding. This allows you to collect your thoughts and avoid rushing into a defensive or unclear answer.

2. Maintain eye contact: look directly at the person asking the question and turn up the corners of your mouth into a friendly smile. This demonstrates your engagement and willingness to address their concerns directly.

3. Use a calm and even tone of voice: avoid getting defensive or aggressive, even if the question seems hostile or unfair.

4. Acknowledge the validity of the question or concern. This shows that you respect your audience's input and are open to discussing different perspectives.

If you feel flustered or emotional, take a moment to regain your composure. You might say, "That's a great question, and I want to ensure I give it the thoughtful response it deserves. I will take a moment to gather my thoughts." Or "Please come and get me at the end of this session, and we can discuss this in more detail." This can buy you time to collect yourself and formulate a clear and confident response, especially if the reply is not relevant to everyone in the room.

Structuring Your Response

When answering a tricky question, I like to provide a clear and concise response directly addressing the issue. This is the structure I follow:

1. Restate the question or concern: this ensures you understood it correctly and allows you to organize your thoughts.

2. If possible, provide a direct answer to the question: if the question is more complex or open-ended, acknowledge that and offer your perspective or insights.

3. Support your answer with evidence, examples, or reasoning: this helps reinforce your credibility and shows that your response is well-thought-out and substantiated.

4. Conclude by reiterating your main point: offer to discuss the issue further after the presentation, if needed.

If you don't have a complete answer to a question, it's okay to acknowledge that. You might say, "That's a complex issue that deserves more time than we currently have. While I don't have a comprehensive answer now, I'd be happy to discuss it further after the presentation or point you towards additional resources on the topic." This shows honesty and humility while still demonstrating your willingness to engage with the question.

Turning Challenges into Opportunities

While tough questions can be intimidating, they also present opportunities to demonstrate your expertise, engage with your audience, and enhance the overall impact of your presentation. Consider the following strategies for turning challenges into opportunities:

1. Use questions as a chance to clarify or expand upon your ideas. If a question reveals a potential area of confusion, provide additional examples or explanations to help your audience better understand your message.

2. Embrace different perspectives and use them to enrich the discussion. If a question challenges your ideas, acknowledge the validity of the alternative viewpoint and explain how it relates to your position. This demonstrates your openness to diverse opinions and can lead to a more nuanced and comprehensive understanding of the topic.

3. Use questions as a springboard for further engagement. If a question sparks a lively discussion or debate, consider allocating more time for audience interaction or inviting participants to continue the conversation after the presentation.

4. Learn from the questions and feedback you receive. Use them to refine your ideas, improve your presentation skills, and better understand your audience's needs and concerns.

Remember, tough questions are not personal attacks or indictments of your expertise. They are opportunities to engage more deeply with your audience, strengthen your arguments, and leave a lasting impact. By approaching these challenges with grace, confidence, and a growth mindset, you can turn even the most difficult questions into powerful moments of connection and learning.

Dealing with Interruptions

In addition to tough questions, you may encounter interruptions or challenging behaviors from audience members during your presentation. These disruptions can take many forms, from audience members arriving late, engaging in side conversations, or phone use to more overt challenges or heckling. The first step in dealing with interruptions is identifying them early and promptly addressing them calmly and professionally.

Depending on the nature and severity of the interruption, you may choose to:

1. Pause briefly and make eye contact with the person or group causing the interruption. Often, a simple, silent acknowledgment is enough to discourage the behavior.

2. Gently remind the audience of the importance of their attention and participation. For example, you might say, "I know this is a complex topic, so I appreciate your full attention as we work through these ideas together."

3. If the interruption persists, address it more directly. You could say, "I'm sorry, but the side conversations make it difficult for others to hear. Could I please ask for your cooperation in keeping the room focused?"

If the interruption is more severe or hostile, maintain your composure and respond respectfully. Acknowledge the person's concerns, but firmly redirect the conversation to your presentation. For example, "I appreciate your perspective, but for the sake of time and staying on topic, let's discuss that further after the presentation."

Public Speaking Q&A Confidence Assessment

I have prepared a questionnaire to help you identify your strengths and areas for improvement in your approach to question-and-answer sessions.

Answer each question honestly. Choose the option that best describes your current experience and feelings.

1. **How often do you incorporate Q&A sessions into your presentations?**
   -Never
   -Rarely
   -Sometimes
   -Often
   -Always

2. **How do you feel when you think about handling a Q&A session?**
   -Very anxious
   -Somewhat anxious
   -Neutral
   -Somewhat confident
   -Very confident

3. **What aspect of Q&A sessions worry you the most?**
   -Not knowing the answer
   -Handling hostile questions
   -Keeping the session on track
   -Managing time effectively
   -Engaging a quiet audience

4. **How prepared do you feel to handle unexpected questions?**
   -Not prepared at all
   -Slightly prepared
   -Moderately prepared
   -Very prepared
   -Extremely prepared

5. **Have you ever been unable to answer a question during a session? If yes, how did you handle it?**
   -Yes, I admitted I didn't know the answer.
   -Yes, I deferred the answer to a later time.
   -Yes, I redirected the question to the audience.
   -No, I've always had an answer.

6. **How much do you prepare for potential questions before your presentations?**
   -I don't prepare at all.
   -I think about a few possible questions.
   -I extensively prepare for many possible questions.
   -I prepare with mock Q&A sessions.

7. **Do you use any specific techniques to engage the audience during Q&A sessions?**
   -No, I don't use any specific techniques.
   -Yes, I use direct questions to prompt participation.
   -Yes, I use interactive tools like live polls.
   -Yes, I encourage audience members to discuss among themselves first.

8. **How do you usually manage hostile or aggressive questions?**
   -I get flustered and struggle to respond.
   -I move on to another question quickly.
   -I address the question calmly and professionally.
   -I invite the questioner to discuss it privately after the session.

9. **What feedback have you received from audiences about your Q&A sessions?**
   -Mostly negative.
   -Somewhat negative.
   -Mixed reviews.
   -Mostly positive.
   -I haven't received any feedback.

10. **What would help you feel more confident during Q&A sessions?**
    -More subject matter expertise.
    -Techniques for managing stress and anxiety.
    -Better strategies for engaging the audience.
    -Training on handling difficult questions.
    -More experience with actual Q&A sessions.

Your answers will paint a clear picture of your current attitude to Q&A sessions and highlight what needs improvement so you can work on that area for future presentations.

Building Long-term Relationships

Effectively handling challenging situations is not just about managing the moment; it's also about building long-term relationships with your audience. You can establish yourself as a trusted and respected speaker by demonstrating your professionalism, expertise, and commitment to their learning and growth.

Here are some strategies for building long-term relationships with your audience:

1. Follow up after the presentation. Send a thank-you email to participants, share additional resources or materials related to your topic, and invite them to connect with you on professional networks like LinkedIn.

2. Seek feedback and use it to improve. Ask your audience for honest feedback on your presentation and use their input to refine your content and delivery for future engagements.

3. Stay engaged and accessible. Remember, it's all about building rapport with the people in the room. The more your audience knows you, the more they will like you. The more they like you,

the more they will trust you. When they trust you, they will listen to you, buy from you, follow you, and write great reviews about you!

Public speaking is a profoundly rewarding experience but also filled with challenges. Embracing the unexpected elements and interacting meaningfully with your audience can significantly enrich your presentation and your growth as a speaker. As mentioned, building rapport creates a foundational connection that enhances receptivity to your message, while thorough audience analysis ensures your content resonates deeper.

By mastering the strategies discussed in this chapter, you will be better equipped to navigate any speaking environment, ensuring that each presentation is effective and a genuine exchange of ideas and perspectives takes place. Remember, every challenge is a chance to shine, and every interaction is a step toward becoming a more impactful and inspiring speaker.

Embrace these opportunities with a positive outlook, and your public speaking journey will be an exciting adventure of continuous learning and connection.

9

EFFECTIVE USE OF TECHNOLOGY AND VISUAL AIDS

"The more striking your presentation, the more people will remember you." P Arden

In his 2006 TED Talk, Swedish physician and statistician Hans Rosling used data visualization to challenge common misconceptions about global health and development. Throughout his presentation, "The Best Stats You've Ever Seen," Rosling used Gapminder, a software tool he co-developed, to display animated bubble charts that illustrate complex data clearly and engagingly. Rosling guided the audience through a compelling narrative by interacting with the visualizations in real time, revealing surprising trends and insights. The dynamic nature of the presentation kept the audience engaged and helped them grasp the key messages quickly.

I share this with you because Rosling's talk, although old, showcases the power visual aids can have to elevate a presentation from merely informative to genuinely influential. When employed strategically, visual aids can capture the audience's attention, reinforce an important message, and forge a deep connection between the listeners and the shared ideas. Each slide or prop you use should be thoughtfully selected to work harmoniously with your spoken words, complementing and amplifying their impact, not distracting or interrupting your flow.

This chapter will examine everything from basic visual aids like photographs to more advanced technologies. You will learn how to choose the right visual aids for your next presentation, understand design principles, and respond when things go wrong with technology.

Optimal Visual Aid

A diverse array of visual aids exist and are at your disposal as a speaker, ranging from simple graphs to intricate animations. The key to success is identifying the type that most effectively conveys your intended message. As mentioned above, a well-designed graph can distill the information into an easily digestible format when faced with complex data. Alternatively, a flowchart or timeline may prove more suitable when explaining a process or sequence of events.

Photographs can inject a personal touch or evoke an emotional response, while diagrams illustrate a whole's components. With their dynamic nature, videos introduce movement and can immediately captivate an audience's attention. The selection of appropriate visual aids requires an understanding of the subject matter and the audience's needs and preferences.

Before settling on a specific visual, it is crucial to consider the takeaway you want the audience to gain from each one. Is the goal to provide clarity, create impact, or leave a lasting impression? This deliberation ensures that the chosen visuals are not mere embellishments but integral elements that enhance and support the narrative.

Design Principles

The impact of a visual aid depends on its design. Fundamental design principles such as balance, contrast, alignment, and repetition significantly influence how the audience perceives and engages with the visuals. A well-balanced design ensures that no single element overpowers the others, allowing the information to be easily absorbed.

Contrast can highlight key points, such as critical data in a chart. Consistent alignment creates a clean and organized appearance, making complex information more accessible to digest. Repetition of style or color across visuals enhances the overall cohesiveness of the presentation, reinforcing the central message (and your brand) through visual consistency.

When designing visuals, it is crucial to prioritize legibility and simplicity. Cluttered visuals with excessive text or data can lead to confusion. Opting for easily readable fonts and appropriate sizes ensures the information is visible even from a distance. Simplicity in design often translates to clear communication, ensuring that the visuals both engage and inform the audience. If design is not your natural talent, I recommend hiring a professional. Once you have a great template, you can use it repeatedly.

An example of effective visual design that comes to mind is Apple, known for its sleek, minimalist presentations. Their iPhone launch event slides are often nothing more than a striking product image against a plain background with a single, powerful phrase. By stripping away irrelevant elements, Apple ensures the audience focuses solely on the product and its key features. The visuals complement the message rather than competing with it.

Ensuring Everybody Can Engage

Inclusivity is vital in presentations. You want everyone in your audience to be able to engage with your visuals, including those with disabilities. By incorporating the following, you respect your entire audience and ensure your message reaches everyone effectively.

1. Provide alternative text for images so screen readers can describe them.

2. Use color schemes that are friendly to colorblind individuals.

3. Caption your videos for those with hearing impairments.

4. Ensure audience seating allows everyone a clear view of the visuals.

Videos and other multimedia can be game changers in presentations, but only when used effectively. Here are some dos and don'ts to keep in mind:

- Do choose multimedia that directly supports your objectives.

- Do ensure the content is high-quality and professionally produced.

- Do consider your audience's cultural and demographic background when selecting multimedia.

- Do introduce each multimedia element with context to integrate it seamlessly into your narrative.

- Do use multimedia to re-engage the audience during lengthy or data-heavy sections.

- Do test your multimedia beforehand. Technical glitches can derail even the best presentations.

- Don't use multimedia just for the sake of it. Each element should serve a clear purpose.

- Don't let multimedia overshadow your main message. It should enhance, not distract.

- Don't rely on multimedia alone. Your presentation should stand on its own, even without the fancy extras.

Here are some tools I've used in the past.

Software:

1. PowerPoint and Keynote: for creating slides and integrating multimedia.

2. Prezi: a cloud-based presentation tool that allows dynamic, non-linear presentations.

3. Canva: a graphic design tool for creating visually appealing slides and infographics.

4. Adobe Creative Suite: for video editing, graphic design, and animation.

Online Platforms:

1. SlideShare: for sharing and discovering presentations, infographics, and documents.

2. Vimeo and YouTube: allow for easy embedding of videos into presentations.

3. Mentimeter and Slido: enable live polls, Q&A sessions, and audience engagement.

4. Piktochart and Infogram: these create interactive infographics and data visualizations.

Re-engagement Through Multimedia

Multimedia can be particularly effective in re-engaging an audience that might be losing focus. A relevant video or an interactive element can revitalize the audience's attention and interest following a deep dive into detailed data or a prolonged speech section. This strategy works by providing a change in stimulus. Interactive elements, such as audience response systems that complement the multimedia, draw attention and actively involve the audience in the presentation, making the experience more participatory.

Multimedia offers a powerful storytelling tool that can evoke emotions and create a strong connection with the audience. Whether it's a customer testimonial, a dramatic re-enactment, or an animated story, these formats can compellingly convey your message, making the underlying concepts more relatable and accessible.

Technical Considerations

No matter how great your visuals are, technical issues can negatively affect your confidence and destroy your presentation. To ensure a smooth delivery, remember the following:

1. Always have a backup: save your presentation on multiple devices and bring printouts of slides, just in case.

2. Test, test, test: check your visuals on the equipment you'll be using, including the projector and sound system. Iron out any glitches before showtime.

3. Arrive early: give yourself ample time to set up and troubleshoot issues before your audience arrives.

4. Know your tools: familiarize yourself with the presentation software and equipment you'll be using. Practice navigating your slides and adjusting settings.

5. Have a plan B: if technical difficulties arise mid-presentation, don't panic. Have a joke or anecdote ready to keep the audience engaged while you resolve the issue.

Even with the best preparations, sometimes things go wrong. I once attended a conference where the keynote speaker's microphone died mid-sentence. Instead of panicking, she stepped forward, looked around, projected her voice, and said, "Well, I guess this is the universe's way of telling me to speak up!" The audience smiled, and she continued without missing a beat. Her quick wit and adaptability turned a potentially disastrous moment into a memorable one. Technical issues will happen. It's how you handle them that matters. You can gracefully navigate any presentation pitfall by staying calm, keeping your sense of humor, and having a backup plan.

Leveraging Social Media

Social media is a powerful tool for enhancing the reach and impact of public speaking engagements. By leveraging social media platforms, you can extend the life cycle of your presentations, from building anticipation before the event to continuing the conversation long after its conclusion. This amplifies your message and strengthens your connection with the audience.

The phase before the presentation offers a valuable opportunity to set the stage and cultivate the audience's interest and excitement. Share snippets of your upcoming talk to spark curiosity and build anticipation. Consider sharing short teaser videos, intriguing quotes, or critical questions the presentation addresses. These serve as appetizers, providing enough information to whet the audience's appetite for the main course. Another great strategy is creating event pages or groups where attendees can RSVP, share the event, and engage in preliminary discussions. This boosts the event's visibility and initiates audience engagement before the presentation.

Integrating live social media interaction into your presentation can significantly enhance audience engagement and participation. Encouraging live sharing of the presentation using a specific hashtag allows online followers to participate in real-time, even if they are not physically present, and enables a broader discussion that can extend the reach of the talk. Displaying live social media posts on a screen beside the presentation fosters more interaction, as participants see their contributions acknowledged in real-time.

After the presentation, social media is an excellent platform to continue dialogue and deepen your relationship with the audience. Start by sharing a thank-you post on various platforms and acknowledging the audience's participation and feedback. Following this, share key highlights or segments of the presentation that were particularly well-received. This serves as a refresher for attendees and provides value to those unable to attend.

To foster ongoing engagement, consider releasing additional content related to the presentation topic over the following weeks. This could be in the form of blog posts, infographics, or follow-up videos. This content keeps the conversation alive, reinforcing the key messages of the talk and providing additional value to the audience. Ensure you actively engage by responding to these posts' comments, questions, and discussions. This will demonstrate a genuine commitment to the audience beyond the presentation itself.

Use this worksheet to plan and execute a social media strategy to increase engagement for your next presentation:

1. Identify key questions or ideas from the presentation to share on social media to generate interest.

2. Create visually appealing content (images, videos, infographics) to promote the upcoming talk.

3. Select appropriate platforms and create event pages or groups.

4. Develop relevant questions for social media polls to gather audience insights.

5. Choose a unique and memorable hashtag for the presentation.

6. Plan to integrate the live social media feed into the presentation.

7. Select suitable tools for conducting live surveys or Q&A sessions.

8. Develop strategies to encourage participation throughout.

9. Identify the main takeaways from the presentation to share on social media afterward.

10. Create additional content (blog posts, videos, infographics) to add value.

11. Develop a promotion strategy to share post-presentation content with the audience.

12. Respond to comments and questions on the shared content.

By strategically leveraging social media platforms, you can amplify the impact of your presentation, foster meaningful connections with your audience, and extend the reach of your message beyond the event itself. I encourage you to embrace social media and use it to engage, inspire, and build a community around your ideas and expertise.

The Future of Public Speaking

Integrating advanced technologies such as Virtual Reality (VR) and Artificial Intelligence (AI) is revolutionizing how we prepare, deliver and personalize presentations. These technologies offer new frontiers in enhancing speaker training, optimizing engagement, and tailoring content to meet each audience member's unique preferences and needs. As we navigate this exciting era, understanding the application and implications of these technologies is paramount for anyone seeking to excel in public speaking.

Virtual Reality provides an immersive environment to hone your public speaking skills. By simulating diverse speaking environments, from a small boardroom to a packed conference hall, VR allows you to practice your delivery in a controlled yet realistic setting. This technology will enable you to rehearse your speech and interact with varied audience types and sizes. VR can also provide real-time feedback on your body language, eye contact, and engagement as you address a virtual audience that reacts like a live crowd. This feedback is invaluable, as it allows for adjustments in performance that traditional practice settings might not. For instance, VR can simulate a distracted audience, allowing you to master techniques to recapture attention. Repeating scenarios within these virtual environments can significantly enhance your speaking confidence and competence.

AI-driven Analytics

Artificial Intelligence transforms public speaking by providing precise and tailored analytics. AI tools can analyze various presentation aspects, from speech patterns and pacing to audience engagement levels. For example, AI can identify parts of the speech where engagement drops, allowing you to refine these areas for a more significant impact. It can also provide feedback on pacing, suggesting adjustments to ensure that the delivery matches the intended emotional tone of each segment. In addition, AI-driven analysis can evaluate the audience's reactions, providing a deeper understanding of how the message is received and what emotions it evokes. This real-time data is so helpful in allowing you to adjust your delivery and enhance the overall effectiveness of your communication.

Personalization and AI

AI excels in its ability to personalize content, ensuring that each audience member receives a message that resonates with them. By analyzing data points from previous interactions, AI can help tailor your presentation to better align with your audience's interests, knowledge level, and cultural background. For example, AI can modify your slide show in real time to include more basic explanations if the audience needs to become more familiar with the terminology. Alternatively, you could adjust the cultural references in your speech to better match the predominant demographics of your audience. This level of customization not only improves audience comprehension but also significantly boosts engagement.

Ethical Considerations

While the benefits of VR and AI in public speaking are substantial, they also present ethical considerations that must be carefully considered. One primary concern is privacy; as AI technologies often collect and analyze large amounts of data, it is essential to ensure that this data is handled in alignment with privacy laws and ethical standards. Transparency with your audience about what data is being collected and how it is used is essential to maintain trust.

Additionally, there is the risk of overreliance on technology, which could diminish your genuine interaction with the audience. While these tools are potent, they should enhance rather than replace the human elements of public speaking.

As you refine your skills in this area, consider each presentation an opportunity to experiment with new tools and techniques to enhance your effectiveness as a speaker. I encourage you to be open to evolving with the changing landscape of technology in this area.

Crafting Engaging Slideshows – A Speakers Guide

Slideshows are a staple in the world of presentations, but let's face it – we've all experienced "death by PowerPoint." So here is a summary of creating slideshows that engage and educate.

> 1. Less really is more: limit text on each slide. Use large, plain font. Use concise bullet points, not paragraphs.

2. Visuals over text: whenever possible, convey information using images, graphs, or charts. Visuals are processed faster and remembered longer than text.

3. Consistency is vital: maintain a consistent theme, font, and color scheme throughout your slides. This creates a professional, cohesive look.

4. Embed multimedia wisely: videos and animations can add interest and break up text-heavy sections. But use them sparingly and ensure they're relevant to your message.

5. Tell a story: structure your slides to follow a logical narrative arc. Each slide should build upon the previous one, leading your audience towards your key takeaways.

6. Practice, practice, practice: familiarize yourself with your slides and the flow of your presentation. This will allow you to focus on engaging with your audience rather than fumbling with technology.

As you move forward in your public speaking journey, remember that visual aids are tools to support your message, not to replace it. Your words, passion, and connection with the audience remain the heart of any excellent presentation. Use these visual techniques to amplify your message, but keep them from overshadowing your unique voice and perspective.

In the end, the most effective presentations strike a balance between compelling content, engaging delivery, and supportive visuals. By mastering the art of visual aids, you're equipping yourself with a powerful tool to captivate your audience and leave a lasting impression.

Your presentations will naturally become more engaging as you refine your skills, embrace new technologies, and experiment with different visual techniques.

10

Tailoring Your Message Across Various Contexts

"If you can't say it, you can't sell it!" A Robinson

As a public speaker, your ability to adapt your message, delivery style, and engagement techniques to suit different purposes can significantly impact your success in achieving your communication goals. This chapter will delve into the unique considerations and strategies for delivering impactful speeches and presentations in various settings, including business pitches, workshops and seminars, social events, and inspirational talks. By understanding the nuances of each context and employing tailored techniques, you can build stronger connections with your audience, convey your message more effectively, and leave a lasting impact on your listeners.

Structuring A Business Pitch

Crafting a successful business pitch goes beyond assembling facts and figures; it involves structuring your content to resonate with your audience and achieve your strategic goals. Begin by defining the purpose of your presentation clearly—is it to inform, persuade, or propose? Once the purpose is clear, tailor your content to align with your audience's interests, emphasizing how your message addresses their needs or solves their problems.

A well-structured business pitch typically starts with an introduction that captures attention and outlines the discussion topics. This is followed by the body of the presentation, where key arguments are presented logically and supported by data and insights. Each main point should seamlessly connect to the next, maintaining a narrative flow that guides the audience through your reasoning. The conclusion briefly summarizes the main points and ends with a solid call to action. It prompts the audience to take a specific step, be it approval, a follow-up meeting, or direct action related to the business proposal.

Frame your business solutions within a story that illustrates the challenges faced, the actions taken, and the results achieved. This will make your presentation more engaging and help the audience visualize your proposals' practical application and impact.

A notable example of a successful business pitch is Airbnb's pitch to investors in 2009. Brian Chesky, the co-founder of Airbnb, crafted a compelling narrative highlighting the problem the company aimed to solve: the lack of affordable and unique accommodation options for travelers. He began by sharing his personal story of struggling to pay rent and coming up with the idea of renting out air mattresses in his apartment to conference attendees.

Throughout the pitch, Chesky uses emotional appeals to connect with investors, describing the frustrations and desires of modern travelers seeking authentic experiences. He supported these emotional appeals with logical evidence, presenting market research and data demonstrating the growing demand for alternative accommodations. Chesky also addressed potential concerns by discussing the company's safety measures and insurance policies, building credibility and trust with the investors.

To further engage the audience, Chesky used visuals, including photos of Airbnb listings and customer testimonials, to illustrate the platform's unique value proposition. He concluded the pitch with a solid call to action, inviting investors to join Airbnb in revolutionizing the travel industry and creating unforgettable experiences for millions worldwide. As a result of this effective pitch, Airbnb secured $600,000 in funding, setting the stage for its future success as a global hospitality platform.

Delivering Engaging Workshops and Seminars

Professional development workshops and seminars are pivotal platforms for interactive learning and knowledge sharing. The success of these events hinges significantly on your ability to deliver content that holds participants' attention, encourages their active involvement, and facilitates real-time learning. This requires a deliberate approach where every element of the workshop or seminar is designed to foster engagement and comprehension.

Interactive elements are the cornerstone of engaging workshops and seminars. They transform passive listening into active learning and foster a collaborative environment that encourages participation. Techniques such as breakout sessions allow participants to delve into specific topics in smaller groups, facilitating deeper discussion and problem-solving. These sessions can be efficient when participants are asked to tackle a relevant challenge or develop a strategy based on the session's content, applying what they've learned in a practical context.

Incorporating gamification elements such as quizzes or competitive team activities can energize participants and make learning fun and impactful. These activities should be closely aligned with the learning objectives of the seminar or workshop, ensuring that they reinforce the core content while also adding an element of enjoyment.

Educational Content Delivery

Educational content delivered in workshops and seminars must be explicit, engaging, and paced appropriately to suit your audience's learning styles and preferences. Start by clearly outlining the session's objectives, what participants can expect to learn, and how to apply this knowledge professionally. This sets the stage for meaningful engagement as participants understand the value of the presented information.

Using a variety of presentation methods can help cater to different learning styles. For example, visual learners benefit from charts, diagrams, and videos, while auditory learners may gain more from discussions and lectures. Kinesthetic learners, who learn best through doing, will appreciate interactive activities that involve physical participation or hands-on experiments. It's also good to intersperse theoretical information with real-life case studies or anecdotes, which can help ground abstract concepts in practical reality. These stories should be relevant and relatable, ideally reflecting professional scenarios that participants might encounter.

Inviting questions and facilitating discussions throughout the session is crucial rather than saving all questions for the end. This keeps the content dynamic and responsive to the participants' needs, allowing for immediate clarification and deeper exploration of complex topics. Encourage participants to share their experiences or perspectives on the content, fostering a peer-learning environment where participants can learn from each other and you.

Participant Engagement

Maximizing participant engagement in workshops and seminars involves creating an environment where participants feel comfortable, curious, and motivated to engage. Begin by establishing a welcoming atmosphere where all participants feel valued and encouraged to contribute. This can be achieved by actively listening to their contributions, acknowledging different viewpoints, and integrating diverse participant experiences into the session's content.

Effective facilitation techniques also play a crucial role in maintaining engagement. This includes managing the room's energy levels by incorporating physical movement or changes in activity type when energy wanes. Techniques such as think-pair-share, where participants first think about a question individually, then discuss their thoughts with a partner, and finally share with the larger group, can stimulate engagement and ensure that more introverted participants also have a voice.

Feedback and Evaluation

Gathering and implementing feedback is essential for continuously improving your workshops and seminars. Provide participants multiple opportunities to give input throughout the session to gauge immediate reactions.

To gather constructive feedback after a workshop or seminar, consider asking the following questions:

1. What were the most valuable insights or takeaways from the session?

2. How relevant and applicable was the content to your professional or personal life?

3. What aspects of the presentation style and delivery most engaged you?

4. Were there any topics or concepts that needed more clarification or depth?

5. How effectively did the interactive elements (e.g., group discussions and exercises) contribute to your learning experience?

6. On a scale of 1-5, how would you rate the overall quality and value of the workshop/seminar?

7. What suggestions do you have for improving the content or delivery of future sessions?

When analyzing the feedback, start by organizing the responses into categories or themes, such as content relevance, presentation style, interactivity, and areas for improvement. Look for patterns or recurring comments that indicate strengths or weaknesses in specific aspects of the workshop or seminar. For quantitative questions, such as rating the overall quality, calculate the average score to gauge general satisfaction levels. Pay close attention to extreme ratings (very high or low) and the accompanying comments to identify notable successes or areas that require significant improvement. Prioritize the feedback based on the frequency and urgency of the comments. For example, if many participants mentioned that a particular topic needed more depth, consider expanding on that subject in future sessions. Similarly, if several people praised a specific interactive exercise, look for ways to incorporate similar activities in other workshops or seminars.

When acting upon the feedback, communicate the planned changes or improvements to the participants, demonstrating their input is valued and taken seriously. This transparency and responsiveness will foster a sense of engagement and investment in the learning process, encouraging participants to provide feedback in the future.

Toasts & Tributes: Speaking from the Heart

Before you start writing a social speech, it's crucial to understand your audience and the occasion. Ask yourself: Who will be attending the event? What is the purpose of the gathering? Is it a wedding, a retirement party, or a milestone celebration? By clearly understanding your audience and the event's significance, you can tailor your message to strike the right tone and connect with your listeners on a deeper level.

When it comes to social speeches, authenticity is critical. Your words should come from the heart, reflecting your genuine feelings and emotions. To ensure your message is heartfelt, take some time to reflect on your relationship with the person or group you're honoring. Think about the moments you've shared, the qualities you admire, and their impact on your life. By tapping into these personal experiences, you'll be able to craft a message that is both sincere and meaningful.

Aim for a balanced structure that combines emotion, humor, and sincerity to create a toast or tribute that captivates your audience. Here's a suggested outline:

1. Opening: begin with a warm greeting and express your gratitude for the opportunity to speak.

2. Personal Connection: share a brief story or anecdote highlighting your relationship with the honored person or group.

3. Admirable Qualities: highlight the qualities or achievements that make the honoree unique. Use specific examples to illustrate your points.

4. Humor: inject humor to keep the mood light and to engage. Choose appropriate and respectful anecdotes or jokes.

5. Heartfelt Wishes: express your hopes and wishes for the honoree's future. Offer words of encouragement and support.

6. Toast or Tribute: conclude by inviting everyone to raise their glasses or join you in paying tribute to the honoree.

Personal stories and anecdotes can make your toast or tribute more engaging and relatable. When selecting stories to share, consider moments that showcase the honoree's character, achievements, or impact on others. Aim for concise, relevant, and emotionally resonant stories. To seamlessly incorporate personal stories into your speech, use transitional phrases like "I remember when..." or "One moment that stands out to me is..." These phrases help to weave the stories into the overall narrative of your tribute, making it feel cohesive and natural.

Delivering a toast or tribute with confidence requires practice. Start by writing out your speech and reading it aloud several times. Pay attention to your pacing, intonation, and emphasis on critical points. As you become more comfortable with the content, practice delivering the speech without relying on your notes. Consider recording yourself or practicing in front of a mirror to observe your body language and facial expressions. Aim for a natural and conversational delivery, making eye contact with your audience and speaking from the heart. Remember, the goal is not perfection but authenticity. Your audience will appreciate your effort in crafting a heartfelt message, even if there are a few stumbles.

Eulogies: Honoring Memories with Words

When tasked with writing a eulogy, gather memories, anecdotes, and insights from those who knew the deceased best. Reach out to family members, close friends, and colleagues to collect stories and reflections that capture the essence of the person's life.

Begin by asking open-ended questions like, "What are some of your fondest memories with [name]?" or "How did [name] impact your life?" Encourage people to share specific stories, quirky habits, or memorable moments that showcase the deceased's personality, values, and achievements. As you gather these stories, look for common themes that can help you paint a complete picture of the person's life. These insights will be the foundation for a eulogy that truly honors their memory.

A eulogy is a delicate balance between expressing grief and celebrating the life and achievements of the deceased. While it's important to acknowledge the sorrow and loss felt by those left behind, it's equally crucial to focus on the person's positive impact during their lifetime. Begin by acknowledging the sadness and pain of the moment, but gradually shift the focus to the joy, laughter, and love that the person brought into the world. Share stories highlighting their kindness, generosity, and unique qualities that made them special. Emphasize how the deceased made a difference in the lives of others, whether through their career, hobbies, or personal relationships.

By celebrating their accomplishments and the love they shared, you create a tone that is both respectful and uplifting, reminding everyone of the beautiful life that was lived.

Structuring the Eulogy

When crafting a eulogy, aim for a flow that seamlessly weaves memories, personal reflections, and tributes together. Here's a suggested outline:

1. Introduction: begin by expressing gratitude for the opportunity to speak and your relationship with the deceased.

2. Early Life and Childhood: share stories or anecdotes from the person's early years, highlighting their upbringing and formative experiences.

3. Personal Qualities and Values: discuss the qualities and values that defined the deceased, using examples to illustrate their character.

4. Achievements and Contributions: highlight the person's personal and professional accomplishments and their impact on others.

5. Memories and Anecdotes: share specific stories and memories that capture the person's essence, evoking laughter and tears.

6. Legacy and Lasting Impact: reflect on how the deceased's life will continue to inspire and influence those they left behind.

7. Closing: offer comfort and support to the grieving audience, acknowledging the collective loss while celebrating the gift of the person's life.

Delivering a eulogy is emotional and challenging, but it's also an opportunity to connect with the audience and offer comfort during a difficult time. When giving the eulogy, prioritize empathy, respect, and sincerity. Speak from the heart, allowing your emotions to show while maintaining composure. Make eye contact with the audience, engaging them with your words and presence. Pause when necessary to gather your thoughts or allow moments of reflection.

Remember, the purpose of the eulogy is to honor the deceased and provide solace to those grieving. By speaking with authenticity and compassion, you create a safe space for everyone to mourn, remember, and celebrate the life of their loved one.

Master of Ceremonies

A master of ceremonies plays a pivotal role in setting the tone, guiding the flow, and ensuring the success of an event. As an MC, your primary responsibilities include:

1. Welcoming and engaging the audience.

2. Introducing speakers, performers, or special guests.

3. Keeping the event on schedule and managing transitions.

4. Facilitating audience participation and interaction.

5. Handling any unexpected situations or changes with grace and composure.

Preparing and organizing the event segments thoroughly ensures a smooth flow and engaging experience. Start by familiarizing yourself with the event's agenda, including the order of speakers, performances, or activities.

Collaborate with the event organizers to understand each segment's purpose and goals. This knowledge will allow you to create seamless transitions and provide context for the audience.

Prepare introductions for each speaker or performer, highlighting their background, accomplishments, and relevance to the event. Practice delivering these introductions with enthusiasm and clarity. Consider adding personal anecdotes or humorous remarks to make the introductions more engaging. Ensure that any humor is appropriate and respectful to the audience and the event's tone.

Energizing the Audience

As an MC, one of your primary goals is to keep the audience engaged and energized throughout the event. Here are some techniques to achieve this:

1. Start strong: begin the event with a warm welcome and a captivating opening remark that sets the tone and captures the audience's attention.

2. Use inclusive language: address the audience as a collective, using phrases like "we" and "us" to create a sense of unity and shared experience.

3. Encourage participation: invite the audience to ask questions, share their thoughts, or participate in interactive activities when appropriate.

4. Inject humor: use appropriate and tasteful humor to keep the atmosphere light and enjoyable. However, be mindful of the event's tone and the audience's sensibilities.

5. Maintain energy: keep your energy level high throughout the event, using vocal inflections, gestures, and facial expressions to convey enthusiasm and engagement.

Building Confidence

Confidence is critical to being a successful MC. To build and maintain confidence, thoroughly prepare and practice your role. Familiarize yourself with the event's agenda, the speakers' backgrounds, and any technical aspects of the event.

Arrive at the event venue early to get comfortable with the stage, microphone, and audio-visual equipment. Practice your introductions and transitions and visualize yourself delivering them with poise and clarity. Despite thorough preparation, unexpected situations may arise during the event. An MC must think on their feet and handle these situations with composure. If a speaker runs over time, politely remind them to wrap up. If technical difficulties occur, keep the audience engaged with impromptu remarks or activities.

Remember, the audience looks to the MC for guidance and reassurance. By maintaining a calm and confident outlook, you can navigate any challenges and ensure the event continues smoothly.

Inspirational Speeches

The foundation of any inspirational speech lies in its central message—a clear, compelling idea that resonates with the audience and inspires them to take action. To identify your central message, consider the following:

1. Purpose: what is the goal of your speech? What do you want your audience to feel, think, or do differently after hearing your words?

2. Audience: who are you speaking to? What are their needs, aspirations, and challenges? How can your message address these factors?

3. Personal experience: what personal stories, insights, or lessons have shaped your perspective on the topic? How can you use these experiences to connect with your audience?

Incorporating Motivational Stories

Personal and others' motivational stories are powerful tools for illustrating key points and inspiring audiences. When selecting stories to include in your speech, look for those that:

1. Reinforce your central message.

2. Demonstrate the power of perseverance, resilience, or transformation.

3. Evoke solid emotions and create a lasting impact.

When sharing personal stories, be vulnerable and authentic. Allow your audience to see the challenges you've faced and the lessons you've learned. This vulnerability creates a bond with your listeners and makes your message more relatable. When incorporating stories of others, choose examples that are relevant and inspiring to your audience. These could be well-known figures or heroes who have overcome adversity or achieved remarkable feats. Use vivid descriptions and sensory details to bring these stories to life, allowing your audience to experience the emotions and lessons vicariously.

An inspirational speech should motivate and mobilize the audience to take concrete steps inspired by your message. As you near the end of your speech, focus on delivering a powerful call to action. Clearly articulate the specific actions you want your audience to take. These could be internal shifts in mindset or external steps towards a goal. Use robust and action-oriented language to convey a sense of urgency and possibility. Paint a vivid picture of the positive impact these actions can have on the audience's lives and the world around them. Help them envision the transformation that awaits them when they embrace your message.

Finally, leave your audience with a memorable and uplifting closing statement that encapsulates the essence of your message and inspires and empowers them.

As you can see throughout this chapter, effective communication is more than one-size-fits-all. A successful business pitch requires a blend of persuasive techniques, data-driven arguments, and a clear call to action. Workshops and seminars demand interactive elements, engaging content delivery, and continuous participant engagement. Social speeches, such as toasts and eulogies, call for heartfelt sincerity, personal anecdotes, and a delicate balance of emotions.

The key to success across all these contexts lies in understanding your audience, crafting a message that resonates with them, and delivering it authentically and confidently. Whether you're presenting in a boardroom, facilitating a workshop, delivering a toast at a wedding, or inspiring a crowd, your ability to adapt your content and style to the situation will set you apart as a versatile and impactful speaker.

As you continue to grow as a public speaker, embrace each opportunity to speak in different contexts as a chance to refine your skills further. With practice, preparation, and a willingness to adapt, you'll find that you can captivate and influence audiences in any setting, making your voice heard and your message remembered.

11

SPECIALIZED TECHNIQUES FOR DIFFERENT AUDIENCES

"Diversity is a fact, inclusion is an act." V Myers

Navigating the complexities of audience diversity is crucial in today's globalized environment. This chapter explores how to adapt your presentations to technical and non-technical audiences while also considering factors like gender, cultural backgrounds, age, disabilities, and the unique dynamics of online environments. Understanding and addressing these elements can dramatically enhance the effectiveness of your communication. There are practical tips and case studies included that illustrate how these strategies are applied in real-world scenarios.

Technical vs. Non-Technical Audiences

When you present, whether it's to a boardroom of executives or a community hall filled with locals, understanding the level of technical expertise in your audience is crucial. This understanding directly influences how you craft and deliver your message to ensure it resonates effectively. Techniques for assessing the technical level of your audience can be as straightforward as conducting pre-event surveys or as interactive as initial probing questions during the presentation itself. These strategies provide a clearer picture of whom you're addressing, allowing you to gauge the familiarity with the subject matter across your audience. For instance, in a technical presentation about cybersecurity, you might start with a question about standard cybersecurity practices to understand how deeply you should dive into the technical details.

Once you grasp the audience's expertise, simplifying complex information becomes your crucial tool in ensuring clarity and engagement, especially with non-technical listeners. Simplification involves distilling information to its essence without stripping away its meaning. This can be achieved through analogies that relate complex ideas to everyday experiences, thus making them more accessible. For example, explaining data encryption in terms of translating a secret language can help lay audiences understand its importance and function without needing to grasp its intricate mathematics. Using clear, jargon-free language is imperative. Replace technical terms with simpler words or, if specialized terms are necessary, define them succinctly at their first use.

Engagement strategies must also be tailored to fit the technical understanding of your audience. For technical audiences, deep dives into the specifics of a topic can stimulate discussion and foster engagement. These audiences appreciate the challenge of complex problems and often value data-driven insights that can lead to innovative solutions. For non-technical audiences, engagement is usually boosted through storytelling that highlights the human impact of the technology or process being discussed. Here, the focus shifts from the 'how' to the 'why' and 'what'—why the topic matters and its implications on a personal or societal level. Creating interactive segments where the audience can ask questions or share experiences can also maintain engagement, providing a platform to connect the dots in a familiar context.

Choosing the right visual aids and examples is pivotal in bridging the comprehension gap for different audience types. Visual aids for a technical audience might include detailed graphs, flowcharts, and schematics that provide in-depth analysis of data or processes. These visuals should be precise and thorough, offering the depth of information that a technically adept audience would appreciate. Conversely, visuals should emphasize clarity and impact over complexity for non-technical audiences. Infographics, highlighting key points, simple charts tracking trends, and images illustrating outcomes or benefits help make abstract concepts tangible. When selecting examples, ensure they are relatable to the audience's experiences. For instance, when explaining a technical product to non-technical users, choose examples that show practical applications of the technology in their daily lives or familiar settings, demystifying complex functionalities and highlighting real-world utility.

Gender-Specific Strategies

Understanding and respecting gender-specific communication styles is essential to crafting presentations that resonate with diverse audiences. Gender can influence how people perceive information, their preferred communication styles, and their interactions during presentations. To communicate effectively across genders, it's vital to recognize these differences and adapt your approach to be inclusive and effective.

Research has shown that communication styles can vary significantly across genders. Men often employ a more assertive and competitive communication style, which is direct and to the point. They tend to focus on independence and achieving tangible outcomes. Women, on the other hand, generally utilize a more collaborative and inclusive style. This approach emphasizes emotional connection, process orientation, and mutual understanding, often focusing on building relationships and fostering group harmony. Of course, these tendencies are not absolute and can vary widely among individuals. However, recognizing the possibility of this spectrum within gender communication styles is important; it involves observing how your audience interacts, listening to the questions they ask, and noting the feedback they provide. This understanding allows you to tailor your presentation to match or complement the predominant communication styles of your audience, ensuring that your message is heard and appreciated across gender lines.

Inclusive language plays a pivotal role in engaging all audience members effectively. It involves using terms and references that do not assume or favor one gender over another. For instance, using 'spokesperson' instead of 'spokesman' or 'chairperson' instead of 'chairman' avoids gender bias and promotes equality. The importance of inclusive language extends beyond mere political correctness. It reflects respect for the diversity within your audience and contributes to a more positive reception of your message. Inclusive language fosters an environment where all participants feel valued and respected, which can enhance their engagement and openness to you and the information presented.

Adapting your presentation style to communicate across genders effectively involves more than adjusting your language; it also includes modifying your delivery and interaction techniques. For example, when presenting to an audience that appreciates direct communication (often associated with masculine communication styles), it might be practical to use a transparent, concise, and goal-oriented approach. This could involve outlining the objectives at the beginning of the presentation, using bullet points to emphasize key information, and focusing on outcomes or solutions. Conversely, for an audience that values relational communication (often associated with feminine communication styles), incorporating storytelling, asking rhetorical questions to stimulate thought and discussion, and providing opportunities for audience participation can be more effective. These strategies cater to the audience's preferences and enhance your presentation's overall impact by aligning with their communication values.

Analyzing case studies where speakers have successfully navigated gender communication preferences can provide valuable insights into the practical applications of these strategies. Consider a scenario where a tech company executive presents a new product to a mixed-gender audience. The executive uses a balanced approach by starting with concise, data-driven points that appeal to a more assertive communication style, then weaving in customer testimonials and team stories that illustrate the collaborative efforts behind the product. This approach conveys the product's technical specifications and the human element of teamwork and customer satisfaction, catering to direct and relational communication preferences.

Another example could involve a healthcare conference where a keynote speaker addresses an audience of medical professionals. The speaker integrates gender-sensitive communication by highlighting statistics and evidence-based practices (appealing to a more direct style) and facilitating breakout sessions where participants discuss these practices in small groups to foster collaboration and consensus (appealing to a relational style). This dual approach ensures the presentation is robust, informative, interactive and inclusive.

Through these examples, it becomes evident that understanding and adapting to gender-specific communication styles is not about reinforcing stereotypes but recognizing and respecting how people communicate and perceive information. Employing strategies that embrace this diversity will enhance your effectiveness as a speaker, ensuring your presentations are heard and resonate deeply with every audience member.

Cultural Sensitivity

In today's globalized world, the ability to effectively communicate across cultural boundaries is not just an asset but a necessity for professional speakers. When you stand to deliver a speech or presentation to an international audience, your sensitivity to cultural nuances can dramatically affect the reception of your message. Building cultural awareness involves more than understanding surface-level differences; it requires a deep appreciation of the values, communication styles, and societal norms that shape how people perceive and process information. This awareness is critical, as it informs every aspect of your presentation, from the examples you choose to illustrate points to the stories you tell to connect with your audience.

To ensure your content resonates with a diverse audience, you must adapt it to reflect cultural relevance and respect. This adaptation process begins with thorough research into the cultural background of your audience. Understand the significant cultural influences, historical contexts, and current issues that may impact how your message is received. For instance, when presenting a new technology in a country with significant technological disparities, consider framing your message to acknowledge these gaps while highlighting the benefits of bridging them.

Adapting your content for cultural relevance means being mindful of local customs and sensitivities—avoid metaphors and analogies that may not translate well across cultures and replace them with locally relevant examples.

Consider the case of a multinational corporation that launched a series of workshops to facilitate better communication between its European and Asian branches. The workshops were designed with a deep understanding of the distinct communication styles prevalent in each region—direct in Europe versus subtle and indirect in Asia. The facilitators adapted their delivery to suit these styles, using clear and concise language for the European participants while employing more nuanced and context-driven explanations for the Asian attendees.

Another example I witnessed involved a global health organization that conducted public health campaigns in multiple countries to raise awareness about diabetes. Recognizing the cultural factors influencing dietary habits and health perceptions in different regions, the campaign managers tailored their messages to align with local values and beliefs. In some areas, this meant focusing on the impact of diabetes on family health, leveraging the family-centric solid values of the target audience. In others, the campaigns emphasized individual health and well-being, resonating with cultures prioritizing personal achievement and success.

Throughout these campaigns, the organizers carefully respected local traditions and customs, using culturally appropriate symbols and language to foster a greater connection with the audience.

These case studies highlight the importance of being culturally aware and adaptable, qualities that are indispensable in today's interconnected world.

Age-Specific Groups

When addressing an audience, the effectiveness of your communication can often hinge on how well you adapt your delivery to match your listeners' age-specific characteristics and preferences. This approach ensures that each audience segment receives your message in the most accessible and engaging manner possible.

For children with shorter attention spans and a developing understanding, the key is simplifying complex concepts and delivering them engagingly and dynamically. Utilize visual aids like colorful charts and images or incorporate props to make the learning experience more tangible. Storytelling is another powerful tool; weaving educational content into stories captures children's attention and conveys information in a naturally engaging format. It's also crucial to use language that is clear, straightforward, and devoid of complex jargon. Keep your sentences short and your terminology simple. When providing examples or scenarios, tie them to environments familiar to children, such as school activities or famous cartoons, making the abstract more concrete and relatable.

Transitioning to teenagers, often characterized by a quest for identity and a desire to be treated as adults, requires a different approach. Make your content relevant to their lives by discussing social media trends, educational challenges, or current events that resonate with their experiences. Foster an interactive environment by encouraging questions and discussions, keeping them engaged and feeling valued and understood. Adopting a respectful yet conversational tone is beneficial when communicating with teenagers and recognizing their growing maturity. Emphasize technology and multimedia in your presentations, as most teenagers are digital natives and respond positively to content delivered through these mediums.

Addressing seniors, on the other hand, calls for a shift in pace and clarity. Deliver your content more slowly to accommodate any cognitive processing needs and ensure that your speech is loud and clear, avoiding slang or idioms that may be unfamiliar or confusing. Focus on topics especially relevant to seniors, such as health care, retirement planning, or leisure activities that align with their interests and lifestyle. Acknowledging their vast experiences is also respectful; encouraging them to share their insights or relate their experiences to the topic at hand enriches the discussion and fosters a greater connection with them.

Audiences with Disabilities

When presenting to an audience that includes individuals with disabilities, it's essential to make your presentation accessible and inclusive. Here are some strategies to accommodate common disabilities:

1. Visual Impairments: provide large-print handouts or electronic copies of materials that can be easily magnified. Use high-contrast colors and legible fonts in your visual aids. Describe images, charts, and other visuals verbally for those who cannot see them. Ensure the presentation space has adequate lighting and minimal glare.

2. Hearing Impairments: use captioning or provide a written transcript of your presentation. Face the audience when speaking and keep your mouth visible for those who rely on lip reading. Use a microphone to amplify your voice and repeat questions from the audience before answering. Provide sign language interpretation, if possible, and when requested in advance.

3. Mobility Impairments: ensure the presentation venue is accessible, with ramps, elevators, and wide doorways. Arrange seating to accommodate wheelchairs and other mobility devices. Ensure the stage or speaking area is accessible with a ramp or lift. Allow for frequent breaks and provide a comfortable, accessible seating area.

4. Cognitive and Learning Disabilities: break complex information into smaller, more manageable chunks. Provide visual aids and

written materials to reinforce key points. Allow extra time for processing information and answering questions. Be patient, respectful, and willing to clarify or repeat information.

By implementing these strategies and being open to individual accommodations, you can create a more inclusive and accessible presentation environment that enables all audience members to engage fully with your message.

Engaging an Online Audience

In today's increasingly digital landscape, delivering effective virtual presentations is crucial for any public speaker. While virtual presentations come with their own unique set of challenges, there are several strategies you can employ to capture and maintain the attention of your online audience.

One of the most important aspects of virtual presenting is ensuring that your setup is optimized for engagement. This includes positioning your webcam at eye level to create the illusion of direct eye contact, ensuring that your face is well-lit with a soft, diffused light source, and selecting a clean, uncluttered background that won't distract from your message. By arranging your physical space properly, you'll be better equipped to connect with your audience and confidently deliver your content.

In addition to your physical setup, leveraging the tools and features available on your chosen webinar platform is essential. Encourage your audience to submit questions via the Q&A feature and use the chat box to foster discussion and gather feedback. For more intimate conversations or collaborative activities, use breakout rooms to facilitate small group interaction and exchange ideas.

When delivering your presentation, speaking directly to the camera and maintaining eye contact as if talking to someone in person is essential. Pay close attention to your body language and facial expressions; these nonverbal cues convey your message and enthusiasm. If you plan to share your screen, ensure that your slides or visuals are clear, legible, and visually appealing, avoiding the temptation to clutter your slides with too much text.

To create a truly immersive and memorable experience for your virtual audience, consider incorporating interactive elements such as polls, quizzes, or collaborative whiteboards. These tools encourage active participation and help break up the monotony of a traditional presentation format. Additionally, feel free to experiment with virtual backgrounds that align with your topic or brand, as this can help transport your audience and add a professional touch to your presentation.

Inevitably, technical issues or delays may arise during your virtual presentation. A backup plan is crucial, such as having your presentation offline or being prepared to switch to a different platform if necessary. By anticipating potential challenges and having contingency plans ready, you can navigate any obstacles gracefully and minimize disruptions to your audience's experience.

Ultimately, the key to mastering virtual presentations lies in your ability to adapt to the unique demands of the digital format while still connecting with your audience on a personal level. By implementing these strategies and continually refining your approach, you'll be well-positioned to deliver engaging virtual presentations.

Audience Adaptation Scenarios

I have created the following activity to encourage you to think critically about audience adaptation. It involves applying the techniques discussed in the chapter to realistic speaking situations. I have listed various speaking scenarios below.

For each one, outline a brief strategy for adapting your presentation to suit the needs of the relevant audience.

1. You're presenting a new technology product to:

-A group of senior citizens at a community center
-A room full of tech-savvy millennials at a startup incubator

2. You're giving a speech on climate change to:

-An international conference with attendees from various cultures
-A high school science class

3. You're delivering a workshop on leadership skills to:

-A mixed-gender group of corporate executives
-A group of young women in a mentorship program

4. You're presenting a new health initiative via a webinar to:

-Healthcare professionals from around the world
-Local community members with varying levels of health literacy

5. You're giving a presentation on financial planning to:

-An audience that includes individuals with visual impairments
-A group of recent college graduates

As you can see from this chapter, public speaking demands a deep understanding of your audience and the ability to adapt your approach to meet their diverse needs. We've explored various strategies for tailoring your presentations to different audiences, technical expertise, gender, culture, age, and physical abilities.

The key takeaway is that effective communication is more than one-size-fits-all. By recognizing the unique characteristics of your audience and adjusting your content and delivery accordingly, you can significantly enhance the impact of your message. Whether you're addressing a group of visual learners, bridging the gap between technical and non-technical listeners, navigating cultural sensitivities in international speeches, or engaging an online audience, your flexibility and adaptability as a speaker will set you apart.

These specialized techniques are not about stereotyping or making assumptions but about being attuned to any group's needs and preferences. By consistently striving to understand and connect with your audience on a deeper level, you'll improve the effectiveness of your presentations and foster a more inclusive and engaging environment for all participants.

As you continue to develop your public speaking skills, challenge yourself to step outside your norm and experiment with different approaches. Embrace the opportunity to learn from each audience interaction and use these experiences to refine your techniques further.

With practice and dedication, you'll become a versatile speaker capable of captivating and inspiring audiences across all walks of life.

12

PURSUING GROWTH AS A PUBLIC SPEAKER

"Communication works for those who work at it." J Powell

This chapter guides you through the evolving landscape of your speaking skills. Understanding and accepting the stages of change everyone goes through when learning something new is pivotal here. You'll discover how to navigate and thrive through these phases, setting realistic goals and cultivating resilience that transforms challenges into stepping stones for success.

When learning any new skill, people typically progress through four stages.[1] Initially, you're unaware of what you don't know—this is unconscious incompetence. As you begin to understand the complexities of the new skill, you enter conscious incompetence, recognizing your limitations. With practice, you reach conscious competence. Finally, after substantial experience, you achieve unconscious competence, speaking effectively without thinking about it. Recognizing these stages can help you stay motivated and understand that improvement will come with persistence and practice.

---

1. The four stages appeared in the 1960 textbook *Management of Training Programs* by three management professors at New York University. Management trainer Martin M. Broadwell called the model "the four levels of teaching" in an article published in February 1969. Paul R. Curtiss and Phillip W. Warren mentioned the model in their 1973 book *The Dynamics of Life Skills Coaching*. The model was used at Gordon Training International by its employee Noel Burch in the 1970s; there it was called the "four stages for learning any new skill".

The Learning Curve

Becoming a great public speaker is like climbing a series of hills; each ascent offers new views of proficiency and insight. Initially, you might grapple with the basics—overcoming nerves, mastering timing, and engaging your audience. This stage, often fraught with challenges, is where you lay the foundational skills upon which your future speaking talent will build. As you climb further, you encounter intermediate challenges, such as refining your storytelling techniques and using body language effectively. Each stage requires different strategies and mindsets, and recognizing where you are in this sequence is crucial.

Growth inherently involves stepping out of your comfort zone and embracing the discomfort of trying new things. Whether experimenting with a different presentation style, injecting humor into your speeches, or speaking to larger, more diverse audiences, each new experience can induce a sense of unease. This discomfort, however, is a powerful indicator of personal development. It signifies that you are pushing the boundaries of your known capabilities and venturing into new realms of potential.

To effectively manage and embrace this discomfort, start acknowledging it as an everyday learning process. Reframe these feelings as signs of growth rather than threats to your confidence. Remembering that this learning curve is not a straight path but a series of ebbs and flows will help maintain your motivation and commitment to continuous improvement.

Setting Exciting Goals

As you work through the stages of learning, setting realistic goals becomes your roadmap, guiding your journey and providing benchmarks for success. You may have heard of SMART goals. This is a method whereby your goals should be Specific, Measurable, Attainable, Relevant, and Time-bound. Here's an example:

Specific: Deliver ten paid speaking engagements on digital marketing to audiences of at least 100 people each.

Measurable: Track the number of engagements delivered, audience size, and income generated from speaking fees.

Achievable: Leverage existing network and gradually build reputation through smaller events to reach more extensive paid engagements.

Relevant: Aligns with career objectives as a public speaker and digital marketing expert.

Time-bound: Accomplish this goal within the next 12 months.

One day, I was walking my dog and thinking about my speaking goals; in my mind's eye, I saw the word 'SMART' backward, which reads 'TRAMS.' I started to think of my public speaking career as a journey. I visualized myself in the driver's seat of a tramcar. I pictured where I wanted to go and which companies I needed to speak to. I had a clear map to guide me in the right direction and a timetable to keep me moving forward. The passengers onboard were my support team, encouraging me to keep going when steep hills seemed impossible to climb. Now, I use my 'TRAMS'™ goal-setting method for everything I wish to achieve. Here's what each letter of the acronym stands for.

Towards: focus on moving forward towards your goal; don't look back.

Relationships: don't try to do everything on your own. Build a team around you. We all need supporters, mentors, speaking agencies, and colleagues who will recommend us.

Attitude: organisations want someone flexible and willing to work alongside their agenda. A positive attitude is everything when it comes to being hired as a speaker.

Meaningful: I want my speaking engagements to be meaningful and memorable for both the audience and me. Finding meaning in my work is very important, so I ensure this is included in all my goals and speeches.

Smile: the thought of every goal should excite you and make you smile. As mentioned in the chapter on body language, this is one vocabulary everyone understands and should be the first thing people see when you step on stage.

Take a moment now and write your TRAMS™ goals. Here are a few suggestions to help you:

Towards:
-Improve delivery skills and confidence
-Develop a more engaging speaking style
-Master various speech structures and formats
-Enhance ability to connect with diverse audiences

Relationships:
-Build rapport with audience members quickly
-Learn to read and respond to audience reactions
-Develop networking skills within speaking circles
-Collaborate effectively with event organizers and fellow speakers

Attitude:
-Cultivate a positive mindset before and during speeches
-Embrace constructive feedback as a growth opportunity
-Maintain composure under pressure
-Develop resilience in the face of setbacks or demanding audiences

Meaningful:
-Craft speeches that resonate with and inspire listeners
-Incorporate personal stories and experiences effectively
-Research thoroughly to provide valuable content
-Align speaking topics with personal values and passions

Smile:
-Use appropriate facial expressions to enhance delivery
-Practice genuine smiling to connect with the audience
-Incorporate humor to lighten the mood when appropriate
-Maintain a pleasant demeanor throughout presentations

You will want to adjust your goals as you evolve. What seemed a stretch goal when you started will soon become the norm, requiring you to set new, more challenging objectives. I encourage you to strive for continual improvement.

Persistence and Resilience

The path to public speaking excellence can be littered with setbacks—speeches that don't go as planned, audiences that don't engage, and feedback that is difficult to hear. Persistence in the face of these setbacks, powered by a resilient mindset, will see you through to success. Resilience in this context means more than just bouncing back; it involves learning from each experience, adapting your strategies, and persisting with renewed vigor.

Developing this resilience can be helped by viewing upsets as invaluable learning opportunities rather than criticisms of your ability. Create a support network of fellow speakers who understand your challenges and can provide insight and encouragement. Remember to celebrate your progress, no matter how small, as acknowledging growth fosters a positive mindset. Continuous improvement is not just about refining your skills but about redefining your potential. Each step forward updates the narrative of your public speaking journey.

Personal Practice Plan

Setting goals and having a plan is one thing, executing that plan and making those goals a reality is something else. In other words, developing your skills hinges not just on the knowledge you acquire but on how you apply this knowledge through deliberate practice. This plan is not merely a schedule; it is a strategic approach to honing your abilities, pinpointing areas for improvement, and consistently pushing the boundaries of your comfort zone.

It is essential to commit to this plan once created. Don't let anyone or anything get in the way of your practice plan; be determined, remain focused, make a promise to yourself, and you will reap the benefits.

The first step in developing this plan is assessing your current speaking skills. This process involves more than introspection; it requires honest and sometimes challenging feedback from trusted colleagues, mentors, or a professional coach. Utilize video recordings of your speeches or presentations to revisit your performance. Watch for flaws and subtler elements like pace, tone, and audience engagement. Are you speaking too quickly when nervous? Do you rely too heavily on your notes? Maybe your strengths lie in your ability to tell compelling stories, but you need help using non-verbal cues effectively. You create a baseline to build your practice plan by identifying these areas.

To truly improve your public speaking skills, it is essential to practice in a variety of scenarios. Each setting, from a formal business conference to an informal team meeting, offers unique challenges and opportunities for growth. Seek out these opportunities actively; volunteer to speak at local community events or offer to lead meetings at work. This variety will help improve your adaptability and build resilience as you adjust your delivery and content to suit different audiences and contexts. Also, consider practicing under less-than-ideal conditions. For example, you might practice speaking in a noisy environment to prepare for unexpected distractions during a presentation.

Keeping track of your progress is vital as it motivates you and provides insight into the effectiveness of your practice strategies. Create a simple log or journal where you record each practice session and note what went well and what didn't. Include details such as the date, the type of speaking engagement, the audience, and personal reflections. Over time, these entries will highlight patterns and trends, showing you where you've improved and where further practice is needed.

Revisit your goals periodically to assess whether they align with your development needs or should be adjusted. This ongoing process of tracking and tweaking ensures that your practice plan remains dynamic and aligned with your evolving skills and objectives.

Seeking Constructive Feedback

Feedback, often seen as daunting, is essential to unlocking profound growth and mastery in public speaking. For you, as a dedicated professional striving to enhance your oratory skills, establishing a productive feedback loop is vital. This involves gathering insights from various sources, understanding them, and implementing them effectively while maintaining emotional resilience. Let's explore how you can transform feedback into a powerful tool for your development.

The first step in establishing a productive feedback loop is actively reaching out to those who have witnessed your presentations—peers, mentors, or audience members—and asking for their honest insights. It's essential to approach this with a specific request; rather than asking whether your presentation was 'good' or 'bad,' encourage detailed comments on aspects such as your delivery, the clarity of your message, or the effectiveness of your visuals. You can facilitate this process by creating structured opportunities for feedback. For instance, after a presentation, you might distribute a quick survey that asks specific questions about various elements of your performance. Alternatively, consider a more informal approach, like inviting a peer for a coffee discussion to reflect on your latest speaking event. Whichever method you choose, the key is to make it easy for people to provide their observations and insights in a way that is structured enough to be helpful but open enough to encourage honest, constructive criticism.

I like to use the following questions.

Questions to Elicit Feedback:

1. What were the key takeaways from my presentation?

2. How well did I communicate my main points?

3. What parts of my presentation resonated with you the most?

4. Were there any areas where I could have provided more clarity or detail?

5. How effective were my visuals and supporting materials?

6. Did my delivery style (e.g., tone, pacing, body language) enhance or detract from my message?

7. What are your suggestions for improving my content, delivery, or audience engagement?

Analyzing Feedback

Once you've gathered feedback, the next challenge is analyzing it to extract actionable insights. This stage is crucial and requires a balanced approach; it's easy to focus on overwhelmingly positive or negative feedback, but actual growth comes from a comprehensive analysis considering all perspectives. Start by compiling the feedback and looking for common themes. If multiple people noted that your speech was inspiring but too detailed, consider how to maintain your motivational edge while simplifying the content. It's also beneficial to categorize the feedback into content, delivery, and audience interaction. This helps you identify which aspects of your speaking are most vital and which need more attention.

To deepen your understanding, cross-reference the feedback with your self-assessment and perhaps video recordings of your performance. Seeing yourself through the lens of your audience can provide new perspectives and highlight discrepancies between your self-perception and how others perceive you. This analysis is not just about identifying flaws but also about recognizing and reinforcing your strengths, which are very valuable for building confidence as a speaker.

Separating Self from Critique

Critique, a word that often sends shivers down the spine of many professionals, is not just a tool to foster improvement but a gateway to profound personal and professional growth. For you, as a public speaker striving to enhance your efficacy and impact, understanding how to process and learn from critique without undermining your confidence is crucial. This involves a delicate balance of detaching your identity from the critique, cultivating a mindset that sees feedback as positive, engaging in constructive self-talk, and leveraging the guidance of mentors.

The art of receiving critique begins with the understanding that feedback on your performance does not reflect your worth as an individual. It's about your actions or delivery, not your identity. To navigate this, start by framing critique as data—neutral, impersonal information you can use to decide how to adjust your behavior or approach. This perspective shift is vital in maintaining objectivity and preventing emotional responses that can cloud judgment or damage self-esteem. For instance, if someone critiques your presentation skills, interpret this as specific to the situation and not as an indication of your overall capabilities. Practicing this separation consistently can transform potentially hurtful experiences into opportunities for growth, allowing you to approach feedback with curiosity rather than defensiveness.

Cultivating a Growth Mindset

Central to learning from critique is cultivating a growth mindset—believing your abilities can be developed through dedication and hard work. Instead of a fixed mindset that sees skills as static and unchangeable, this mindset empowers you to view critique as a necessary part of learning. Embrace the idea that each piece of feedback is a stepping stone to greater mastery and that setbacks are not a sign of failure but a part of the learning process. Embedding this philosophy into your practice involves regular reflection on how you respond to feedback and consciously choosing to see each critique as a chance to evolve. For instance, after each speaking event, instead of focusing solely on what went wrong, ask yourself, "What can I learn from this?" and "How can this help me improve?" This approach enhances your resilience and keeps you motivated and engaged in your developmental journey.

Constructive Self-Talk

Your dialogue with yourself in response to critique can either be a powerful tool for growth or a destructive force that impedes your progress. Negative self-talk, where you might tell yourself that you're not good enough and you'll never improve, can erode your confidence and skew your perception of your abilities. To counter this, engage in constructive self-talk that is supportive and objective. Replace critical thoughts with affirmations and statements that encourage learning and improvement. For example, if you think, "I messed up that presentation," reframe it to, "I have an opportunity to learn from this." Another good one is, "I am proud of myself for stepping up and facing the challenge, regardless of the outcome." By consciously adjusting your internal narrative, you reinforce a positive self-image and build resilience against the potentially disheartening effects of critical feedback.

Finding Mentors and Coaches

Navigating the critique terrain can be significantly enhanced by the guidance of a mentor or coach who can provide expert feedback and emotional support. These individuals act as sounding boards, offering perspectives and insights you might not know. They can help you see your blind spots, interpret feedback constructively, and implement changes effectively. Additionally, mentors serve as models of receiving and using critique positively, providing real-life examples of resilience and adaptability. Establishing relationships with mentors involves reaching out to experienced individuals whom you respect and whose feedback you value. Regularly engage with them to discuss your progress, challenges, and feedback you've received, and be open to their guidance and suggestions.

Through these strategies—separating your self-worth from critique, fostering a growth mindset, practicing constructive self-talk, and engaging with mentors—you create a robust framework for turning critique into a dynamic personal and professional development tool. This structure facilitates your growth as a speaker and enriches your resilience, ensuring your confidence remains intact and even strengthened through every feedback you encounter. As you continue to implement these practices, remember that each critique is not just a reflection of where you are but a signpost pointing toward where you can go, offering insights essential for your journey of continuous improvement and success in public speaking.

Peer Review Groups

In public speaking, where personal improvement is as crucial as the applause at the end of a speech, peer review holds great value. Engaging with a group of fellow speakers who review each other's practices not only enhances individual skills but also fosters a community of continuous learning. Forming or joining a peer review group can seem daunting, but its benefits are profound. Start by reaching out within your existing networks—professional associations, speaking clubs, or even among workplace colleagues who share a keen interest in refining their public speaking abilities. The goal is to gather a diverse group of individuals who bring varying levels of expertise and perspectives to the table, as this diversity will enrich the feedback and learning experiences for all members.

When forming these groups, it's essential to establish clear guidelines that underscore the importance of constructive and respectful feedback. It is necessary that all group members feel safe and valued, as this will encourage open and honest communication. As mentioned earlier, effective peer reviews should focus on specific aspects of speaking, such as delivery, content clarity, and audience engagement, rather than veering into personal critiques that can be discouraging. It's also beneficial to rotate the roles of speaker and reviewer within the group, ensuring that each member receives balanced feedback and the opportunity to observe and critique others. This rotation not only enhances the learning experience but also keeps the group both dynamic and engaging.

Balancing the art of giving and receiving feedback within these groups is essential. When receiving feedback, approach it with an open mind, recognizing that each piece of feedback is a gift that provides insights into how you can improve. Conversely, when giving feedback, do so with kindness and precision. Aim to be specific in your critiques and always offer suggestions for improvement. For instance, instead of saying, "Your speech was unclear," you might say, "I think your message would be clearer if you outlined your main points at the beginning." This specific feedback is more valuable to the speaker and demonstrates a supportive approach to peer review.

You'll often find the advice you give is just as applicable to your own practice. Moreover, discussing different approaches and techniques within the group can spark new ideas and inspire you to try techniques you might not have considered before.

Remember to celebrate your successes along the way and embrace the ongoing journey of growth and development as a speaker. With dedication, perseverance, and a commitment to continuous learning, you'll unlock your full potential as an influential communicator and thought leader.

13

SETTING YOURSELF APART AS A PUBLIC SPEAKER

"The world says fit in; the universe says stand out."
M Dhliwayo

Every speaker brings a distinct set of traits to the podium, and understanding these can transform your public speaking from standard to standout. Personality assessments like the Myers-Briggs Type Indicator (MBTI), DISC, or the Big Five personality traits provide insightful frameworks for understanding your natural talents. Are you an extrovert who thrives on interaction or an introvert who excels in thoughtful deliberation? Do you respond to stress with a calm pragmatism, or do you harness the energy of stressful situations to enhance your dynamism? Understanding these aspects of your personality can help reveal your inherent strengths and potential weaknesses as a speaker.

Personality undeniably shapes every facet of our behavior and interactions; public speaking is no exception. The nuances of your personality influence how you perceive and are perceived by your audience, impacting everything from your choice of words to your body language. For instance, an extroverted speaker might naturally enjoy engaging with large audiences, thriving on the direct feedback and energy of the crowd. In contrast, an introverted speaker might excel in delivering detailed, thoughtful presentations to smaller groups where a more profound connection can be formed. Understanding this intrinsic link between personality types and speaking styles is crucial for leveraging your strengths and addressing any inherent challenges.

Adapting your natural speaking style to meet various audiences starts with a keen awareness of your personality traits. This awareness is not about altering who you are but optimizing your approach to communication in different contexts. For example, suppose you are naturally introverted and must engage a large audience. In that case, you might incorporate more structured audience interaction into your presentation, such as planned Q&A sessions, to help manage and direct audience engagement more comfortably. Conversely, if an extrovert needs to engage in more detailed and nuanced discussions, practice focusing your energy on listening and providing thoughtful responses rather than dominating the conversation. This adaptability broadens your effectiveness as a speaker and significantly enhances your audience's experience by ensuring that your delivery method matches the content and setting.

Persuasive Techniques

The ability to persuade effectively is about delivering a message and moving your audience to action. This requires a deep understanding of the principles of persuasion: ethos, pathos, and logos. Ethos refers to the credibility of the speaker. By establishing yourself as a credible source, you gain the trust of your audience, making them more open to your message. Conversely, pathos appeals to the audience's emotions, tapping into their values, desires, and fears to create a connection that transcends the intellectual content of your speech. Lastly, logos involves the logical structure of your argument, ensuring your points are coherent, well-supported, and compelling.

Building credibility, or ethos, begins long before you step onto the stage. It starts with your reputation and the respect you command in your field. However, within the context of your presentation, credibility is often established in how you introduce your topic and yourself. It's about demonstrating your expertise and authority on the subject. This can be achieved by citing relevant qualifications, experiences, or even anecdotes highlighting your depth of knowledge and commitment to the field. Moreover, the clarity and confidence of your delivery play a crucial role; a speaker who seems unsure or unfamiliar with their material will quickly lose the audience's trust. Therefore, thorough preparation and a deep understanding of your topic are fundamental.

The key lies in understanding your audience's values and emotional triggers regarding pathos or emotional appeal. This requires a nuanced approach, as what moves one audience may not resonate with another. Your message's emotional core should align with your audience's interests and passions. For instance, if you are addressing a group of entrepreneurs, emphasizing themes of innovation, risk-taking, and the thrill of building something new can be particularly effective. Emotional appeal can also be strengthened through personal stories or vivid descriptions that allow the audience to visualize the impact of your message on real life. These stories should be chosen carefully to evoke specific emotions such as empathy, pride, or even righteous anger, driving the audience to feel deeply about the subject, which is crucial to motivating action.

Crafting a compelling call to action is the culmination of your persuasive efforts. This part of your speech must be clear, urgent, and feasible, providing the audience with concrete steps to take in response to your message. The effectiveness of your call to action depends significantly on how well you've managed to establish credibility and evoke emotions. It should feel like a natural next step, an opportunity for the audience to act on the feelings and convictions your speech has inspired. For example, suppose your goal is to persuade your company to adopt a new sustainability initiative. In that case, your call to action might involve inviting your audience to join a pilot project or attend a workshop on the initiative.

Whatever the action, it should be framed so that the audience feels empowered and eager to participate, seeing it as a way to be part of a solution or movement that aligns with their values and emotions discussed throughout your presentation.

Incorporating these elements of persuasion into your speeches transforms them from mere presentations of ideas into powerful calls to action that have the potential to inspire and mobilize your audience. As you continue to refine these techniques, remember that the goal of persuasion is not just to convince but to connect, not just to argue but to inspire. Each speech is an opportunity to share knowledge, forge relationships, and create movements reflecting your audience's aspirations and values. Mastering this skill will help you rise above the norm.

Using Humor to Differentiate

Incorporating humor into your public speaking can significantly enhance the engagement and memorability of your presentations, transforming even the most mundane topics into delightful entertainment for your audience. Understanding the various types of humor and their strategic application is crucial for ensuring that your humorous content resonates well and contributes positively to your objectives.

Humor comes in many forms, each serving different purposes within public speaking. Anecdotal humor, for example, involves personal stories or observations that are amusing and relatable, making your presentation more personable and down-to-earth. On the other hand, situational humor arises from the context or circumstances described during the speech, offering a light-hearted take on potentially complex or dry subjects. Then, there's topical humor, which relates to current events or trends, connecting your speech to broader, contemporary themes. Each type of humor has its place and can be incredibly effective when matched appropriately with the topic and audience demographics.

However, the key to successfully incorporating humor lies in choosing the right type and mastering the timing and appropriateness of its use. Timing in humor is everything. A well-timed joke or humorous remark can serve as a perfect icebreaker or punctuate a section of your speech, providing a mental break for your audience. It's essential to deliver the punchline when it can be most appreciated – typically after a build-up of context or following a poignant point, giving the audience a chance to digest the information while enjoying a light-hearted moment.

Appropriateness, meanwhile, involves ensuring that the humor aligns with the audience's values and expectations and remains sensitive to diverse perspectives. This is particularly crucial in today's globalized world, where cultural sensitivities must be navigated carefully. Avoid humor that might be divisive or offensive, which can alienate parts of your audience and detract from your message. Instead, opt for inclusive and respectful humor, enhancing your rapport with the audience without undermining the seriousness of your topic when necessary.

Practicing the delivery of your humorous content is as important as the content itself. The impact of a funny story or joke often lies in the delivery – the timing, tone, facial expressions, and body language. Pay attention to your intonation and pacing, as these can dramatically affect how the humor is perceived. A backup plan is also beneficial; if a particular piece of humor does not seem to land as expected, be prepared to smoothly transition back into your main content without dwelling on the miss.

Analyzing examples of effective humorous speeches can provide valuable insights. Consider the speeches of professional speakers who skillfully integrate humor into their presentations. Observe how they set up an amusing story, the cues they use to signal a joke, and how they tie the humor back to the central message of their speech. Many seasoned speakers use humor to make complex information more accessible, to disarm the audience, or to refresh the attention span during longer sessions.

In your next presentation, try integrating humor by starting with small, safe jokes or universally relatable anecdotes. As you grow more comfortable and receive positive feedback, gradually introduce more nuanced humor that plays off the deeper content of your speech.

Remember, the goal of using humor is to entertain and create a memorable, engaging experience that enhances the audience's connection to your message and sets you apart from other speakers.

Building Your Brand

In the competitive arena of public speaking, your brand guides audiences and collaborators toward your unique message and style. Think of your brand as your professional signature—a blend of your experiences, expertise, values, and personality that you consistently present to the world.

Defining this brand requires introspection and strategy. It starts by asking yourself key questions: What am I passionate about? What do I want my audience to remember about me? What differentiates me from other speakers? The answers to these questions form the foundation of your brand, encapsulating what you stand for and how you wish to be perceived professionally.

As you hone this personal brand, consider how it enhances your public speaking endeavors. A strong, clear brand can transform the way your audience perceives you. It acts like a thread connecting diverse speaking engagements, ensuring your identity and message remain coherent and compelling, whether addressing an intimate seminar or a large conference. This consistency builds trust and amplifies your authority as a speaker. For example, if your brand is centered around innovative leadership, your presentation should echo this theme through content, speaking style, or the stories you share. This clear branding helps your audience understand and relate to your message more deeply, enhancing the impact of your presentations.

Consistency across all platforms is essential in today's digitally connected world. Your brand should be unmistakable, whether someone is viewing your LinkedIn profile or sitting in the audience at one of your talks. Each platform offers a unique opportunity to reinforce your brand attributes. Use social media to share insights and stories that reflect your brand, publish articles or blog posts that delve into your areas of expertise, and ensure that your visual branding—from the design of your PowerPoint presentations to your profile pictures—aligns with the brand you are building. This consistent presentation helps solidify your professional image and makes you more recognizable and relatable to your audience, fostering a sense of familiarity and loyalty.

Leveraging your brand effectively opens numerous doors for professional opportunities and engagements. Begin by identifying platforms and forums where your brand's message will most likely resonate. Engage actively with these platforms— industry conferences, workshops, or online webinars.

Networking plays a crucial role here. Connect with other professionals who share or value your brand attributes. This networking can lead to collaborative opportunities, speaking engagements, or guest appearances on podcasts and webinars that reach your target audience. Additionally, consider teaching or mentoring, which allows you to give back to the community and reinforces your position as an expert in your field. Each strategy extends your professional reach and embeds your brand more deeply in public speaking.

Your choice of dress and overall appearance is a powerful tool for reinforcing your brand. Every element, from clothing to accessories, should reflect your brand's attributes. If your brand emphasizes creativity and innovation, you might incorporate unique or artistic elements that signal creative thinking and modernity into your attire. Alternatively, classic styles and colors can subconsciously communicate these qualities to your audience if your brand is built on trust and reliability. This strategic alignment of appearance with the brand helps make a memorable impression and create a consistent image that audiences can relate to across different speaking engagements.

I know a motivational speaker who dresses in vibrant colors and eclectic patterns when addressing audiences at creative leadership conferences. This deliberate choice makes her instantly recognizable and mirrors her message of thinking outside the box and pushing boundaries. Her distinctive style complements her vibrant delivery and engaging content, making her presentations memorable and her brand distinctive. Audience feedback often highlights the inspiration they derive from her talks and how her appearance and energy make her messages more impactful and relatable.

A friend of mine who is a financial advisor speaks at retirement planning seminars and often opts for a conservative, meticulously tailored appearance that communicates trustworthiness and attention to detail—qualities highly valued in his field. His suit, tie, and overall grooming are chosen to project an image of stability and reliability, reinforcing his expertise in financial matters. Attendees at his seminars often note how his professional appearance made them more receptive to his advice on economic security and investments.

These examples underscore how effectively aligning your appearance with your speaking context and brand can significantly enhance your credibility and the impact of your message. They also illustrate that while content is paramount, visual elements, including your appearance, play a crucial role in how that content is perceived and received. Hence, thoughtful consideration of how you present yourself visually is not just about making a good impression—it's an integral part of your communication strategy that can amplify your influence and help you achieve your speaking goals.

Your brand is not just about how you are seen—it's about making an indelible mark on your audience, ensuring that your message reaches and resonates meaningfully.

Your Speaker Profile

Consistently using social media to share your speaking engagements, insights, and professional reflections can significantly enhance your profile as a speaker. Each post, share, or interaction contributes to building a knowledgeable, approachable persona and engaging with current trends and discussions. Highlighting your speaking engagements, sharing behind-the-scenes content, and discussing your preparation process can make your public persona more relatable and accessible, attracting more followers and enhancing your credibility.

Regularly update your social media profiles with upcoming speaking engagements, feedback from past events, and professional accolades. This keeps your audience informed and showcases your active involvement and success in the speaking arena. Engaging with other speakers, thought leaders, and professional groups on social media platforms can further broaden your network and influence.

By strategically leveraging social media before, during, and after your presentations, you transform each speaking engagement from a finite event into an ongoing conversation that continually enhances your relationship with your audience and strengthens your position as a thought leader. This dynamic interaction ensures that your message resonates far beyond the immediate confines of your presentation, creating lasting impact and ongoing engagement.

Organized and Prepared

The devil lies in the details when preparing for a public speaking engagement. Ensuring thorough preparation not only boosts your confidence but also significantly enhances the quality of your delivery. A meticulous preparation checklist is indispensable, serving as your roadmap through the myriad tasks that lead to a successful presentation.

Let's delve into what such a checklist should include, ensuring that every presentation aspect is polished and poised for success.

Firstly, the checklist should begin with a review of your speech objectives and audience analysis. This ensures that your content is aligned with the goals of the presentation and tailored to the audience's interests and needs. Following this, a detailed content review is crucial. This includes verifying facts, refining key messages, and ensuring a logical flow of ideas. Each of these steps helps construct a coherent and compelling narrative.

Next, consider the technical aspects—check the compatibility of your presentation with available equipment and familiarize yourself with the setup. This is particularly important to avoid last-minute hiccups that could disrupt your flow.

Another critical entry in your checklist should be the preparation of backup materials. This includes having extra copies of your speech, backup slides, and alternative equipment like clickers or adapters. Such foresight can be a lifesaver when technology fails or materials are misplaced. Lastly, set aside time for several dry runs of your presentation. These practice sessions are invaluable as they help you fine-tune your delivery, adjust your timing, and become comfortable with your material. This part of your checklist ensures that when you finally step onto the stage, you are familiar with your content and confident in your ability to deliver it effectively.

Public Speaker's Checklist

Before the Presentation:

1 Define the purpose and key message of your presentation

2. Analyze your audience and tailor your content accordingly

3. Develop a clear structure and outline for your presentation

4. Create engaging and visually appealing slides or materials

5. Rehearse your presentation multiple times, focusing on timing and delivery

6. Test all technical equipment (microphone, projector, computer) in advance

7. Arrive at the venue early to familiarize yourself with the space and setup

8. Ensure you have backup copies of your presentation materials

9. Dress appropriately for the occasion and audience

10. Take a few moments to relax, breathe, and center yourself before starting

During the Presentation:

1 Start with a strong opening that captures the audience's attention

2. Maintain eye contact with your audience, scanning the room

3. Use clear, concise language and avoid jargon or technical terms

4. Speak at an appropriate pace, allowing time for pauses and emphasis

5. Vary your tone, pitch, and volume to keep the audience engaged

6. Utilize gestures and body language to enhance your message

7. Incorporate storytelling, examples, and anecdotes to illustrate your points

8. Engage the audience with questions, polls, or interactive elements

9. Manage your time effectively, ensuring you cover all key points

10. Navigate any technical issues or disruptions calmly and professionally

After the Presentation:

1 Conclude with a robust and memorable closing that reinforces your main message

2. Invite the audience to ask questions and engage in discussion

3. Provide your contact information for follow-up questions or feedback

4. Thank the audience for their attention and participation

5. Gather feedback from the audience through surveys or informal conversations

6. Reflect on your performance, noting areas for improvement

7. Follow up with any promised resources or materials for the audience

8. Share your presentation slides or materials online if appropriate

9. Update your portfolio or website with any photos, videos, or testimonials from the event

10. Celebrate your success and use the experience to refine your skills for future presentations

Using this checklist, you can ensure that you are well-prepared, confident, and ready to deliver an engaging and impactful presentation while taking steps to improve your skills and grow as a speaker continuously.

Organizational Tools and Apps

Many digital tools and apps can help you organize and prepare for your presentations. These resources can streamline your preparation process, enhance productivity, and ensure you are fully equipped for your speech.

One such tool is Evernote, a versatile app that allows you to organize your research, draft your speeches, and store all your speaking notes in one accessible place. Its ability to sync across devices ensures you can work on your speech at your desk or on the go.

Another invaluable tool is Trello, which offers a visual overview of your preparation process through customizable boards, lists, and cards. This tool is handy for managing large projects or collaborating with a team, as it allows you to track the progress of each task and assign responsibilities.

For speakers who want to refine their delivery, tools like Orai come in handy. Orai provides detailed feedback on your pacing, clarity, and energy, allowing you to polish your delivery by identifying areas for improvement through AI-driven insights.

Choosing the correct set of tools that align with your needs ensures that every aspect of your speech, from content creation is meticulously crafted and ready for the stage.

If you get stuck at any stage in the process and would like assistance or coaching, get in touch with me, see QR code on page 166.

14

FINAL WORD

"Speakers who talk about what life has taught them never fail to keep the attention of their listeners." D Carnegie.

I sincerely hope you have enjoyed this book and learned a lot. However, reading the advice on these pages is only the start. Putting what you have learned into practice is what will achieve success. I firmly believe anyone willing to put in the time and effort can learn and master the skill of public speaking. This powerful tool can open doors to countless personal and professional opportunities.

Throughout this book, we have explored the various aspects of public speaking, from the initial stages of overcoming stage fright and self-doubt to more advanced persuasion techniques and well-timed humor. We have seen how public speaking can inform and inspire, help individuals and organizations achieve their goals, and positively impact the world.

Storytelling is essential in public speaking, as it allows you to harness the power of narrative to make your messages more memorable. By weaving personal anecdotes, case studies, and metaphors into your presentations, you can create an emotional connection with your listeners, making them more receptive to your ideas and more likely to act based on your words.

Body language and nonverbal communication reinforce your message and help build rapport with your audience. By using confident, open postures, maintaining eye contact, and using gestures to emphasize key points, you can convey a sense of authority and enthusiasm that can be infectious.

Vocal techniques are another vital aspect of effective public speaking. Enhancing your vocal delivery through proper breathing, pacing, and intonation can captivate your audience and keep them engaged from start to finish. Whether speaking to a small group or a large auditorium, the ability to project your voice and vary your tone can make all the difference in how your message is received.

Effective use of technology and visual aids can also be a powerful tool in public speaking, particularly in today's digital age. By incorporating multimedia elements such as slides, videos, and interactive polls, you can create a more engaging and dynamic experience for your audience. However, it is essential to use these tools wisely and keep them from overshadowing the substance of your message.

Public speaking is not always painless, and there will inevitably be challenges and obstacles along the way. Handling challenging situations with poise and confidence is a hallmark of a skilled public speaker. Whether navigating tough questions, managing interruptions, or dealing with difficult audience members, remaining calm and composed under pressure is crucial to maintaining credibility and authority.

I'm sure you will agree that one of the key takeaways from this book is the importance of authenticity and finding your unique speaking style. By embracing your strengths, passions, and experiences, you can develop a genuine, relatable, and compelling speaking persona. This authenticity allows you to connect with your audience on a human level, building trust and rapport that can lead to lasting relationships and ongoing opportunities.

Ultimately, the key to setting yourself apart as a public speaker is continually striving for growth and improvement. You can become a more confident, effective communicator by seeking feedback, setting goals, and consistently practicing your skills. This may involve stepping outside your comfort zone, trying new techniques, and learning from your mistakes, but the rewards of becoming a skilled public speaker are well worth the effort.

So go out confidently, let your voice be heard, and know that your words can change lives. The journey of a thousand miles begins with a single step, and by taking that first step into the world of public speaking, you are embarking on a path of growth, discovery, and endless possibility.

I'm excited for you!

Anne

PS: Whether you're preparing for a big presentation, aiming to improve your pitch, or just looking to feel more comfortable speaking in public, I can help you. I offer personalized coaching tailored to your specific needs and goals. Scan the QR code below to get in touch and let's talk.

Make a Difference with Your Review
Unlock the Power of Public Speaking

Kindness is never wasted; it always makes a difference. B De Angelis

Public speaking is a skill that can transform your and your audience's lives. But something even more powerful binds this world together: the magic of sharing. Just as your words can inspire, so can your voice make a positive difference.

My aim with "*Public Speaking: From Stage Fright to Spotlight*" is simple: to make the transformative power of public speaking accessible to all. The only way to truly accomplish this is to spread the word.

And that's where your voice comes into play—most people judge a book by its cover, but even more by its reviews.

Would you be kind enough to leave a review of this book for the aspiring speaker, the eager learner, or the curious reader you've never met?

Your review, which will take no more than one minute, could...

...ignite a passion in a young communicator.
...inspire a professional to enhance their speaking skills.
...help an educator find a resource for their students.
...bring together communities through powerful stories.
...make one more person step confidently onto the stage.

If the magic of sharing resonates with you, you truly understand the spirit of public speaking. Welcome to the world of effective communication. Scan QR code on next page to leave your review. You're one of us!

With immense gratitude,

Anne

Scan the relevant QR code on the next page to leave your review.

USA

AUSTRALIA

UK

www.ingramcontent.com/pod-product-compliance
Lightning Source LLC
Chambersburg PA
CBHW071955290426
44109CB00018B/2028